Advance Praise

for *From Battlefield to Boardroom*

"Dr. Laurie has delivered another engaging and insightful look at managing in an increasing global marketplace. Management strategy contrasted against a backdrop of history's great battlegrounds makes for fascinating reading."

—Bryan Bergsteinsson, Group Vice President,
University of Toyota, Toyota Motor Sales USA, Inc.

"War and global business competition have much in common: the struggle for existence and dominance, the mobilization of human resources and especially the setting of strategy. Using abundant examples from history, *From Battlefield to Boardroom* brings winning military strategies to today's business arena. The book should be of great value to corporate strategists around the world."

—Setsu Mori, L.A. Bureau Chief, The Nikkei Newspapers

"Wow!! What a great way to study business strategy! There are two memorable features to this book: First, it is fun to read. Second, it stresses my principal tool which is FOCUS. All his strategies and tactics emphasize that successful business focuses on what is critical to its success."

—Mark E. Buchman, President, PacRim Financial Consultants, Inc.,
and former president and CEO of Government National
Mortgage Association ("Ginnie Mae")

Laurie's *From Battlefield to Boardroom: Winning Management Strategies y's Global Business* is a management book unlike any you have ever read. rie's view the requirements for successful leadership in the corporate om can be deduced from the strategic principles that guided the great leaders of history. In this highly original book we learn a great deal oth warfare and business. But most of all we learn that the fundamental tance of strategic thinking in waging war successfully is little different its role in business success in the competitive marketplace."

—Archie Kleingartner, Ph.D.
UCLA Professor of Management and Policy Studies

"Dr. Laurie has provided us with an interesting linkage between business, the battlefield and strategy. His historical examples underscore the truism that winning strategies must build upon the challenges, opportunities and circumstances at hand."

—Rodney N. Lanthorne,
President Kyocera International, Inc.

"Two thumbs up! Energy! Insight! Good to see that Dennis Laurie is back with another tight, thoughtful piece on global business strategy."

—Jack G. Lewis, Ph.D., Director,
International Executive Program,
Marshall School of Business,
University of Southern California

"This book reinforces the important role of strategy in today's fiercely competitive, war-like business environment. It is of great help to the business manager looking to design and execute winning strategies."

—David Haight, Vice President, AT&T Wireless

FROM BATTLEFIELD TO BOARDROOM

Winning Management Strategies
for Today's Global Business

Dennis Laurie

palgrave

To Jessica, Krista, Becky, Garret and Josh,
their parents and grandmother.

 FROM BATTLEFIELD TO BOARDROOM
Copyright © Dennis Laurie, 2001. All rights reserved. No part
of this book may be used or reproduced in any manner whatso-
ever without written permission except in the case of brief
quotations embodied in critical articles or reviews.

First published 2001 by
PALGRAVE™
175 Fifth Avenue, New York, N.Y. 10010 and
Houndmills, Basingstoke, Hampshire, England RG21 6XS.
Companies and representatives throughout the world.

PALGRAVE is the new global publishing imprint of St. Martin's
Press LLC Scholarly and Reference Division and Palgrave
Publishers Ltd. (formerly Macmillan Press Ltd.).

ISBN 0-312-23647-6 hardback
     0-333-94990-0 (UK)

Library of Congress Cataloging-in-Publication Data
Laurie, Dennis.
     From battlefield to boardroom : winning management
strategies for today's global
   business / Dennis Laurie
   p. cm.
   Includes bibliographical references and index.
   ISBN 0-312-23647-6
   1. International business enterprises—Management. 2.
Strategic planning. I. Title.
HD62.4.L38 2001
658'.049—dc21

                                        2001021294

A catalogue record for this book is available from the British Library.

Designed by planettheo.com

First edition: August 2001
10 9 8 7 6 5 4 3 2 1

Printed in the United States of America.

Contents

Acknowledgments

Over the years I have come to know some outstanding business people. They have successfully led their respective organizations in the face of brutal competition. Indeed, they have confronted first-hand many of the strategic issues raised in the following pages. I am indebted to all of them for their many insights and their friendship. Special thanks to Bryan Bergsteinsson, CEO, Lexus; Mark Buchman, President, Ginnie Mae (Ret.); David Haight, SVP, AT&T Wireless; Eric Kuramoto, Director, Canon USA; Rod Lanthorne, CEO, Kyocera; Tom Orbe, CEO, Infiniti; and Hideaki "Don" Iwatani, chairman and CEO Matsushita America (Panasonic).

My business career as a manager and executive was played out at two fine companies. I was at Hughes Electronics for 12 years. The company is now part of Raytheon. I also spent 20 years at Arco which is now a subsidiary of British Petroleum. I am much appreciative of the opportunities provided me during those years. I owe much to many people at Hughes and Arco. Lod Cook, Arco's CEO and Chairman was always supportive.

The Internet is no doubt a wonderful thing as an information source. I, however, have relied primarily for this work on the *Wall Street Journal, Fortune* and the *Harvard Business Review* as well as the rich bibliography of books found in this work's closing pages. Credit should go to the men and women of all business news gathering organizations who provide such timely and valuable information. I want to recognize here two outstanding journalists, Mike Tharp and Setsu Mori, from *U.S. News & World Report* and the *Nikkei Journal* respectively, for their help.

While the methods dealing with strategy developed in this book are aimed at business, they are in fact perfectly applicable to certain non-profits including law enforcement organizations. I am honored to have worked with Mark Kroeker, Chief Portland Police Bureau, who has been able to bring strategic principles to bear on the organizations he has headed.

The United States is blessed with many fine institutions of higher learning. I have greatly benefited from three of them: UCLA, USC and the Drucker School of Management. I want to acknowledge here some of the excellent professors that I have studied under including Fred Weston, Richard Ellsworth, David Drew and of course Peter Drucker. I want to add special thanks to Dean of the Drucker School Cornelis de Kluyver, Archie Kliengartner at UCLA and Jack Lewis at USC. All of my education from BS to MS, to MBA and Ph.D. came while working full time. The programs of these schools made that possible.

The publishing of a book is far more collegial than an outsider might expect. The writing here is mine but you would not be reading this without the work of the professionals at Palgrave. I especially thank Toby Wahl, Sarah Schur, Roee Raz, Meg Weaver, Sabahat Chaudhary and Debbie Manette. And special praise to Alan Bradshaw.

Business professionals today, both men and women, are forever torn between their families and the demands of their work life. There really is no resolution. Time spent salvaging some crucial business account is time not spent watching your child score his or her first soccer goal—only years later does it become vividly clear which was more important. A supporting and understanding family is crucial for business success. Mine has been both. I thank them for that.

Prologue

strat • e • gy ('stra-tə-jē), n., -gies 1. the science and art of assembling and deploying large military units in operations against an enemy that cover a large geographic area and extend in duration over a protracted time period. 2. the who, what, where, when and how unifying organizational action plan for achieving a specific military mission. 3. a crucial determinant of military victory. Descended from Greek *strategia* 350 B.C. ref. to generalship or military commander.

Revised addendum circa 2001 A.D. 4. directly applicable to businessmen and women in the emerging world global economy, at the corporate, division or department level—ref. *From Battlefield to Boardroom.*

CHAPTER ONE

Reconnaissance

Overview of Book's Content and Purpose

> *To assure victory, always carefully survey the field before battle.*
>
> —Sun Tzu

> *No war should be begun until it is first determined what is to be achieved and how it will be conducted.*
>
> —Carl von Clausewitz

> *If we first knew where we are [in this Civil War] and whither we are going we could better judge what to do and how to do it.*
>
> —Abraham Lincoln

Strategies, well crafted and boldly executed, are the linchpin of a successful company and the determinants of ultimate victory or defeat. They provide the guiding architecture for achieving the most audacious of corporate missions. There is Nike's sports celebrity marketing strategy, Coca-Cola's brand strategy, Disney's cross promotions strategy, Dell's customer-direct sales strategy, Microsoft's top people hiring strategy, GE's six-sigma quality strategy, Cisco's acquisition strategy and FedEx's hub-and-spoke logistics strategy. Strategy is an underlying competitive advantage for each of these companies just as it is for any prosperous business enterprise, domestic or global, no matter its size or industry. And there is this essential fact: *Every* business strategy has its genesis on one of history's battlefields of war.

There are two dimensions to war. There is the actual combat between warriors who battle to capture or destroy key enemy positions and wound or kill their adversaries. It is a brutal, bloody, stinking and filthy affair. Separate from that there is the strategy for waging war—the who, what, where, when and how organizing blueprint for a war's execution. In sum, there is the primordial violence and carnage of physical war and there is the coldly, intellectually calculated strategy for waging it. This book deals with the latter: military strategy and its extension from the battlefield to the world of business.

War brought us the very word "strategy." It originates from the Greek *strategia*, referring to the leadership role of the general, and is best exemplified by Alexander the Great, Macedonia's brilliant and intrepid military leader. Using strategic principles taught to him by his father Philip and his tutor Aristotle, he conquered and forged a vast empire stretching from what is now Gibraltar eastward to Iran and even beyond to the borders of India, all while still in his twenties—a Gen-Y prodigy of his time. Alexander was born to war; it has been said that he wept upon discovering that there were no more worlds to vanquish. But warfare neither began nor ended with him. Long before Alexander and during the 2,300 years since, indeed to the present day, the killing fields of war, somewhere on the planet, have been a constant. And where there has been war there has been strategy for carrying it out.

War and strategy, then, are not new. What is new is the increasing introduction, over the last few years, of strategy into the business arena. This has happened largely without reference to, or awareness of, strategy's military origin. There is no such oversight here. Indeed, this book's underlying theme is that the strategies of war are also the strategies of business. Every business strategy hammered out today in the offices of some European, Asian or American company, whether at the corporate, division or department level can be traced back to some battlefield of a war past. A few examples.

In the early 1960s, the now-legendary Sam Walton began executing a strategy of opening retail stores in small towns not served by the then-Goliath Sears. When attacking Sears' weakness in small-town America, Walton was using the wisdom of ancient China's revered military philosopher and practitioner Sun Tzu: "To be certain to take what you attack is to attack a place the enemy does not protect." "Mr. Sam," as many referred to him, did just that and the Wal-Mart empire was born.

When the *Wall Street Journal* initiated a London edition to fend off the U.S. foray of the salmon-colored *Financial Times*, it was practicing the military strategy of Scipio Africanus. That Roman general, rather than confront the invading forces of Hannibal on Italian soil, crossed the Mediterranean and launched a counter-offensive against Carthage itself, Hannibal's homeland. That strategy forced Hannibal to abandon his attack and return to defend Carthage. Rome was saved.

When Nordstrom recently established a magnificent new flag-ship store in Houston, the decades-long impregnable citadel of its nemesis Nieman Marcus, it was executing the strategy used by the Japanese at the dawn of WWII: "To capture the baby tiger you have to go into the mother tiger's lair." For the Japanese, the prize—the baby tiger—was the anchored American fleet and the mother tiger's lair was Pearl Harbor. For Nordstrom, the baby tiger is the upscale customer, the mother tiger is Nieman Marcus and the mother tiger's lair is the city of Houston.

When Coca-Cola cajoled Venezuela's only bottler to defect from Pepsi and join its own ranks, it exploited the strategic lessons of one of history's most successful covert ops, the Israeli attack on Entebbe. That coup de main was marked by minutely detailed planning, lightning-fast execution, a shroud of secrecy, superb intelligence and the use of elite shock troops.

In 1999, Carly Fiorina, Hewlett-Packard's newly appointed CEO, moved strategically to spin off all of the company's operations except for computers, printers and Web devices. Her intent was to bring focus to HP's business and to exploit the military verity of Prussia's Carl von Clausewitz that "There is no higher, or more basic, military strategy than keeping one's forces concentrated at the point of attack."

Over 2,000 years ago, a small force of 300 Spartans held off Persia's King Xerxes and his 400,000-man army by controlling a narrow mountain pass at Thermopylae in northern Greece—a crucial choke point. Microsoft has used this choke-point strategy by controlling a key technology, its PC operating system, to become one of the world's largest market cap companies at some $350 billion.

Without the strategic alliance among the United States, England and Russia during WWII, Hitler and his Nazis may well have triumphed. AMR, parent of American Airlines, has learned the lesson of that successful military alliance—its global strategy is based on it. It now has an extensive international reach with its alliance partners Qantas, Cathay Pacific, Finnair, Iberia and Canadian Airways.

The singular focus in the pages ahead is on strategy. At the book's core are ten chapters, four through thirteen, each depicting a classic historical battle and the key winning military, and by extension business, strategy involved. In those chapters, military strategies of attacking strength, alliances, force concentration, choke-point control, relentless attack, revitalizing a shattered command, combat-readiness and more are taken from history's great battlefields and brought to today's business arena. Color and realism will add to the telling, noting the scores of today's companies that have already begun executing these military-originated strategies. Thermopylae, Napoleon's Russian invasion, Gettysburg, Little Big Horn, Guadalcanal, Vietnam, Desert Storm, Somalia—these conflicts are fittingly taught at our military academies. Appropriately, they might also be taught at graduate business schools for the lessons they provide about winning strategies.

Since the mid-1980s much corporate attention has been given to operational efficiency. That has been a good thing. But its focus on the immediate here and now is becoming recognized as not enough. A company vying amid ever more intense global competition must also have tailored strategies that provide the framework for a long-term future plan. Chapter 3 demonstrates, with a practical and easy-to-use format, a strategic planning model that will allow any business organization unit, from department to division to entire company, to develop winning strategies—strategies tested on the battlefield.

The great wars have been chronicled in vast tomes by military scholars. In the minutest detail, every aspect of a particular battle has been carefully analyzed. By way of example, scores of books have been written about the Crimean War with an emphasis on the courageous, and suicidal, charge of an English light cavalry brigade against entrenched Russian forces. That's fitting and useful. But sometimes the entirety of a battle can be distilled into a few trenchant words; Gen. Pierre Bosquet, an observer of the attack, said of it, "It is magnificent but it is not war." Recognizing the power of such succinct insights, some 100 carefully chosen maxims and quotes, ascribed to renowned scholars, military and business figures, are woven into the book's message and are conveniently summarized after the last chapter. They serve to concisely capture the essence of the presented strategic principles and are themselves of great value.

The ghosts of military leaders of the past including Alexander, Sun Tzu, Caesar, Nelson, Marlborough, Clausewitz, Napoleon, Wellington, Lee, Grant, Pershing, Rommel, MacArthur, Yamamoto and Patton are still with us. Indeed, they are here in the following pages. They whisper to their business-world kindred spirits of their battles and the strategies executed to win them. The strategies of wars past have become the strategies of corporate leaders like Jack Welch, Carly Fiorina, Bill Gates, Meg Whitman, John Chambers, Steve Case, Rupert Murdoch, Jaq Nasser, Shelly Lazarus, Lois Juliber, Andrea Jung, Michael Dell and more. It will be shown here exactly how the military strategies of the former have become the business strategies of the latter. With this book, they can also become the reader's.

Some executives and managers have been heard to say that the pace of their business is simply too rapid for them to have a meaningful strategy. Such a view is naive, intellectually lazy and terribly dangerous for the organization. To paraphrase Albert Camus, Not to have a strategy, is also a strategy. Such a default strategy means quite literally that there will be no long-term commitments or major human and capital resource allocations, no targets will be set or efforts made to discern future competitor initiatives, and there will be no overarching mission, indeed no apparent mission at all. The business climate five years hence, or three, or even one need be of no concern. In fact, there is no need even to plan for tomorrow. Every day will be taken, ad hoc, as it comes. *That* is the strategy of those who say they have none. Alvin Toffler, the futurist, writes, "If you don't have a strategy you will be permanently reactive and part of somebody else's strategy."[1] The result is nonstop fire-fighting until the organization, overcome by frustration, stress and fatigue, simply collapses as individual fires merge to become an all-consuming conflagration. Having no strategy is inevitably a strategy of defeat. But strategies, indeed winning strategies, are to be readily found in military history.

Late in the afternoon of a blistering summer day, an exhausted runner staggered into the Spartan camp with terrible news—a Persian army, 400,000 strong, was marching southward to crush the young Greek states including Sparta itself. The Spartan king, Leonidas, immediately gathered around him the hero Dienekes and several other veteran officers to plan strategy. Well into the evening they sat before their tents on crude camp stools crafting a strategy that would allow their own vastly outnumbered forces to hold off the great locust-like invasion juggernaut. There was much discussion and heated debate. Sticks were used to draw maps and troop deployments in the dirt. Mighty Zeus, Apollo and Nike, as well as the lesser gods, were called upon for counsel and benediction. Finally there emerged a consensus—what would become the winning choke-point strategy at a mountain pass known as Thermopylae. The actual battle, fought a few days later, was a bloody affair of atavistic violence, but Spartan bravery and, most important, a brilliantly conceived strategy saved the Greeks and with it the seedlings of Western Democracy. It was the year 480 B.C.

From that battle at Thermopylae fast forward through the millennia to the present and the dawning of the twenty-first century.

Members of a small task force of business executives and managers from a leading corporation, perhaps even the reader's own, are sitting in their high-backed black leather chairs around a mahogany table in a communications-rich boardroom. They are aiming PowerPoint presentations at one another, gulping mega-dosed caffeinated drinks and arguing convincingly for what each believes to be the most effective competitor-directed strategy for their company, division or department. Large-screen liquid-crystal wall displays, not unlike those in Pentagon war rooms, show the current state of the ever-unfolding business crisis: The competitor, with a bold new product launch and advertising initiative, has suddenly begun seizing market share around the globe. Cell phones and Web-based teleconferencing keep the strategists instantly informed of changes in the field. Professional careers, millions of dollars of stock options, thousands of employee jobs and indeed the viability of the corporation itself are all at stake. Probably unknown to the businessmen and women of this task force is that the counterstrategy they are hammering out in that boardroom, whatever form it might eventually take, originated on one of history's thousands of battlefields of war, possibly even Thermopylae. The book's title captures the essence of this: *From Battlefield to Boardroom: Winning Management Strategies for Today's Global Business.*

The Sun Tzu, Clausewitz and Lincoln quotes at the beginning of this chapter point to the importance of reconnoitering a battlefield before actual combat has begun. Similar counsel holds for any intellectual endeavor, including the reading of this book. Recognizing that, this chapter has served as something of a reconnaissance or overview of the content and purpose of the chapters to come. The final chapter will provide a backward look, a debriefing and quick summary of the book's critical points.

A note about references. To underscore various issues dealing with business strategy, the pages that follow are filled with real-world examples and the related views of involved executives, managers, analysts, consultants or academics. In most cases, the information is drawn from *The Wall Street Journal,* or *Fortune,* or *Harvard Business Review* or one of the books listed in the bibliography. Stories that broke as the book was going to press, in the period November 2000 to March 2001, are noted by the designation NEWSFLASH!

This book targets two audiences: senior business executives and managers whose responsibilities include the setting of corporate or business unit strategy and, secondly, those business professionals who aspire to such leadership positions. This book's content should help both groups advance their individual careers as well as greatly benefit their respective companies. That is especially so for those businessmen and women who have not known war directly and have not realized the benefit of studying it.

Military victory comes from thinking and acting strategically—so does victory in business. Designing and executing winning business strategies—strategies that originated on the battlefields of war—is what this book is all about.

———————

Chapter 2 draws more tightly the nexus between war and business—especially and specifically the recognition that the strategies of the former are becoming the strategies of the latter.

"Annihilate the Red Army of Coca-Cola"

Waging Business as War

We're in a war right now [with Microsoft].
—Carl Yankowski, CEO, Palm Pilot[1]

Shoot them in the belly and cut out their living guts.
—Gen. George S. Patton

I am a no-holds-barred, take no prisoners, shield and sword, go-to-war executive.
—Debby Hopkins, CFO,
Lucent Technologies[2]

Now our mission is to kill Cisco.
—David Bishop,
Director of Electronics, Bell Labs[3]

It makes no difference what we think of war. War endures.
—Cormac McCarthy, author[4]

War and commerce are entirely alike in terms of human conflict, strategy and sought objectives.
—Carl von Clausewitz

Sculpted Glass Hand Grenades

Pepsi's Brazilian operations head, Luis Suarez, swaggered onto the stage at a recent company sales rally. He wore battle fatigues, carried an assault rifle and had camouflage paint covering his face. Defiantly he roared to his people, "We, the Blue Liberation Army of Pepsi, will annihilate the Red Army [of Coca-Cola]."[5] The impassioned crowd responded with wildly supportive shouts, stamping feet and fists pumping the air.

Andy Grove, Intel's bellicose chairman, speaks the military argot when saying "To deal with the Pentium processor flaw crisis we built a war room with people bringing reports from the front and returning to execute agreed-upon courses of action."[6] Grove's combat-readiness is captured by his motto, "Only the paranoid survive." Nor is he forgiving of an enemy—after a bitter lawsuit, Grove adamantly refuses to reconcile with AMD's President Jerry Sanders.

To avoid a handshake or a cordial greeting, Nike's CEO, Phil Knight, will not appear at an industry social event if Reebok's CEO, Paul Fireman, is expected to be present. Knight seeks to maintain a focused, laserlike enmity toward his competitor. That animus serves as a powerful motivating driving force for him as well as the men and women of Nike.

David Hancock heads Hitachi's U.S. computer business. Describing his company, he says, "We are not defenders. We are predators. It's war here and we love war."[7] Hancock knows that there are no conscientious objectors or pacifists in the PC business.

With a string of acquisitions over a span of less than a decade, Hugh McColl has taken NationsBank, recently renamed Bank of America, from twentieth-largest to *the* largest of U.S. banks with assets over $600 billion. Reflecting the company's fierce, no-holds-barred competitiveness, McColl, an ex-Marine, awards sculpted glass hand grenades to his highest-performing managers. The prizes are most highly coveted.

A few years ago Dell was blindsided by Compaq's unexpected announcement of heavy PC discounting. Michael Dell, the company's eponymous founder and CEO, responded by immediately calling a meeting for the following day of his top 1,000 or so people.

His intent was to encourage and exhort them to confront the competitive challenge. The next morning, as Dell stepped to the podium at the front of a large conference room and looked out at his people, he was both very pleased and surprised to see that everyone was wearing camouflage fatigues. No order had been issued to dress in military garb; word had simply spread. The symbolism was clear to all who were there: This was war, business war.

Pepsi has been moving aggressively into noncarbonated drinks, including fruit juices, tea, coffee and water. Future offerings will be fortified with vitamins and nutrients. For a decade now the company has been referring to itself as the "Beverage Company." How is Coca-Cola responding to that? Coke's president of North American operations, Jeffrey Dunn, says, "The cola wars are going to be played now across a lot of different battlefields."[8]

These are but a few examples of America's top companies and their executives who approach business as if it were war. Today, just past the new millennium's beginning, with trade accounting for some 25 percent of world GDP, there are no safe harbors, no sanctuaries from the rigors of global competition. To excel in this worldwide coliseum of intense business competition, more and more companies are taking on the trappings of war. For such companies business has become simply war by another means. Evidence of that is seen in a recent *Wall Street Journal* story that dealt with the furious, warlike competition between AMD and Intel in semiconductors. Here are some of the actual words and phrases the reporter used: rally the troops, attack, battle, potent weapon, enemy, guerrillas and chain of command. That is the language of war. It isn't just that story; a comparative cover-to-cover reading of any issue of, say, *Fortune* and a recent *VMI Military Journal* will show a striking commonality of vocabulary, including recruiting, training, alliances, esprit, espionage, tactics, reconnaissance, beachhead, early-warning system and logistics.

Surely it is not coincidental that business and war share a common vocabulary. That they do so must be because the two have striking similarities. Both entail organizing and directing large numbers of personnel and vast resources against an opponent. Both war and business have become global in scope and are conducted over long periods of time. And at the most fundamental level, they both involve deadly serious, high-stakes, adversarial human conflict oftentimes carried out by those having a certain zest for challenge and a compulsion to test themselves against others.

Some 1,500 years ago Genghis Khan, the great Mongol warrior-chieftain, reflected to his son that "Man's highest joy is to conquer his enemies, to deprive them of their possessions, to make their beloved weep [and embrace] their wives and daughters." Although speaking of war and why men fight, he could have been speaking of business today; although a contemporary Genghis, recognizing the reality of the ever growing number of mentally tough and more than capable women coming to dominance in corporate America, would surely adjust his remarks to include his own daughters.

Much silliness has been written of late that encourages kissy-kissy, I win, you win, we all win approaches to business. It is inane psychobabble. New Agers, with their tender senses and little actual business experience, might author some books, but they don't fight the business wars. "It makes no difference what we think of war. War endures,"[9] writes the author Cormac McCarthy. Like it or not, there is war, and, like it or not, the essence of war and the essence of business competition is the same. The barely literate Gen. Nathan Bedford Forrest, one of the Civil War's finest cavalry officers, observed that "War means fightin and fightin means killin." Well, business is war without the killin—at least killin in its strictest sense. When Palm Pilot's CEO, Carl Yankowski, grimly says, "We're in a war right now [with Microsoft],"[10] or when David Bishop of Bell Labs publicly affirms "Now our mission is to kill Cisco,"[11] their words are to be taken almost, but not quite, literally.

Even after all of the above examples, a reader may still choose to reject the premise of business as war, although there is much career benefit in embracing, rather than rejecting it. But what cannot be rejected is the verity that battlefield strategies of wars past translate directly to the world of business competition. The evidence is irrefutable.

War, Business and Strategy

War and business: The fundamentals of waging both are the same. One of the most important of those fundamentals—strategy—is at the core of this book. Clausewitz wrote as long ago as the early nineteenth century that "War and commerce are entirely alike in terms of human conflict, strategy and sought objectives." He was one of the first to recognize the linkage among war, business and strategy.

More recently, Gen. Robert Wood also recognized the application of military strategy to business. Wood, a graduate of West Point, brought his military skills from WWI to the world of business, becoming CEO of Sears in 1928. Sears, founded some forty years earlier, was about to begin a period of uncontested retail dominance. Under Wood's disciplined leadership, Sears was transformed from a modestly successful mail-order firm to a mammoth, and enormously profitable, retailer. Strategy was fundamental to the transformation. Wood once observed that "Business is like war ... If the grand strategy is correct, any number of tactical errors can be made and yet the enterprise proves successful."[12] Once again—war, business and strategy. Winning in war, winning in business depends on a well-crafted strategy.

The role of military strategy in the world of business was further advanced by Robert McNamara and the so-called Whiz Kids. The term referred to a group of about a dozen young Air Force officers who during WWII developed highly effective mathematical approaches to create and execute a number of strategic initiatives against the Nazis. After the war, in the late 1940s, they were recruited en masse by Ford Motor Company. McNamara, probably the brightest of the group, used military strategies, learned and refined in the Air Force, against Ford's competitors. He rose quickly through the Ford executive ranks and within a decade became the company's highly successful CEO. McNamara demonstrated that military strategy did indeed translate perfectly to the world of business. He later joined the Kennedy administration as Secretary of Defense. McNamara went from war to business and back to war. The transitions were easy for him.

From the time of McNamara's first coming to Ford until the late 1960s, strategic planning began to make inroads at a few score other companies scattered around the country. By the early 1970s, strategic planning had gained broad acceptance in the corporate world. It became the business management fad du jour, gaining as much attention as reengineering or outsourcing or core competencies would a decade or so later. However, largely because strategic planning was still poorly understood and not well executed, by the late 1970s it had fallen into corporate management limbo. But then, in 1990, strategic planning began making a quiet comeback. It has grown in usage ever since. Today, the enormous complexity of domestic and global business, the warp speed at which it operates and its intense competition make strategy, and strategic planning, absolutely crucial.

Now, in 2001, a mere step across the threshold of the twenty-first century, the important role of strategic planning in business is reasonably well established if not always effectively carried out. Interestingly, however, while strategy has recently become ever more important in business, its battlefield origin has been all but lost or forgotten. This book rediscovers that origin and accentuates it simply because there is so much to be gained for a business professional from doing so.

Since about the time of Alexander the Great, 356 to 323 B.C., warfare has required strategy to wage it. Strategy, as a cognitive discipline, originated on the battlefield as warfare advanced from its primitive beginnings involving only a few men and little more than rocks and clubs for weapons. The more complicated battle became—involving a greater number of combatants, more lethal and diverse weapons, covering more ground and extending over a longer time frame—the greater the need for strategy to plan, coordinate and direct it all against the adversary. Modern warfare has become far too complex to be fought without a detailed and sophisticated strategic plan as a means of waging it. And now there is the reality that business also has become far too complex to be conducted without a strategic plan.

The argument that military strategy readily transfers to the business arena is unassailable. It is supported by both examples and fact. Some of those examples were noted in the last chapter. Recall Sam Walton's first Wal-Mart stores in small-town, rural America where Sears had no presence and the Sun Tzu military strategy "To be certain to take what you attack is to attack a place the enemy does not protect." Scores of other examples will appear in later pages. Beyond the examples, which are proof enough that military strategies have become business strategies, there are the facts . . .

Military strategies are dependent on the current and projected circumstances that are part of, and surround, the battlefield. The weather, enemy deployment, highground, available weapons, river-crossings and much more are circumstances that must be factored into the choice of a particular strategy. Prevailing circumstances—competitor, economic, market, technological, regulatory and more—are also determinants of business strategy.

Military strategy is directed at an enemy. Business strategy is directed at one or more competitors.

The purpose of a military strategy is to accomplish a crucial mission. A company's business strategy is intended to fulfill its corporate mission.

A military strategy must take account of, and be consistent with, all available resources: manpower, equipment and weaponry. Available resources, human and capital, are also basic to a business strategy.

An effective military strategy sets performance targets and milestones against which progress can be measured. Business strategy requires exactly the same thing.

A military strategy involves vast resources and is adhered to for long periods of time—years, even decades. The same is true of business strategies.

Military strategic plans should not include more than roughly ten major initiatives, simply because more would be too difficult to implement. Experience has shown the same to be true for business. Indeed, the best companies have no more than five or six strategic initiatives.

Leadership is crucial to the design and execution of military strategy. It is no less crucial for business strategy.

Warfare, at least from the twentieth century on, with WWI and WWII, has extended over nearly the entire globe. Military strategy must account for that. So, too, must business strategy today when firms have to compete in a global business arena.

A military strategy determines the who, what, where, when and how action blueprint for the entirety of an armed force. It is the unifying entity for otherwise disparate command elements. A business strategy plays the same invaluable role within a corporation.

The success of an overarching military strategy depends on successful tactical operations carried out by front-line personnel in the field. Tactics are no less important in business.

It is an army's general, senior officers, noncoms and recruits who breathe life into a military strategic plan. It is they, by their ability, knowledge and drive, who will determine the strategy's success or failure. The same holds in a business organization, from CEO, to senior and middle management to entry-level personnel.

Still more facts demonstrating the business-war-strategy nexus will be cited in later pages. But for now, the factual evidence is clear and strong enough. The setting of strategy in warfare is no different in substance from the setting of strategy in business. Warfare, over the centuries, could not have been waged successfully without carefully crafted guiding strategies. Neither can business today be effectively conducted, domestically or globally, without well conceived strategy for doing so. What generals and their senior officers have done in setting military strategy, CEOs, senior and middle management now do in the world of business. The methods and approaches are identical; war, business and strategy are inextricably linked.

The Camry-Taurus War

War over the millennia has been a near-constant thing. Indeed, Plato wrote some 2,000 years ago, "Only the dead have seen the end of war." War is still with us today. Because that is so, it is not surprising that quite sophisticated means have developed to wage this ever-present circumstance in our lives. Those sophisticated means center around strategy, which organizes and directs the waging of war.

Beginning in the mid-1800s a new powerful force began to dramatically influence mankind: business. While business is far more benign than war, with far-reaching benefits, it can also be brutally harsh to those who fail. Still, it is no doubt better to have France's Renault exchanging sports car advertising broadsides with Germany's DaimlerChrysler than to have WWI trench warfare with the French *poilu* and the German *soldaten* lobbing mortar shells and hand grenades at one another. And it is assuredly better to have the Toyota-built Camry bitterly compete with the Ford-built Taurus for best-selling four-door sedan then to have Mitsubishi-built Zeroes over Midway in deadly aerial combat with Lockheed-built P-38s during WWII. In any case, business has become enormously complex and, like warfare, must have a guiding strategy to be conducted effectively. Easing the challenge of developing winning strategies for a CEO, divisional vice president or department manager is the fact that the same strategies that have proven effective in warfare are equally effective in business—and those military strategies are well known.

————

The following chapters develop ten specific winning military strategies for direct application by the business reader to his or her own management challenges, whether at the department, division or corporate level. But first, some precise definitions and a simple and ready-to-use strategic planning model are introduced.

CHAPTER THREE

Strategy

Key to Victory

Battles are won by slaughter and [strategy]. The greater the general, the more he contributes in [strategy], the less he demands in slaughter.
—**Winston Churchill**

If you don't have a strategy you will be . . . part of somebody else's strategy.
—**Alvin Toffler**[1]

We have made a big mistake in overlooking the strategic planning process; we have been way too seat-of-the-pants.
—**Jeff Bezos, Chairman, Amazon.com**[2]

Setting the strategy at Cisco . . . that's one of the top three things I do.
—**John Chambers, CEO, Cisco**[3]

"I Shall Return"

The powerful deep-throated rumble of the PT boat's idling Pratt & Whitney engines broke the predawn quiet. The sleek, high-speed, eighty-foot craft tossed impatiently in the choppy waters; it awaited the boarding of Gen. Douglas MacArthur, who was about to begin a daring escape from the Japanese-besieged, craggy island of Corregidor in the Philippines. Much against MacArthur's will, President Roosevelt had ordered him to take on a new command with headquarters in Australia. He would have to leave behind the men of his joint American-Filipino army. A bitter fate awaited them. Hoping, futilely as it turned out, for reinforcements, within weeks they would be forced to surrender. Thousands of the men would die on what became known as the Bataan Death March or, surviving that, would perish while in Japanese prisoner-of-war camps.

Perhaps MacArthur foresaw what the terrible days ahead would bring to his abandoned army and the people of the Philippines themselves. In the moments just before embarking, the tall American general turned to the small-statured Philippine president, Manuel Quezon, who stood beside him on the dock. MacArthur placed his hands on the man's shoulders and gazed deeply into his eyes as he emotionally vowed, "I shall return." It was March 12, 1942. The United States had entered World War II only a few months before and had suffered one terrible reversal after another. MacArthur's optimism seemed incongruous.

Ten days later, first by PT boat, then by B-17 aircraft and finally by a rickety old train drawn by an ancient wood-burning locomotive, MacArthur's odyssey ended at Melbourne, Australia. There he was put in command of the beleaguered Australian, British and American forces in the Southwest Pacific. He faced a Herculean challenge. The Japanese occupied much of Southeast Asia and nearly all the habitable North and South Pacific islands. Australia, the last redoubt, itself was threatened.

Sometimes—rarely—the grand sweep of history turns upon one individual. So it was here with MacArthur whose immediate decisions and actions would have repercussions impacting millions of lives. Calmly, deliberately, his military-trained mind turned automatically to strategy as the starting point in confronting the challenge before him. In solitude, the general paced the confines of his study, his signature corn-cob pipe jutting from between thin lips, hands thrust in back pockets as was his practice, thinking. Periodically he looked up to the map that covered an entire wall of the otherwise book-lined room. What he saw might have dismayed and overwhelmed a lesser man. Scores of tiny "Rising Sun" flags were thrust into the map, designating islands and archipelagoes that had been seized by Japan in the days just after Pearl Harbor and then strongly reinforced: New Guinea, Tarawa, Guadalcanal, Wake, Rabaul, Tulagi, Saipan, Peleliu, Guam, Truk, Kwajalein and more. Far to the north, some 5,000 miles across the horizon from MacArthur's Australian headquarters, and nestled safely behind those strongholds, was Japan—a vibrant, stoic, hardworking, emperor-worshipping monolith of ninety million souls that only a century before had, by sheer grit, raised itself from an isolationist feudalism. Within the veins of the Japanese military, industrial and government leaders pulsed centuries of samurai blood. Those leaders were calling for Japanese East Asian hegemony. The United States faced a formidable enemy.

Limited resources precluded MacArthur from a conventional strategy of frontal attacks that would drive the Japanese first from one island and then another seriatim; nearly three-fourths of American manpower and materiel during WWII was deployed in Europe to be used in battle against Hitler. MacArthur, and his Pacific campaign stepchild, would have to make do with what was available. How then to deal with an entrenched and fanatic enemy? Slowly, a crucial strategy took form in his mind.

Gathering his staff officers before him, MacArthur, using his pipe stem as a pointer, tapped the map at a dozen or so Japanese strongholds, including the bastion at Rabaul, and told his officers that they would simply be bypassed and left to wither away. The wisdom of the strategy became immediately apparent. Naval forces, under regional command of Adm. Thomas Kinkaid, would assure that those strongholds were not resupplied. Hundreds of thousands of Japanese, expecting to die gloriously for Emperor Hirohito while bravely fighting Americans, would instead die ignominiously and wretchedly of starvation, disease and broken morale without ever having seen an American. Where Americans did attack, the Japanese fought tenaciously, holding every inch of land and launching suicidal counterattacks when that was no longer possible.

For three years the war raged throughout the Pacific. Gradually at first, and then more rapidly, the miniature Japanese flags were taken down from war-room maps and were replaced with the American red, white and blue. Finally, on January 10, 1945, MacArthur waded ashore at Lingayen Gulf in the Philippines. In a quickly arranged radio communiqué to the Filipino people he began simply, "People of the Philippines, I have returned." A few months later, the Philippines were retaken. The war itself ended in August with the atomic bombing at Hiroshima and Nagasaki. MacArthur's strategy of bypassing Japanese strongholds had significantly contributed to winning the war.

The Churchill quote at the beginning of the chapter underscores the greatness of generals who minimize the slaughter of their own forces through the execution of sound strategy. In the Philippine operation, MacArthur lost just under 1,100 GIs; the Japanese dead numbered some 25,000. That comparative casualty ratio characterized nearly all of MacArthur's Pacific battles. He could have ordered his men forward in the face of enemy guns, knowing that many of them would have been killed, but also coldly calculating that in the process some of the Japanese would be killed as well . . . war by attrition and statistics. But that was not the MacArthur way. He relied on strategy far more brilliant than that.

Strategy

A complex of factors explain the victory of the Allies in the Pacific during WWII. Leadership, training, morale, resources, logistics, communications and more—all were important, but strategy was fundamental. The crucial importance of strategy in warfare did not begin with MacArthur and the great world conflict during the years 1941 to 1945. It began long before.

It is a summer afternoon in 346 B.C. A ten-year-old boy, named Alexander, sits at the feet of two great men: the philosopher Aristotle and his own father, King Philip of Macedonia. They are teaching him much about what came to be the beginning of modern warfare, with emphasis on *strategia*, the recently coined Greek term referring to generalship and the art and science of war. Taking the principles he had learned, Alexander would later go on to slash, burn and destroy his enemies and in the process forge a vast empire stretching from what is now Gibraltar at the mouth of the Mediterranean eastward to Persia, today's Iran and beyond to the very gates of India. He would come to be called Alexander the Great. Having consolidated his empire, he died at age 33, some say of malaria, leaving behind an extraordinary legacy of waging war on a strategic scale. The killing fields of war did not end with Alexander. Indeed, click to CNN to see that, somewhere on this planet, at this very moment war goes on: Lebanon, Eritrea, Chechnya, Serbia, Sierra Leone and a dozen more torn and tormented lands. And where there has been war, there has been strategy for waging it. Indeed, strategy historically has been a primary determinant of military victory or defeat.

The Spartan defense at Thermopylae; double envelopment, or flanking, of Roman forces by Hannibal at Cannae; Russian biding of time against a massive French invasion in 1812; the Union's blockade of Confederate ports during the American Civil War, U.S.-England-Russia alliance against Hitler in WWII; MacArthur's surprise Inchon landing in the Korean War; lightning strike of Israeli armor across the Sinai in the Four Day War—all and more were strategies leading to military victories. Those and other winning strategies carry over directly to the world of business. From battlefield to boardroom: the winning strategies of war have become the strategies of business.

Harvard, Stanford, Wharton, UCLA, the Drucker School of Management and other major U.S. business schools now offer dozens of executive courses labeled strategic this or strategic that. Consulting firms, large and small, are making certain that their PowerPoint presentations are generously peppered with the word "strategic." Browse the business section of a Barnes & Noble bookstore or Amazon.com's equivalent in cyberspace and you will see the many titles with the word "strategic" preceding an array of business functions: strategic marketing, strategic logistics, strategic finance, strategic purchasing, strategic manufacturing, strategic human resources and so it goes. This growing awareness of strategy's importance is a good thing. Too often, however, the word "strategy" has been used inappropriately. Here is a precise definition for all that follows in this book:

> Strategies are courses of action involving vast resources that are
> critical to a mission's fulfillment, complementary to one another,
> projected years into the future, relatively few in number and rarely

changed. They serve as a guiding who, what, where, when and how unifying organization-wide action blueprint for confronting adversaries.

Strategy is still better understood by contrasting it with tactics.

Tactics

Carl von Clausewitz observed that "War . . . divides itself into strategy and tactics." Strategy then is not tactics. Still, the two terms are sometimes confused and mistakenly used interchangeably. They shouldn't be. Both play a vital role in military, and business, campaigns but are quite different from one another.

One of MacArthur's key Pacific War strategies, the bypassing of certain Japanese strongholds, was limned above. But in the remote jungles of New Guinea, Tulagi and Guadalcanal, MacArthur's GIs and marines fought the Japanese largely unaware of, and caring very little about, grand strategy. The dogfaces and leathernecks were hundreds or thousands of miles away from where strategy was being set and monitored in comfortable air-conditioned war rooms. There, campaign maps covered the walls and graying generals with their well-fed and neatly uniformed staff officers were bustling about. No, these American young men, kids really, many not yet or barely out of their late teens, were at the front lines. Their world, their nightmare, was one of fetid, slimy and cloying mud; venomous reptiles; rotting vegetation stench; mosquito swarms; stifling, oppressive wet heat; recurrent malaria and dysentery attacks; suppurating skin ulcers; mind-numbing fatigue; and of course the ever-present, but mostly invisible, implacable enemy that sought to kill them. Their survival, let alone their victory, depended not on strategy but on battlefield tactics.

Tactics are immediate actions taken by individuals or small units at the very point of combat. The actions are flexible and innovative, often discovered by trial and error and designed to meet any newly arising exigencies. A tactical operation may last not much more than a minute and seldom more than twenty-four hours. Military tactics look to capturing a hill, radar site, half-track, river or road crossing, supply cache, airfield, tank, sniper or gun emplacement. Each small tactical victory chips away at the enemy's strength until finally, by the hundreds, thousands and tens of thousands, the victories combine to achieve the strategic objective. Tactics in the Pacific War, against the Japanese, took a myriad of forms.

To deal with Japanese dug into underground bunkers, the flame-thrower was developed as a brutal but effective tactical weapon. Satchel charges and Bangalores were used to blow apart Japanese-laid barbed wire. In the predawn hours of an island's D-Day invasion, rubber-suited navy Underwater Demolition Teams (UDTs) removed mines and other obstacles from approaches to the landing beaches. Naval bombardment preceded a landing to hammer Japanese beach defenses. Foxholes were dug on the reverse side of slopes to reduce the danger of enemy artillery bombardment. To keep a hand grenade dropped into a Japanese underground bunker from being tossed right back out, a buddy's accompanying rifle fire was used to confuse the enemy. Passwords with lots of Ls that the Japanese could not pronounce were common: Lorelei, lollapalooza, lollipop, lily. All of these were tactics.

Two business examples will make even clearer the distinction between strategy and tactics.

When Kodak's chairman, George Fisher, recently announced the beginning of a ten-year and multibillion-dollar program to dominate China's photographic film market, he was articulating a strategy. When a Kodak expatriate manager in Beijing, in order to win government friends, helps to arrange an education visa at Michigan State University for the son of a ranking Communist official, that is tactics.

A second example of tactics versus strategy in the business world involves Wal-Mart. Its initial decision in the early 1960s to open stores exclusively in small towns not served by the mighty Sears or any other major retailer was a strategy—in hindsight an empire-building one. But when a Wal-Mart store manager in Bend, Oregon, population 9,752, notices a large number of out-of-state fishermen with camper-trailers passing nonstop through town and sets aside a designated overnight parking area with free electrical hookup for them just

Table 3.1

	STRATEGIES	TACTICS
TIME FRAME	Long term: years	Short term: days or less
REQUIRED RESOURCES	Vast	Minimal
SCOPE OF INVOLVEMENT	Entire organization	Front-line unit
NUMBER	Ten or less	Countless
RESPONSIBILITY	Senior management	Front-line personnel
COMMAND	Centralized	Decentralized
ENCOMPASSING SPACE	Large, even global	Local

outside the store, tacitly encouraging them to come in, shop and buy, that is tactics—darn good tactics.

Table 3.1 above summarizes the distinctions between strategies and tactics for a military command as well as any business operation, be it a department, division or entire corporation.

Tactical efficiencies can be built into a modern-day business operation. The best companies do so: Southwest Airlines, Wal-Mart, Nordstrom, Saturn, Disney, Cisco, Home Depot and FedEx with their outstanding recruiting, training, team-building, esprit, empowerment and highly qualified mid-level managers, the equivalent of the military's noncoms, come immediately to mind.

The great American tank commander Gen. George Patton, never known as a strategist, held tactics in high regard, often saying, "Good tactics can save bad strategy and bad tactics can ruin even the best strategy." In fact, arguing the merit of strategy as opposed to tactics is misdirected. Both are necessary for victory in war and business—especially business. From a Dell customer rep to a Southwest Airlines baggage handler, from a Nordstrom salesperson to an AT&T long-distance operator, from a Saturn service mechanic to a Sears furnace installer: the tactics of front-line people can make or break a company.

Effective tactics are indeed vital. But they have been introduced here not for their importance as such but to draw the differences more sharply between them and strategy. Having done that, return now to strategy: the focus of this book.

Strategic Planning Model

Beginning with chapter 4, specific strategies, the cornerstone of a strategic plan, are presented. Their creation, execution and monitoring require much effort. That effort can be guided and facilitated with a simple but comprehensive strategic planning model. Such a model follows here. While military in origin, it is equally fitting in the business arena. It is straightforward and immediately available for application at the corporate, division or department level. Its six elements are mission, satellite snapshot, future scan, strategic building blocks, performance targets and required resources.

Mission

The business-is-war metaphor is, in most ways, quite accurate but it is not perfect. For one thing, military wars are generally waged over a limited period of time while business competition continues for the life of a company, which, in theory, could be forever. After one or ten or a hundred battles over a few days or even a few decades, wars eventually grind to an end. Peace is restored and armies are demobilized. The war is over. Not so for the business wars, where a company must be prepared to compete in perpetuity; even if a competitor is driven from the field, another quickly emerges to take its place. General Electric, Exxon, Aetna, Corning, Ford, J. P. Morgan, Levi's, Procter & Gamble, Brinks, Union Pacific, Chase Manhattan, Du Pont and dozens of other American companies have been waging their respective competitive business wars for 100 years and more. Thus a military mission is usually achievable in a measured time frame of months or at most a few years; MacArthur's defeat of Japanese forces in the Pacific and his return to the Philippines took three years to accomplish. But the mission of a business must look to an endless future as if the firm were immortal. Its words must reflect that sense of perpetuity. Part of Microsoft's published mission is an example: "Empower people through great software, any time, any place and on any device." That should be good for centuries.

A lost mariner looks to the North Star for guidance, knowing that its place in the heavens is unchanged. The mission of a corporation or smaller business unit is like that. It is an-all-but immutable beacon that serves as a guide for strategy setting. It is the starting point of any strategic plan. Apple, founded in 1977 by Steve Jobs, rocketed to industry leadership and enormous investor profitability. But without a clear mission, internal arguments over the company's direction began to paralyze decision making. By 1985, the company was foundering and Jobs was forced to resign. In a strange twist of business fate, after being exiled for nearly fifteen years, a more experienced Steve Jobs has returned to Apple as interim CEO. It remains to be seen whether this time around he can sculpt an enduring corporate mission.

Almost fifty years ago, Thomas Watson Jr., the son of IBM's founder, said, "I believe that we must have a set of beliefs that serve as premises for all of our strategies and actions."[4] That set of beliefs formed IBM's mission in its years of greatest growth, during which time it was establishing itself as a premier company of the twentieth century. A company's mission, usually articulated in broad strokes, typically addresses bedrock issues that might include products, services, customers, technology, employees, markets, ethical standards, core competencies, stakeholders and social responsibility. It outlines the role and importance of each of these and articulates what the company aspires to, its ultimate objective, how it wants to be known, what it is and equally what it is not, as well as its very raison d'être. Peter Drucker refers to all of this combined as the "theory of the business."

Johnson & Johnson's page-long, single-spaced mission statement underscores the company's devotion to the well-being of healthcare providers and consumers to whom its products are sold. The men and women of the company live the document. It has served them wonderfully for nearly a century, particularly during times of crisis. In

1982, Tylenol capsules in several bottles in half a dozen Chicago retail outlets were found to be laced with cyanide. Seven people died. When the news broke, J&J people at all levels of the company, throughout the country, and on their own, immediately responded by pulling Tylenol from the shelves. There was no need for a headquarters order to do the right thing. J&J people, suffused with their corporate mission, knew automatically what actions to take. There is a postscript: The recall cost the company $100 million and ushered in the tamper-proof bottle cap. The public applauded the actions of Johnson & Johnson, its brand name was strengthened and Tylenol sales have since more than doubled. The poison-wielding murderer has never been found.

The current crisis facing Microsoft offers another example of the important role of mission. The Justice Department has called for a break up of the company, threatening its very future. Asked about how he is dealing with this crisis, Steve Ballmer, Microsoft's CEO, responded, "I must assure that we refocus upon clear goals, keep good people and give them a mission."[5] There's mission again. It is at the very core of a company and is always turned to, especially during difficult times.

A detailed statement of mission like J&J's is not necessarily required. McDonald's founder, Ray Kroc, built his company on only four, albeit robust, pillars: "Quality, Cleanliness, Service and Value." Implicit in those four words was the entirety of the McDonald's operation and the essence of its mission. Lexus captures an important aspect of its mission with "The relentless pursuit of excellence." Sun's Scott McNealy has "The network is the computer" as the underlying premise of his company. Dick Kovacevich, CEO of Wells Fargo, tells his people that their mission is "To be the best customer service bank in the world."[6]

Except for rare modest amendments or adjustments, once set, the mission is all but immutable. Strategies, to achieve the mission, are somewhat more prone to change, still they have years, sometimes decades, of duration. Tactics, as has been discussed, are constantly changing to accomplish strategic targets.

For nearly a century, Kellogg's cereals have appeared on American breakfast tables. The understood Kellogg mission was to be the leading breakfast food cereal company. Fruit Loops, Corn Flakes,

Rice Krispies, Frosted Flakes and the rest have been family staples—
have been. Changing lifestyles, with single parents, or dual working
parents, child day care and long commutes, are rendering breakfast,
as grandma and grandpa knew it, a relic. A new era is passing Kellogg
and its mission by. Kellogg's sales have been falling, and in the bull
market of 1999 its stock declined 45 percent. Carlos Gutierrez, the
Kellogg CEO, is attempting to reinvent the company as a snack food
provider. He says, "That's the way the world is moving and we will
move with it."[7] Be clear about this. Kellogg is not simply changing
strategy from breakfast food to snacks—that is far too great a leap
because the two businesses are so different from one another. Kellogg
is in essence founding an entirely new company with a different
mission and an entirely new strategic plan. An important first step has
been taken: in late 2000 Kellogg acquired the snack food company
Keebler in a multibillion-dollar deal. The company is evidently quite
serious about transforming itself. The odds against it successfully
doing so are great.

It was noted earlier that a firm's mission is fixed. The only
exception to that is when a company, like Kellogg, transmutes itself
into something totally different from what it had been. The original
company has de facto died, taking its mission with it to the corporate
graveyard. Such a company has not merely changed strategy, it has
undergone an entire metamorphosis that calls for a quite different
mission and a correspondingly new strategic plan. There is no greater
management challenge than this born-again transition. Changing
strategy is hard enough; successfully changing mission is much harder
still. It is difficult to identify even half a dozen examples of companies
that have successfully done so.

Strategic errors then trace back to missions that are either too
vague—think Apple—or, paradoxically, too precise—think Kellogg.
If too vague, they provide inadequate strategic guidance. If too
specific, they circumscribe strategic choice. Missions may also simply
be wrong for the times: too early or too late. In any case, an
inappropriate mission leads to a firm's demise. There is nothing more
fundamental than the mission—it is the starting point for the strategic
plan of any business enterprise and serves to keep the firm centered
and anchored as storms of market vicissitudes sweep across it. Yet too
often the mission is given short-shrift. Clausewitz wrote that "No war

should begin until it is first determined what is to be achieved and how it will be conducted." He was referring specifically to mission and the overall strategic plan. Going to war without a clearly defined mission in Somalia and Vietnam led to serious problems for the United States. In the former conflict, captured Rangers were dragged naked through the streets of Mogadishu and eighteen American lives were needlessly lost. And in Vietnam, a lack of agreement on mission resulted in Presidents Kennedy, Johnson and Nixon leading a divided nation, much to the detriment of the grunts in the jungles and rice paddies of Southeast Asia, where thousands of them died. The problem in both cases was an ambiguous and all-too-vague military mission. In war or business, the setting of the mission is crucial to the strategic plan. But once established, attention turns to the satellite snapshot.

Satellite Snapshot

"To assure victory, always carefully survey the field before battle," wrote Sun Tzu. That is easier to do for a military commander today than it was for Sun Tzu, 2,500 years ago. With orbiting satellites overhead, military commanders today can obtain a comprehensive and near-perfect snapshot of a potential battlefield in order to determine strategy well before the guns begin to fire. Once a strategy has been set and the battle has been joined, future satellite snapshots track the strategy's effectiveness. Modest adjustments over time may be necessary. Bill Gates, for one, has allowed, and indeed encouraged, Microsoft's strategies to adjust slowly and evolve as circumstances change.

A business equivalent of the military satellite snapshot at the least should include detailed competitor, customer, industry, technology, macroeconomic, legal, demographic, political and government quantitative and qualitative information. In addition, the "satellite lens" should be turned inward to deeply probe and audit the organization's own strengths and weaknesses—its technology, manpower, assets, allies and more.

Mentally underscore "competitor" in the above list. For a decade now the corporate focus has been on the customer. That has been a good thing, but not enough attention has been given to the competitor and the competitive environment. Michael Porter, of Harvard, has written: "A strategy not grounded in competitive rivalry will fail."[8] A marketing, financial, manufacturing or any other strategic plan must take the competition into account; indeed, strategy should be *directed* at the competition. Focusing only on the customer is far too one-dimensional. Customer *and* the operating environment *and* especially the competitor need full attention. "We should have done a better job of predicting the strength of our competitors,"[9] said Cynthia Trudell, head of the Saturn Division at GM. She was referring to the greatly disappointing launch of Saturn's midsize S series. Saturn did detailed consumer research but did not adequately consider its competitors' counterstrategies. The consumer is the prize to be won, on an ever-changing battlefield, with the competitors as adversaries standing in the way of the prize.

The legendary Sam Walton pioneered his version of the satellite snapshot at Wal-Mart. During the company's early years, from Monday through Friday, senior Wal-Mart people, including Mr. Sam himself, would crisscross the country prowling the aisles of their own as well as competitors' stores. They would come together Saturday mornings back in Bentonville, Arkansas, to review their findings. As effective as that approach was, it isn't good enough now when companies need to operate in real time 24-7-365—24 hours a day, 7 days a week, 365 days a year. Today, details of every Wal-Mart customer purchase in every store across the country are instantly transmitted from the optical scanner at the cash register to a satellite feed atop the store building and finally to corporate headquarters—literally a satellite snapshot. Nevertheless, while leading-edge Information Technology has replaced some of Wal-Mart's early methods, the underlying process remains. The company's two top executives, David Glass and Lee Scott, still spend considerable time on the road visiting their stores and checking out the competition. Wal-Mart's top people know that insights derived from the sight, sound and touch of firsthand experiences can be obtained in no other way.

GE, a believer in benchmarking and taking sound ideas from others, has adopted the Wal-Mart approach as its own. Then there is Sony's CEO Nobuyuki Idei, a kind of Japanese Sam Walton, who likes to wander through Tokyo's electronics stores on the weekends talking to salespeople and customers about his, and the competitors', products. Finally, Cisco, probably the most wired company on the planet, provides its CEO John Chambers and other senior people with constantly updated information that is cut, diced and chopped in any way that is useful. For Wal-Mart, GE, Sony, Cisco and a growing list of other strong companies, the satellite snapshot has become invaluable.

The sources of competitor intelligence that feed into a company's satellite snapshot are manifold. They include debriefing employees hired away from competitors, visiting trade shows, tracking patent filings, benchmarking, reverse engineering and consumer research as well as readily available media information. Truth be known, there is also more than a little clandestine, quasi-legal industrial espionage going on. All of this gathered information must be compiled and made readily accessible. The military's organization structure includes so-called G2, or intelligence, units that are responsible for gathering and analyzing information about the enemy. With very few exceptions, a formal or at least informal business equivalent is a necessity. Indeed, most of the *Fortune* 500 today have competitor intelligence units.

In the first months of the Civil War, the Union armies were defeated by the Confederates in battle after battle. Abraham Lincoln, flailing about for a strategy, poured his frustrations into a letter to a friend: "If we first knew where we are and whither we are going we could better judge what to do and how to do it." The satellite snapshot tells us "where we are." It describes in detail the current state of the battlefield. It is a prerequisite for setting, and later monitoring, military or business strategy.

Future Scan

Having a detailed understanding of the existing battlefield is crucial in setting strategy—but only a beginning step. Strategy setting certainly takes account of the present but, more important, it is largely based on perceptions of the future—it is there that strategy will play itself out. Craig McCaw, billionaire CEO of Teledesic and a pioneer of wireless telephony says, "You have to think like an anthropologist about what people will soon want, and build for that future."[10] Paul Allen, Microsoft's cofounder and megabillionaire, always asks before investing in a new company: "What is this going to look like five years from now?"[11] Even if they are tacit, or subconscious, perceptions and assumptions about the future are the bases on which strategy is decided. Although not detailed here, regression, sensitivity, decision and Monte Carlo analysis, game and chaos theory and a variety of other statistical and nonstatistical methods can be helpful to scan the future; however, they are limited in recognizing coming revolutionary changes. Something more is needed. Schopenhauer wrote that "Each of us takes the limits of our own field of vision for the limits of the world." Following from this is the exhortation to "Think out of the box"—that is, the limited box of one's own vision. MTV seems able to do that.

For two decades now, MTV has stayed ahead of competitors in the fickle and impulse-oriented youth entertainment market by successfully assessing the future. MTV's CEO, Tom Freston, explains some of his approach: "We do a tremendous amount of questionnaire and open-end consumer research, we go to clubs, hire many young people, read youth magazines, watch the competition . . . all that serves as an early warning system for newly breaking trends."[12]

In another example of the future scan there is Duke Energy Corp. At a recent planning session in Houston, strategists laid out three scenarios for the upcoming two years. The scenarios dealt with GDP growth, energy prices, interest rates and some twenty other indicators. "We try to predict regulatory trends, technology, environmental issues, Wall Street signals and other factors and then war game the various scenarios," says CEO Richard Priory. "We especially look at our primary competitor, Enron, and what it might do to determine how we will be impacted."[13]

The future scan should include the same issues as those discussed for the satellite snapshot: What will customers, markets, demographics, the economy, technology and especially competitors be like years from now? Accurately identifying a trend before anyone else is key to developing a winning strategy. Here's a Bechtel story.

Bechtel, one of the world's largest privately held construction companies, has long been a leader in hydroelectric, highway, bridge, pipeline and refinery projects. That business has been profitable but of relatively modest growth. In the late 1990s, the company had been looking for new opportunities. Perhaps because of its headquarters' location in San Francisco, right next door to Silicon Valley, the future scan of Bechtel's strategic planners picked up on the inchoate e-commerce boom. The result: In the year 2000, Bechtel signed $3 billion in construction contracts for distribution centers and ware-houses with e-company clients Webvan, Equinix and iMotors.

It has been said that every great drama has its foreshadow. True, but shadows are often difficult to discern, their shapes are vague and indefinite. How can one judge or determine amid the clutter and fog of war, or business, what is truly a harbinger of an unfolding future that calls for strategic change? Intel's experience sheds some light.

In the early 1980s, Intel was among the recognized world leaders in research, design and manufacturing of electronic components. Its specialty was dynamic random access memory (DRAM) chips. But slowly at first, then more rapidly, the Koreans and the Japanese invaded the market with better and cheaper products. Andy Grove, then Intel's CEO, and his people constantly monitored the situation. Nearly two centuries ago, Clausewitz wrote that "A great part of information obtained in war is contradictory, a still greater part is false, and by far the greatest part of a doubtful character." Business information is often just as problematic. Was what the Intel people saw an actual structural change in the industry or just another market fluctuation, part of the perpetual chaos and false signals emanating from everyday business activity? For two gut-wrenching years of lost profit margins, debate raged within Intel regarding the industry's future. "We agonized over this,"[14] says Grove. Finally he and his people concluded that a radical marketplace change was indeed occurring that called for a significant alteration in strategy. Grove dubs strategic inflection points like these "10X events"—events that completely alter the status quo. Intel responded in 1985 by shifting product strategy to the more sophisticated, higher-value-added semi-conductor microprocessor devices. It was a wise decision. Intel has since come to dominate the PC chip market, the omnipresent *Intel inside.*

Merrill Lynch is facing a 10X event with the recent exponential growth in online trading led by Charles Schwab—$29.95, not $250.00 trading commissions are becoming the norm. It is not yet clear how Merrill Lynch will respond but it is clear that it cannot stand still, not with the industry at a crossroads.

Toys "R" Us was shocked by Internet upstarts attacking its market. Wayne Huizenga's AutoNation is a threat to traditional auto dealerships. Comcast Cable is being challenged by the sudden appearance of satellite TV companies like EchoStar and DirecTV. Newspapers that earn as much as 25 percent of their revenues from classified ads are being carpet-bombed by e-commerce start-ups. The leading supermarket chains, Kroger and Albertson's, find themselves menaced by the sudden entry of Wal-Mart into the grocery business. Motorola, once the leader in cellular phones, was dethroned in only a few years by Nokia with its digital technology. The near-century-old recorded music industry has seen its very foundation shaken by new MP3 Internet downloading technology and brash upstarts like Napster that provide free musical offerings. Kodak's hundred-year film business may disappear under a coming avalanche of digital photography. No business is immune.

Fed Chairman Alan Greenspan has said that "The best forecast is made with the freshest data."[15] That data is needed to detect 10X events that are often on, or just over, the horizon. Failure to constantly future scan and adjust strategies accordingly can be fatal. Encyclopaedia Britannica offers a case in point.

Only five years ago the highly respected Encyclopaedia Britannica held a near monopoly in its field. The excellent resource work, even at a price of $1,500 per set, could be found in millions of homes and libraries in the United States. For generations these volumes were the sole source of general factual enlightenment and a quite adequate starting point for more serious research. Then came Microsoft's $49 Encarta software attack—a 10X event that went unchallenged by Britannica. Within three years, over 80 percent of Britannica's annual sales were lost. It might be too late for a counterattack. The company may well find itself utterly destroyed simply because its future scan did not pick up the Encarta blip. Or perhaps the company—that is, its senior management—*did* detect the Microsoft presence but fantasyland-like wished it away. Arizona Senator John McCain knows about that.

The American prisoners of war held in Vietnam were always looking for signs and clues that the war was winding down and that they would soon be freed. For five terrible years, John McCain was one of those prisoners. He recalls, "In Hanoi, inmates would spot a tiny change in routine and think the war was over. 'I got a piece of carrot in my soup today!' they'd say. 'We're going home!' But they weren't and it didn't, for years. I swore then: I'm not going to get excited until I see an American in uniform."[16] It is difficult not to be influenced by our hopes and fears in evaluating the future scan.

It is often a difficult challenge for an organization to objectively foresee the future. Denial is rife. Illusion an anodyne. GE's Welch says, "Optimism has an important place, but you must face reality."[17] Change brings with it a fear of the unknown future; inertia and paralysis are often the result. Individual and organizational reputations built on past successes resist change and cling to the status quo. Jurgen Schrempp, chairman of DaimlerChrysler, has told his people to "Be excited about change—don't fear it. Be part of it."[18] Failure to adhere to that maxim leads to disaster on the battlefield as well as in the marketplace. When the need to act is finally recognized, the competitive battle may already have been lost. The future scan then, and what it detects, is crucial to setting strategy: A future perceived to be quite unlike the present likely will call for strategies quite different from those currently in place.

Strategic Building Blocks

Completing a strategic plan as outlined here requires much hard, slogging compilation of data and information followed up with painstaking analysis. But something substantially different is needed in crafting the strategic building blocks that together comprise the overall strategy and are the essence of the strategic plan. What is required is the quality of genius and intellectual reason. Clausewitz believed that war was a "paradoxical trinity" of primordial violence, chance and reason and that only genius could provide the reasoning power necessary to design exactly the right strategic building blocks for a given set of current and projected circumstances. While "genius" might be something of an exaggeration, strategy setting surely must be the province of very smart and experienced people.

Strategic building blocks are at the heart of a strategic plan. In designing them, several factors must be taken into account. The more important of them are listed below.

They should number roughly between three and seven, certainly not more than ten. "You have to be very sparing in the number of strategic initiatives undertaken,"[19] says Scott McNealy, Sun's CEO.

Each building block is mission-critical. If the strategy fails, the mission will not be realized. In addition, each building block must be mission-consistent, no strategy can be contrary to the mission's language or intent.

Each building block should be targeted, directly, or at the least indirectly, at the competition.

Each block requires substantial financial and human capital resources including concerted management attention. Limitations on that attention explain why strategic building blocks must be relatively few in number. Steve Case of America Online says, "We trounced Microsoft in online services because for us it is a basic strategy while for them it is just one other thing, of many, to worry about."[20]

Each building block is projected to remain largely unchanged far out into the future, for years, even decades. Only 10X events significantly alter them. Jack Welch has made only half a dozen strategic changes in nineteen years at General Electric.

Each is complementary to the others.

Each is determined by the organization's top management.

Finally, and of great importance, carefully crafted strategic building blocks combine to provide a who, what, where, when and how organizational action blueprint. Upon implementation they are intended to neutralize and overcome the competition.

Setting strategy, as noted earlier, calls for experience and the reasoning power of genius. Gen. Douglas MacArthur had both.

MacArthur's victorious WWII Pacific campaign was made up of six strategic building blocks: Bypass certain enemy strongholds; coordinate air, sea and ground forces; concentrate forces at the point of attack; leadership mystique—a mix of arrogance, intimidation, symbols and an almost Shakespearean writing and speaking style; use of captured islands to launch air attacks against future targets; and finally, co-opt superiors, especially President Franklin Delano Roosevelt and Chief of Staff Gen. George Marshall.

To implement any one organization-wide strategic building block requires lower-level divisions and departments to develop their own organization plans and detailed operational orders—a cascade of them. These plans and orders also all complement and reinforce one another and contribute to the execution of the larger building block. Thus MacArthur's strategic building block of sea, air and land coordination became the mission for his subordinate commanders' strategic plans. In turn, their building blocks became missions for those reporting directly to them. Not more than two, or certainly three, levels of this should be necessary. In a similar way, a corporation's strategic building blocks must have implementing divisional and departmental finance, human resources, manufacturing, marketing, information technology and other plans. GE Capital, by way of one example, assures those plans are developed by involving hundreds of people from various business units throughout the organization in its planning process.

Well-crafted and boldly executed strategic building blocks are the linchpin of a successful military campaign. They provide the entire armed force with the guiding architecture for achieving the most audacious of missions. What holds on the battlefield also holds in the business arena, where strategies often are the deciding determinants of success or failure. Later chapters explore the Lexus strategy of attacking Cadillac's strength, Boeing's strategy of patience against Air Industrie, Procter & Gamble's strategy of containment against Unilever, Wal-Mart's strategy of attacking Sears' weakness, Microsoft's choke point control strategy and more. Strategy is the underlying competitive advantage for any prosperous company, domestic or global, no matter its size or industry.

Performance Targets

A MacArthur island invasion plan had a targeted D-Day, or initial landing date, as well as a forward timetable of targets: beach secured D-Day plus two, landing strip captured by D-Day plus nine, mop-up D-Day plus twenty-three and so on. As the battle unfolded, progress toward those targets was tracked to discern the need for strategic, or more likely tactical, adjustment. Performance targets, including milestones to be achieved along the way, are basic to a strategic plan but there are problems in presetting them.

Strategies that are unclear or misdirected lead to performance targets that are too ambitious or not ambitious enough or simply wrong. Unintended, and often disastrous, consequences are the likely result. A classic military and then a business example follow.

The Vietnam battlefield was kaleidoscopic. It changed from day to day with no, or only vague, battle lines. Often there was no front. The enemy, the Viet Cong, or VC as they were known, had infiltrated from the north and intermingled with the general population of South Vietnam. The VC attacked in small numbers and then melted back into the surrounding villages and farms—guerrilla warfare at its best. With no physical geographic performance targets available, the Americans opted for "body count" as their scorecard, which proved to be a terrible mistake. A dead Viet Cong was indistinguishable from a neutral civilian farmer. While under fire, the Americans were understandably often not terribly scrupulous about drawing a distinction. The unfortunate civilian massacre at My Lai by an American infantry platoon under the command of Lt. William Calley was an unintended consequence of the body-count performance target. Similar events, although generally far less lethal in result, occur all too often in business.

In spite of a venerable past, few companies have been more poorly managed over the last few decades than Sears. Many of a series of unending debacles have stemmed from Sears' flawed strategies and linked performance targets. In the late 1980s top management felt that the Sears auto repair and maintenance operations had unsatisfactorily low profit margins. Targets were substantially and unreasonably raised and great pressure brought to bear on local managers to achieve them. At the Sears auto service centers around the country, front-line staff, seeing they were given an impossible task, responded. "The suits want more profit? We'll give them more profit." Work orders were falsified, unnecessary repairs were made on customer vehicles and overcharging became the norm. When the story of consumer fraud eventually came to light, dozens of state attorneys general sued Sears for hundreds of millions of dollars. That loss was minor compared to the tarnishing of a once-sterling brand name. Then, in another Sears example, in 1997 the company was forced to write off half a billion dollars in credit card receivables. Corporate senior management had, a year before, set a target of greatly increasing the number of Sears credit card holders with the intent of bringing more customers into the stores. Cards, a blizzard of them, were made available to people with problematic credit history. This was manna for many of the happy recipients who rushed to their nearest Sears, spent extravagantly, ran up big bills . . . and did not pay. Sears compounded the problem by using illegal methods to pressure debtors for payments. Once again the company paid multimillion-dollar fines. Unintended consequences of performance targets have badly hurt Sears; they can hurt any company.

Gen. George Marshall once wrote that "If you get the objectives right, a lieutenant can write the strategy." He was no doubt overstating to make a point. But it is a good point. Performance objectives or targets must be carefully drawn. They should be quantitative with an eye to unintended consequences. Time dimensions should be included and a responsible individual or organization must be assigned. AOL's chairman, Steve Case, has set a dated performance target for his company: "We will have the world's largest market cap by 2004."[21]

Conventional budgets, as well as financial targets including ROE, Ebitda, EPS, EVA and a dozen more acronyms so beloved by senior management in general and chief financial officers (CFOs) in particular are important but not enough. Equally, perhaps more, important are process targets that, for example, relate to the company's customer service, product quality, new product development or on-time delivery. It can be argued that these process targets are more important than financial and outcome targets because they are determinants of the latter.

Business performance targets then fall into three broad categories indicated by the following examples in Table 3.2.

Table 3.2

Type	Target	Date	Responsibility
Financial	ROE 17%	6.1.03	CEO
Process	Six sigma standard	8.4.02	Plant manager
Outcome	43 new store openings	3.1.04	Business development dept.

Target monitoring should be ongoing with key targets reviewed at the most senior levels. In the two Sears debacles just noted, top management claimed ignorance of the situation. The CEO, in each case, was astonished to discover what had occurred, truly astonished. In sharp contrast to this, at a recent senior management Wal-Mart meeting, CEO David Glass led a spirited half-hour discussion of the problem of empty pegs at women's in-store hosiery displays. Sears problems never would have escaped the panty-hose monitoring eyes of Wal-Mart's management.

Required Resources

Over the centuries, war has seen many incompetent generals—butchers really. In WWI, for example, the French general Ferdinand Foch following a German attack against his army told his superiors, "My centre is giving way, my right is in retreat, situation excellent. I attack." Attack he did, right into the Germans' waiting machine guns that scythed the advancing French *poilu*s. Wave after wave of infantry fell. At Verdun, the Somme, Ypres, St. Mihiel and Amiens, Foch applied apparently the only strategy he knew: advance directly into enemy fire. This approach was perhaps appropriate for earlier wars, before the advent of the machine gun, barbed wire, mortars and Krupp cannon, but not for this one. Foch stubbornly contended that "Machine guns are overrated, airplanes are silly and tanks are mere toys." With that leadership and that kind of strategic thinking, some 2 million Frenchmen died in the war and another 5 million were wounded. It was a terrible, flagrant and wanton waste of the most precious of resources.

In warfare, resources take two forms: materiel and manpower. Materiel includes weapons, shells, ground transport, ships, aircraft, communications gear and the entirety of the armamentarium of war. The second resource, and far more precious, are the lives of the military's young men and, more recently at least in American history, young women. Availability of required resources is a necessary and crucial part of the strategic plan.

There are two antipodal approaches to determining the number and amounts of those human and financial resources. The first is to finalize the plan, as outlined above, proceeding sequentially from mission to performance targets, and then, as a last step, simply tote up the corresponding human and financial resources required for implementation. Then, one way or another, obtain the resources. In the case of warfare, a nation-state typically calls for volunteers or drafts required personnel and generally borrows the needed financing. A second approach reverses this process. Given the satellite snapshot and the future scan, it *begins* with the available resources and works backward to set the mission, strategic building blocks and performance targets. The mission and performance targets, so determined, are likely to be far more modest, and strategic building blocks far more innovative, than those obtained using the first approach. In practice there is much give-and-take between the two approaches. In the end, a precise head count and capital and operating dollar figures are obtained. By way of example, the Gartner Group, a leading authority on Information Technology, is adding an e-business strategy. "It will require 100 new personnel and $70 million for hiring, training and compensation funding,"[22] said a spokeswoman.

MacArthur once observed, "I will not take by sacrifice of men what I can take by strategy." However they are obtained, resources are always limited. A government that depletes its treasury and kills off large numbers of its young people in warfare faces internal revolt. Examples of this include: the murder of the Aztec chieftain Montezuma by his people following their disatrous defeat and subjugation by the Spaniards, the forced abdication of Kaiser Wilhelm II from his throne following Germany's costly WWI defeat and Lyndon Johnson's stepping down from the presidency because of his badly flawed Vietnam policy. In the business arena, equity or debt capital is always available but at a price that constrains and circumscribes action. If that capital is wasted, the inevitable result is bankruptcy, takeover or, at the very least, stockholder and board insurrection and the CEO's forced resignation. Al Dunlap of Sunbeam, Robert Allen of AT&T, Jill Barad of Mattel, Doug Ivester of Coca-Cola, Gil Amelio of Apple, Roger Smith of GM and Durk Jager of Procter & Gamble are among the last decade's guillotined corporate leaders whose fall can be traced directly to failed strategy and in many cases squandered resources.

Process

The key elements of the strategic planning model from mission to required resources have now been summarized. One additional point needs to be made. Strategic planning is an *ongoing* process. It must be because the world is not static. As the satellite snapshot and future scan change, so, too, do the underlying assumptions upon which the strategic plan is built. Companies conventionally deal with change by holding annual planning sessions in which a three-, five- or ten-year plan is revised. The frequency of the plan's updating and the period over which the plan is projected is a function of the business and the industry. For General Electric, the company's top 500 people meet annually just after the New Year holiday at Boca Raton to discuss strategic planning issues. John Chambers, CEO of Cisco, says, "Today, we still do most of our [planning] in the two-year scenario."[23] Disney plans longer into the future—a coming Hong Kong amusement park will take five years to complete. Royal Dutch/Shell looks even further ahead—half a century.

The importance of the strategic planning process itself, involving responsible management from throughout the company, cannot be overemphasized. Indeed, the process is nearly as important as the completed plan. The hammering out of positions, insights into what the future might bring, the eliciting of opinions, the occasional eureka, the assurance that all divisions of the organization are coordinating their efforts—all this and more comes out of the process.

Scheduled periodic planning sessions must of course be augmented by unscheduled meetings during times of crisis. The purpose of these crisis resolution meetings is to, first, stave off disaster, perform triage and stabilize the situation. Once that has occurred, attention must again turn to strategy. Paul Saffo, director of the Institute for the Future, is but one expert who has argued the importance of long-term thinking in periods of rapid change. The planning process, carried out in the often chaotic present, should include a look to the past from which lessons can be learned as well as a look to the future where ultimate destiny is to be found.

"We Made a Big Mistake"

Akamai is one of the many new companies born of the febrile Internet era. It designs software for Web downloading. In late 1999, with Akamai's stock reaching new highs, its CEO, George Conrades, was quoted as saying "Everything moves so fast that we don't plan strategy for more than ninety days at a time."[24] Perhaps he was being facetious, perhaps not. As has been noted earlier, strategies must stay in place for years, even decades, not 90 days. By that definition, according to its president, Akamai really had *no* strategy. That may have been all right until the business world turned for the company. Akamai, a Nasdaq-listed company, once at $345 a share, is, at the time of this writing, trading at $12. The precipitous stock decline reflects the company's difficulties. Perhaps meaningful strategic planning might, after all, be a good idea.

Harvard's Gary Hamel estimates that American senior management, in general, spends about 3 percent of its time thinking about the long-term future. While 3 percent may be adequate for a start-up Internet company whose leader's tacit mission is an Initial Public Offering (IPO), cash in and early exit, it is not good enough if senior management is intent on building a company that will endure.

A well-crafted strategic plan brings to a company, division or department a measure of control over an uncertain future and its own destiny. Sony, since its inception, has tried to create its own future. The Sony Walkman is an example of that. Without prior market research, the device was designed, manufactured and then sold to a public that suddenly discovered it just *had* to have one. Masaru Ibuka, Sony's honorary chairman, says "Our emphasis has always been to make something out of nothing."[25] A strategic plan, as described in this chapter, is the first step in doing that. Belatedly, fine companies, even those in the fast-moving world of the Internet, such as Amazon.com, are recognizing that truth. "We have made a big mistake in overlooking the strategic planning process; we have been way too seat-of-the-pants,"[26] says the company's chairman Jeff Bezos.

The essence of the strategic plan are the strategies themselves. Albeit with a multitude of variations, there exist a surprisingly small number of winning strategies for military and, by extension, business campaigns. The following ten chapters present some of the most important of them, one per chapter.

Each military strategy is introduced and then brought to the business arena, beginning, in chapter 4, with the ancient but still much practiced Japanese military strategy of attacking strength.

CHAPTER FOUR

Tora! Tora! Tora!

Attack Strength

To capture the baby tiger you have to go into the mother tiger's lair.

—Japanese military maxim

Our strategy for going after this [Iraqi] army is very, very simple. First we are going to cut it off and then we are going to kill it.

—Colin Powell[1]

When you strike at a king, you must kill him.

—Ralph Waldo Emerson

Gibraltar of the Pacific

At precisely 7:55 A.M., local time, hours of radio silence were suddenly shattered with the crackling of a thrice repeated Tora, or tiger, code message. It was the signal from the dashing young Cmdr. Mitsuo Fuchida to his 216-plane air armada to begin bombing, torpedoing and strafing the sought after prize: America's Pacific Fleet. A few hours later the attack was over. The Japanese victory was nearly complete. The U.S. toll was massive: battleships, destroyers, cruisers, minesweepers and auxiliary ships sunk, burning or capsized; oil depots and shore facilities destroyed. Among the 3,581 casualties were hundreds of the crew from the sunken battleship *Arizona*, who, unable to escape, were trapped belowdecks where their bodies remain to this day. The Japanese had successfully attacked Pearl Harbor, thought to have been the Gibraltar of the Pacific, impervious to attack. It wasn't—not on that early morning of December 7, 1941.

"To capture the baby tiger you have to go into the mother tiger's lair," goes a Japanese military maxim. The Japanese had moved to strategically attack America's strength, the mother tiger's lair, at Pearl Harbor. They had taken the prized baby tiger that was the Pacific Fleet. A great battle had been won.

Pearl Harbor was the centerpiece of a brilliantly choreographed and perfectly synchronized Japanese assault against a score of enemy strongholds spread over nearly one-quarter of the world. Near-simultaneous attacks were unleashed against British, French and Dutch fortresses in Malaysia, Indochina and Indonesia respectively. It was a masterful stroke. In a single day, American and European colonial powers that had dominated much of the Far East for centuries were suddenly thrown on the defensive and barely holding on. The Japanese had used a strategy of boldly attacking strength—and had triumphed.

This attack-strength strategy has led to military victory countless times over a thousand years and more of warfare. The Duke of Marlborough, the most successful of early eighteenth-century British military commanders, became renowned for it. It was the practice as well of Sweden's Charles XII and the North's Civil War hero, Ulysses S. Grant. In the Gulf War, United Nations' forces attacked and destroyed Saddam Hussein's strength, his vaunted Republican Guard. Desert Storm was won. And now this winning strategy has come to the highly competitive world of business.

UPS and FedEx

The strategy of attacking strength has been employed with extraordinary effectiveness in the business wars. Starbucks practices it by opening coffee shops in proximity to established competitors—next door or across the street. Nordstrom is assaulting Nieman Marcus in the latter's powerful Dallas home base. A decade ago, Lexus took on Cadillac and Lincoln in the U.S. luxury car market where the two American companies had a near monopoly; in 1999 Lexus outsold both of them. Rupert Murdoch's News Corp. has contested the entrenched Big Three networks, CBS, NBC and ABC. In the late 1990s, AT&T shook the cable industry with its multibillion-dollar acquisitions of TCI and MediaOne; almost overnight AT&T grabbed 40 percent domestic market share from powerful industry leaders. In 1989, Irwin Jacobs, CEO of Qualcomm, took on the established wireless technology standards TDMA in the United States and GSM in Europe with his own CDMA standard—from a standing start he now has some 20 percent of the market and might just take it all. As a final example, the high-margin overnight air delivery business, long the well-protected fortress of FedEx, is being challenged by the brown-clad men and women of UPS. In each of these cases, the aggressor attacked the competitor's strength as a winning strategy.

Strategic Choice: Prevailing Circumstances

"Strategy . . . takes [circumstances] as it finds them," wrote Clausewitz. First there are the circumstances, and then the strategy to best deal with them is developed. The effectiveness of the attack-strength, or any other, strategy depends largely on current and projected prevailing circumstances. A strategy that is highly successful in one situation may well fail abjectly in another.

The circumstances surrounding every military battle are different, as they are for every business situation. Strategies must therefore be chosen accordingly. For an armed forces commander to select an attack-strength strategy, the prevailing circumstances should include three specific conditions: his own current state of affairs is untenable, his enemy is strong but vulnerable and finally, that time is working on the enemy's side. Look at each of these in some detail.

Current Situation Untenable

The first circumstance on a checklist for choosing an attack-strength strategy is that one's current situation is untenable. For the Japanese prior to Pearl Harbor, the American, British, French and Dutch powers were stubbornly protecting their own Pacific interests and blocking Japanese expansionism. The Westerners threatened to embargo oil, rubber, tin and other crucial raw material shipments to resource-poor Japan unless it ceased and indeed reversed its imperialist ambitions. Thus if the Japanese continued their military aggression, an embargo would put at risk their economic survival. But at the same time, it was impossible for Japan, steeped in the warrior code of Bushido with its attendant pride and honor, to back down, genuflect to the *gaijin*, or barbarians, of the Western powers and accept the humiliation of a secondary place among the nations of the world. Japan could not retreat and the status quo could not be sustained. Japan's situation in 1941, prior to Pearl Harbor, was untenable.

Enemy Strong but Vulnerable

A second prevailing circumstance that suggests choosing the attack-strength strategy is that while the enemy may indeed have a powerful stronghold, overall he is complacent, unprepared and lacks the will to fight. That is a largely accurate description of America's vulnerability during the decade just before the Japanese attack on Pearl Harbor.

It was a far different America at the turn of the century, when, in 1901, President Teddy Roosevelt coined the phrase, "Speak softly and carry a big stick," referring to the country's considerable military strength following land and sea victories in the 1898 war against Spain. But at the precipice of WWII, the reverse held true: America swaggered quite loudly through the geopolitical corridors of the world but carried no stick at all. Throughout the 1930s and into 1941, America's army ranked sixteenth in the world with barely 190,000 men. Lacking equipment, infantry training was sometimes carried out using cardboard cutouts of tanks and broomsticks for rifles. The air force lacked planes that could even begin to approach the speed, maneuverability and armament of Japan's Mitsubishi-built Zero; even if planes were available, there were no trained pilots to fly them. The navy was relatively strong but was deficient in aircraft carriers and was itself susceptible to enemy air attack—just how susceptible, the world was about to discover.

The vulnerable state of the military was a reflection of the American people's isolationist sentiment. President Woodrow Wilson had told the country during WWI that their sacrifices were necessary because "The world must be made safe for democracy." Well, in retrospect, the sacrifices were in vain. The world was at risk once again, and Americans were reluctant to be drawn into yet another war, certainly not when the oceans of the Atlantic and Pacific, to the east and west respectively, provided barriers that could not be breached. Pearl Harbor was the smash to the mouth that taught them otherwise. So from the Japanese viewpoint, their enemy was strong, certainly at Pearl Harbor, but overall quite vulnerable.

Time Working Against You

Third in the set of circumstances is that time is working for the enemy. Every day the enemy becomes relatively stronger while you become weaker. Again, back to 1941, the American president, FDR, was making every effort to stir the country to military preparedness. Here and there responsible people were quietly joining him. Slowly, reluctantly, Americans were beginning to accept the inevitability of war.

The Japanese realized they could not contend with a fully armed and combat-ready United States. Unlike their own country the United States was rich in natural resources, with a vast industrial capacity nearly ten times their own, a landmass twenty-five times greater and a population twice their size. Once awakened, America would be a formidable foe. From the perspective of the Japanese, time was on the side of the Americans.

In summary then, the Japanese deemed the prevailing three circumstances necessary to select an attack-strength strategy to be in place. So, too, for the companies noted earlier that have adopted the same strategy. Consider News Corp. as just one example.

A decade ago, the conventional wisdom was that network television would forever be dominated by the Big Three: CBS, NBC and ABC. Rupert Murdoch, with his modest cable and local television holdings, realized that unless he acted, that conventional wisdom would prove to be true. He knew his existing situation was untenable. It was only a question of time until the networks themselves expanded into cable and in the process bulldozed his own operations. The Big Three, with half a century of dominance, had some 70 percent of the viewing audience and were financially more than strong enough to fend off a new competitor. At the same time their very dominance had led to complacency with its attendant unimaginative programming and high advertising rates. Their ownership problems also made them vulnerable. NBC was part of GE, which had many other things on its plate; ABC was still grappling with its new parent Disney; and CBS was looking around for someone to buy it. Still, given time, the three networks could be expected to overcome their difficulties. The prevailing circumstances for attacking strength were in place. Murdoch struck: *The Simpsons*, *X-Files*, NFL football, *Married With Children*, Fox News and *King of the Hill* have enjoyed high Nielsen numbers. Murdoch attacked strength . . . and won. The Fox Network is now a profitable reality. The Big Three has become the Big Four and Murdoch has only begun to fight.

NEWSFLASH! (January 10, 2001) *Temptation Island* has just begun airing on Fox. The program involves buffed and half-naked young people, not actors, capriciously changing love partners—or something like that. At work here is a kind of Gresham's Law with bad taste driving out good taste. It is wonderful for ratings.

Factors of Success

Given that the prevailing circumstances just discussed have been largely met and the attack-strength strategy has been chosen, what design and execution factors are necessary for its success? Whether dealing with a military enemy or a business competitor, the factors are the same: diligent reconnaissance, exhaustive preparedness, dedicated leadership, concentration and coordination of resources, surprise and a detailed strategic plan. These are all critical when attacking an adversary's power base and destroying his or her forces, weaponry, morale and willingness for further combat. Consider each of these factors in some detail.

Satellite Snapshot

For nearly two years prior to the Pearl Harbor attack, lax American security allowed Japanese spies, operating out of their consulate in

Hawaii, to surreptitiously photograph and diagram every aspect of the harbor as well as surrounding army and air force ground facilities. Ship movements in and out of the harbor were carefully monitored . . . not difficult since naval ship arrivals and departures were helpfully printed in the local newspaper, the *Honolulu Advertiser*. American fleet firepower, ground antiaircraft and land-based fighter planes were diligently counted and cataloged by Japanese intelligence agents masquerading as typical tourists with their gaily colored shirts and ubiquitous cameras. Daily wind, tide and weather reports were tracked. It was noted that security levels were at their lowest on Sunday mornings because large numbers of American servicemen spent Saturday evenings on leave too heavily sampling the offerings of Honolulu's red-light district.

All of this comprehensive reconnaissance yielded vast amounts of information that was forwarded to Tokyo and fed into the satellite snapshot of the Japanese strategic plan. The Japanese success at Pearl Harbor was significantly due to the detailed accuracy of the plan's satellite snapshot—attacking forces knew in advance what likely would be encountered.

A company or smaller business unit adopting this attack-strength strategy must be as assiduous in gathering competitor intelligence as the Japanese were in gathering enemy intelligence in those ominous days just before the outbreak of WWII. In business or war, one does not successfully attack strength without the advantage of the detailed information supplied by the satellite snapshot.

Exhaustive Preparedness

The Roman Publilius Syrus wrote, "War should be long in preparing in order that you may conquer the more quickly." The Japanese understood that principle. Almost a year before the actual Pearl Harbor attack, intense training and preparation had begun. Over and over again Japanese pilots took off, simulated attacks and then returned to their carriers—methodically, incessantly honing their skills. The training, carried out in remote Kagoshima Bay, among the southernmost of the main Japanese islands, far from prying Western eyes, was continuous, hour after hour, day after day, month after month. Finally, men, machines and munitions were thoroughly tested and ready. They waited only for the signal to attack.

Contrast that with Iridium's 1997 launch of its sixty-six satellite-based wireless phone system that was to provide voice, data, cellular pager and Internet capabilities. It was intended as a challenge to the strength of established international and domestic telcos, but Iridium's preparedness was abysmal. An unexplained scheduling mishap resulted in the entire $180 million advertising budget being depleted six months prior to the system's first day of service. Whatever favorable initial impact the advertising might have had on the consuming public, it was dissipated by the time the system made its market debut. The phones themselves had the bulky appearance and weight of a brick, and it was belatedly discovered that they did not work very well inside buildings. At a selling price of $3,000 per phone and with a minimum $4-per-minute calling rate, the system was out of reach of all but a few oil sheiks, millionaires, self-important politicians, entertainers and athletes. Satellite linkage from dozens of different countries around the world had not been finalized. Little thought was given to customer service queries. Not surprisingly, the first day of operations was problem-plagued. Things never really improved. Indeed, in many ways they became worse. Iridium, with some $5 billion in liabilities, has recently filed for bankruptcy protection from its creditors. Motorola and its Iridium partners should be sent to their room for the whole sorry mess.

On the battlefield or in the business wars, an attack-strength strategy requires exhaustive preparedness if victory is to be obtained.

Leadership

Admiral Isoroku Yamamoto was the driving force behind Japan's Pearl Harbor attack that was intended to knock America out of the Pacific. He had spent years in the United States as a naval attaché, even taking courses at Harvard. Yamamoto was well aware of America's immense industrial might even though much of it lay slumbering beneath the oppressive weight of the still-lingering 1930s Depression. He realized that a quick victory would have to be won before that might was brought to bear against Japan. There was much opposition to the Pearl Harbor attack plan among his army and navy colleagues, but, by his intellectual and physical presence, confidence and perseverance, Yamamoto prevailed.

Yamamoto, with his burly build, perpetual scowling war face and shaved head, personified the ideal military leader. That exterior was an enlarged replica of the inner man, a man of enormous courage. It was a special kind of courage that Napoleon more than a century before had referred to as 2 A.M. courage. It is at 2 A.M., the darkest part of night, when—alone, unable to summon the calm of sleep—military commanders, and today's senior executives and managers, confront the most terrible of enemies: their own fears. Yamamoto was able to overcome those fears and project his courage to those around him. No strategy of attacking strength as bold as the Pearl Harbor strategy could have been dreamed of and brought to reality without a leader of Yamamoto's stature. Unfortunately for Japan, from the zenith of his career at Pearl Harbor, the fifty-six-year-old admiral had but sixteen months to live.

It is impossible to imagine a military committee designing and executing an attack-strength strategy. Individual leadership matters greatly in war and perhaps even more so in business, where it is a crucial factor of success for any strategic initiative, especially this one of attacking strength. Return briefly to the Iridium debacle.

Iridium's leader and CEO, Edward Staiano, was a tough, hard-charging, twenty-five-year veteran of the telephone industry. He appears to have tried to stem the disaster as it was unfolding. There is a story of him being brought an unwieldy prototype of the phone along with its attendant cumbersome antennae and other attachments, looking briefly at it all and then flinging the Rube Goldberg contrivance across the room. "You really expect business travelers to carry all this s____?"[2] he roared. Perhaps it was not Staiano's leadership so much as the company's complex, multipartner organizational structure that was the root of the problem—he may not have had the authority to make crucial decisions and hold people to their performance targets. The whole story of Iridium may never be told. What is clear is that, as good as Staiano's leadership might have been, it was not good enough to overcome all of Iridium's inherent faults.

Concentration and Coordination of Resources

Pearl Harbor was indeed an American stronghold. But the Japanese achieved victory by successfully concentrating and coordinating a powerful sea and air force at the exact point of attack: an almost literal spearhead of ships and planes. Hours before dawn, Cmdr. Fuchida and his men had taken off from aircraft carriers several hundred miles from Pearl Harbor. Upon arriving in the skies above the anchored and sleeping American fleet, Japanese dive bombers, high-level bombers, torpedo planes and fighters worked in a near-perfect synchronization that might have been called beautiful had the results not been so terrible. All but a handful of Japanese planes returned safely to their carriers.

This concentration and coordination is one of the most fundamental of military principles, going back to Caesar and his battles in Gaul and back further still to Alexander the Great, and is vital to a successful attack-strength strategy. It is also a basic principle of business that is all too often overlooked at a firm's great peril. More of this later in chapter 7.

Surprise

Hawaii's military commanders, Adm. Husband E. Kimmel and Gen. Walter Short, were caught largely unprepared by the surprise Japanese Pearl Harbor attack. In the aftermath, both were publicly pilloried for their negligence and relieved of duty. Clearly there was American carelessness. Fuchida's squadrons, launched from six large aircraft carriers hours of flying time away, homed in on their objective using signals from a Honolulu-based radio station that was playing popular music. American radar, primitive then but still functional, did not pick up the incoming swarm of Japanese planes, and no American aircraft patrolled the skies over Hawaii. No torpedo nets protected the ships anchored in the harbor. No American ground, air or sea personnel had been placed on war alert.

Partly the surprise was due to Japanese treachery. Tokyo's leaders took to heart Sun Tzu's admonition that "Warfare is a matter of deception." The Japanese ambassador to the United States at the time was Kichisaburo Nomura. He was well aware that the decision to launch the Pearl Harbor attack had been made and that it could not be rescinded. Nevertheless, on December 7, just minutes before the bombs began to fall, he was in Washington, where it was late morning, pretending to talk peace with Secretary of State Cordell Hull. This was deceit at its most brazen.

Well before WWII, General MacArthur had written, "Surprise is the most vital element for success in war." Yet, ironically, MacArthur, in command of American-Filipino forces, was caught entirely unaware by the Japanese assault on the Philippines shortly after Pearl Harbor. It was his most grievous mistake in his fifty-year career as a soldier.

Surprise, feints and misleading signals can only come with secrecy. The Japanese succeeded for more than a year in surrounding the planned Pearl Harbor attack in a shroud of secrecy. It is more difficult to maintain secrecy in business, when employees can resign at any time and hire on with a competitor, taking proprietary information with them. Investor analysts and business news reporters are also on the prowl looking for telltale information about coming strategic initiatives. Companies themselves give away information when they trumpet their future plans in press releases, television interviews, analyst conferences and industry speeches.

One way or another, companies need to do a better job of maintaining the secrecy of confidential strategic issues; a strategy of attacking strength demands it. Silicon Valley, the cauldron of high-tech hypercompetition, may lead the way in this effort; its companies are becoming far more adept than in the past at monitoring competitor information while at the same time safeguarding their own. Former CIA and FBI agents can be found consulting or working directly for nearly all the major high-tech companies on matters of information protection and acquisition. Even trash isn't safe—Oracle took a public relations hit with the breaking news that a detective agency it hired, IGI, had been going through the waste baskets of a Microsoft facility mining for nuggets of information.

Detailed Strategic Plan

Finally, success for the attack-strength strategy depends on the entire organization knowing exactly what is to be done at the signal to attack. The highly detailed strategic plan does indeed provide the necessary directions. But it does much more. The very process of the joint development of the strategic plan by all those involved helps assure that crucial issues have been vetted, contingencies have been provided for and implementation will be relatively trouble-free. To thoroughly test, or war game, a strategy before its execution, many companies, such as Intel, encourage participants in strategic planning review meetings to be hard-hitting, even confrontational in their devil's advocacy. Once in place, the plan serves as the who, what, where, when and how organization-unifying action blueprint for the attack-strength strategy.

As the countdown began for the Pearl Harbor attack, the Japanese, from fleet admiral, to pilot, to radio operator, to the lowly ship deckhand, knew precisely what was to be done and when, where and how to do it. It was all laid out in advance. The role of every man, every machine, every weapon was predetermined. Like actors reading from a script, their actions were directed by a detailed strategic plan. Events then simply played themselves out, as written. The extraordinary power of a strategic plan is at the very heart of this book. The strategic plan—a mere abstraction of words, graphs and diagrams—has life breathed into it by those who follow its direction. The results, in military warfare or in the world of global business, can be profound.

"You Must Kill Him"

Put before your mind's eye a map of the entire Pacific Ocean and Southeast Asia as it existed on December 7, 1941. An explosion of red, designating Japanese-held areas, bursts forth from Japan. Within one year, the red covers nearly the entire regional map; the British Empire's Australia and New Zealand are among the few nations and territories that still hold out. The rest—Taiwan, Korea, Manchuria, Philippines, Singapore, Java, Sumatra, Borneo, Malaysia, Guam, Indonesia, Burma and the scores of islands and archipelagoes of the Pacific—are overlaid in the blood-red of the Greater East Asia Co-Prosperity Sphere, as the Japanese grandiosely call it; the occupied peoples call it something else entirely. The Japanese rule the Pacific. But then the gods of war shrug. In the next six months the map is altered with an ever so slight receding of scarlet. Then as the months pass the red recedes still more and then more—a cancer in accelerated remission. By the fourth year that initial crimson burst has retreated to the Japanese home islands from whence it began. Then in August 1945 come the American atomic bombs: Fat Man at Hiroshima and Little Boy at Nagasaki. The red is instantly vaporized and disappears entirely.

After an initial, nearly complete Japanese victory had come defeat—devastating and complete. Japan's cities lay in ruins, with buildings turned to rubble and water- and electricity-generating systems destroyed. Its people faced a freezing winter and starvation. Some 2 million sons and husbands had died in battle; nearly a like number of innocent civilians had perished. For the first time in its 5,000-year history the country was occupied—Douglas MacArthur had become Japan's proconsul. Seldom in history has a nation been so utterly ravaged by war. How can this have happened after but four years and such an auspicious beginning?

The American essayist, Ralph Waldo Emerson once wrote, "When you strike at a king, you must kill him." To the Japanese strategy of attacking strength at Pearl Harbor must be appended Emerson's warning: Unless the initial assault strikes a death blow, the now-provoked enemy may well recover and retaliate with furious intensity. The Japanese, with one bold stroke, had counted on ending the war at Pearl Harbor—expecting in the attack's aftermath that the shocked Americans would simply collapse and negotiate a face-saving peace. But Japan's future scan was terribly flawed in its judgment of America's fighting spirit. Indeed, Pearl Harbor galvanized what had been a passive and isolationist United States. The day after the bombing, President Roosevelt delivered his "Day of Infamy" speech to the Joint Congress and called for a declaration of war. With howling, rabid, jingoistic shouts and florid-faced fury, 530 of 531 senators and congressmen gave it to him. This was the same Congress that, a few weeks before, had voted down an increase in the existing paltry military budget and had strong reservations about a civilian draft. Now, in a complete about-face, the American military was given carte blanche. Hundreds of billions of dollars were made available for a cornucopia of planes, tanks, ships, artillery, munitions and even a clandestine, top-secret undertaking called the Manhattan Project. America's vast industrial potential, the greatest in the world, was unleashed and converted to war production, millions of men were drafted and Rosie the Riveter went to work. The full power and fury of the United States, and the combative spirit of its people, would be brought to the war. Japan had no strategy to deal with that; indeed, few among the Japanese leadership had even given it any thought.

For four blood-soaked years, until the apocalyptic atomic ending, the Japanese fought on with no follow-up strategy—except that of a tenacious and suicidal defense of terrain seized in the first few months of the war. Typical was Iwo Jima. In March of 1945 the Americans landed on that heavily fortified, Japanese-held, pork chop–shaped, eight-square-mile island. Thirty-six days of brutal combat ensued. One bit of war film footage shows an American tank spewing napalm into a Japanese bunker. A few moments later a Japanese officer, engulfed in flames and with a sword raised above his head, staggers from the bunker. Grotesquely, but magnificently, he charges the American tank until, after a few yards, he simply dissolves into a pile of charred ashes—and then, with a gust of wind, into nothingness. That vignette epitomized the overall Japanese strategy following Pearl Harbor. When the fighting on Iwo Jima ended, the Japanese dead in that battle numbered some 21,000; only a few hundred, sick and wounded, were captured or surrendered. A *Life* magazine photographer indelibly caught the evocative spirit of American victory, and the savagery of the fight to gain it, with a snapshot of U.S. Marines raising the tattered Stars and Stripes atop Mount Suribachi.

At Okinawa, in the war's last battle, barely trained Japanese teenage pilots were ordered to crash planes loaded with explosives into American ships. While the *kamikaze*, or divine wind, pilots, did a good deal of damage, their attacks were hardly a strategy. Thus, belatedly the Japanese learned the necessity of a follow-up contingency strategy if the initial assault against strength fails to end the war.

Yamamoto did not live to see the climactic whirlwind that he had sown at Pearl Harbor. In a samurai-like coda to his career, on April 18, 1943, he was shot from the skies above Rabaul by a squadron of sixteen American P-38s. Yamamoto had been on a regional inspection tour evaluating Japanese defenses in the face of the ever-encroaching enemy. But the Americans, having cracked the Japanese secret radio code, knew exactly where he would be and when he would be there. In some sense his death was by American assassination, but it did not really matter. One way or another, Yamamoto could not have survived the war's end. "When you strike at a king, you must kill him"—

Yamamoto knew the truth of Emerson's words. He also knew, by late 1942, that the blow struck at Pearl Harbor, which he had championed, had not killed the enemy and that thus Japan was doomed. The shame and burden of that was more than a Japanese warrior could live with. Some related business examples follow.

In the 1970s, Sir Freddie Laker's Skytrain electrified the international air passenger industry with slashed prices—a direct assault on the established carriers TWA, PanAm, United and British Air. The four veteran companies were briefly staggered but, within little over a year, recovered and combined to drive the upstart into bankruptcy. Like the Japanese of WWII, Sir Freddie had no strategy beyond the initial attack against strength.

In a more recent example, Packard Bell was founded in the early 1990s by a one-time Israeli tank commander, Beni Alagem. He took the defunct Packard Bell brand name and began producing PCs and selling them through generously rebated retailers at slashed prices. Packard Bell attacked the strength of established industry powers and quickly gained market leadership; IBM, Dell, Compaq and Hewlett-Packard were unprepared for the assault. But again, Packard Bell had no follow-up plan. Its product reliability was poor, its customer service was terrible and its distribution system was in shambles. That and the counterattack of reinvigorated and aggressive veteran manufacturers combined to hammer Packard Bell. The company took hit after hit and began to reel. In 1996, Japan's NEC attempted a financial rescue with a large cash infusion. It was too late. Early in 2000, NEC Packard Bell, as it came to be known, announced its withdrawal from the American market.

Contrary to these two failures, however, there is the classic case of Lexus briefly noted earlier. In 1990, Lexus launched an attack on the strength of Cadillac's and Lincoln's U.S. luxury car market. The attack was not a one-time thing. Lexus has followed up, for a decade now, with a well-thought-out strategy of securing, and expanding, its initial beachhead. The results are consistently top J. D. Powers quality ratings, superbly designed and engineered products, unparalleled customer service and scores of premier dealers. Cadillac, quite literally once a synonym for sterling excellence, appears too old, arthritic and tired to fight the younger, more lithe and muscled Lexus. The average Cadillac owner is sixty years old. Without a strategy of change,

TORA! TORA! TORA! 61

Cadillac risks becoming the geriatric Sun City manufacturer for geriatric Sun City residents. The Lexus attack-strength and follow-up strategy against Cadillac has been a winning one although the final battle is not yet at hand. Cadillac still has a chance. More of this in chapter 6.

Carl von Clausewitz observed that "There is an imperative need for pursuit after victory." Beyond the initial attack against strength, then, there must be a follow-up contingency plan immediately ready for implementation should the enemy not capitulate quickly and totally. As applied to the business wars, think Lexus by way of example.

Mirror-Image Strategy

Assuming the attack-strength strategy is consistent with the prevailing circumstances set forth earlier and that the six factors for success have been attended to, there is a high likelihood of victory. There is of course no certainty of victory; the vagaries of war and business render nothing certain. The greatest uncertainty is the enemy's, or competitor's, response to being attacked. War, like chess, like the martial arts, like business, has moves and countermoves, strategies, counterstrategies and counter-counterstrategies.

Implicit in the strategy of attacking strength is the appropriate strategy of *defending* strength. What should have been the strategy, not of Japan as described earlier, but of the United States in the period prior to December 7, 1941? What should be the strategy today of Carly Fiorina, CEO of Hewlett-Packard, the industry's leading PC and printer company? Or what should be the strategy of John Chambers, CEO of Cisco, whose company dominates the Internet infrastructure business? The answer is a mirror image, or role reversal, of the attack-strength strategy.

The defend-strength strategy calls for a defense in depth and the availability of reserves to immediately counterattack an enemy assault. It requires maintaining constant satellite snapshots to track competitor movements as well as war-gaming the future scan in order to be prepared for a surprise attack. A preemptive strike against the competitor may also be part of the strategy—the Israelis launched such an attack against an Iraqi nuclear facility under construction at Ossirak in the 1980s, and Microsoft attacks potential competitors preemptively as a common practice. Defenses should be hardened. In business that means raising barriers to entry by reducing one's own prices, raising quality, stepping up research and development (R&D), improving service, building alliances, burnishing brand names and developing cadres of motivated and capable people. The strategy might also include counterattacking the home base of the attacker, as Scipio did against Hannibal's Carthage and FedEx is doing against the ground delivery system of UPS. Most important, it means maintaining the company-wide combat-readiness captured by Intel's "Only the paranoid survive" business philosophy—more of that in chapter 13. This then, is the mirror-image defend-strength strategy.

Nine more strategies are presented in the following nine chapters. In each case there exists a mirror-image counterstrategy as just outlined. But this is the last reference that will be made to the issue. Introducing counterstrategies unnecessarily complicates the telling, but readers, with a little work, can determine them on their own. The best generals, the best business leaders can see moves and countermoves far in advance. That is the stuff of genius, intellect and reasoning.

Raw intelligence is usually missing from lists of business leader attributes. It shouldn't be, not today, when strategy has become so complex and so essential for a company. Individual or group intelligence makes possible thinking concurrently along multiple dimensions, anticipating competitor counterstrategies and simultaneously holding many contingencies in mind—it matters greatly for strategy setting. Microsoft, for one, with its legions of whip-smart and tough-as-nails people, recognizes this and hires accordingly. Expect strategic thinking, and the intellect and reasoning it requires, to become ever more important among *Fortune* 500 CEOs and their senior and middle-level managers. Their companies' futures depend on it.

This chapter has focused upon attacking strength as a winning strategy. It has been successful on the battlefield and in our world of business, finance and industry. Given a fitting set of prevailing circumstances, the reader may choose to adopt it as his or her own. But, seemingly paradoxically, in the next chapter another winning strategy is considered: attacking *weakness*.

CHAPTER FIVE

Patton's Morocco Initiative

Attack Weakness

To be certain to take what you attack is to attack a place the enemy does not protect.
— Sun Tzu

Sears ignored us in the early years and in the end we simply blew right by them.
— Sam Walton, chairman, Wal-Mart[1]

Operation Torch

Nearly a year had passed since Pearl Harbor and America's declaration of war against the Axis powers: Japan, Germany and Italy. During that time, the Nazi juggernaut had overrun nearly all of Europe and much of North Africa. Except at sea against German submarines, the United States had yet to directly grapple with Hitler's forces; time instead had been spent training men and gearing up factories for war production. But that was about to change as the United States sought to take the offensive. For reasons of both military imperatives and home-front morale, an initial, even nominal, victory was needed. To achieve that, the Joint Chiefs and Pentagon planners turned to the writings of ancient China's revered military genius Sun Tzu for the strategy of attacking weakness. They chose one of the most poorly protected of Hitler's outposts—Morocco in the eastern Mediterranean. The attack, set for November 8, 1942, would be code-named Operation Torch. After a difficult landing and some bitter, but brief fighting in the streets of Casablanca, an assault force, led by Gen. George Patton, overwhelmed the small and ill-equipped enemy garrison made up of second-rate German and Vichy troops. It was an unquestioned triumph—America's first over Hitler.

Shortly after the Moroccan victory, Winston Churchill, Britain's grandiloquent prime minister, proclaimed, "This is not the end [of the war]. It is not even the beginning of the end. But it is perhaps the end of the beginning." In the ensuing months, American and British forces successfully used the strategy of attacking Nazi weakness twice more—gaining victories first at Sicily and later at Anzio in Italy. By 1944 the American troops were well-bloodied and confident veterans. America's industrial power was, by then, running at full capacity and had produced a bounty of vastly superior ground, air and sea weaponry and disgorged it in prodigious, almost profligate, amounts. It was only at that point, in June of 1944, after North African, Sicilian and Italian beachheads had been secured, that the Allies completely reversed strategies and attacked strength by crossing the storm-tossed English Channel and assaulting Hitler's powerful fortifications on the French coast of Normandy. Final victory in World War II against the Nazis would come a year later.

In the early part of the war, Sun Tzu's attack-weakness strategy contributed greatly to the ultimate defeat of Hitler's vaunted and feared *Wehrmacht*. Sam Walton used the same winning strategy against the omnipotent Sears as did Jeff Bezos against the retail book-selling fortress that was Barnes & Noble.

From Walton to Bezos

The year 1962 seemed to be a wonderful one for Sears. Sales were strong and profits high. The Sears name stood supreme among the score or so of retailers targeting middle America. It was then that a tall, reedy young man named Sam Walton opened his first retail store in Newport, Arkansas—a quiet town of barely 10,000 people. The choice of locations was not arbitrary. Walton had discovered a Sears weakness: its lack of presence in small-town America. Since the 1920s, Sears had opted to build stores only in medium-size to large cities; its catalogs, however imperfect, had reasonably met the needs of rural and small-town America. But a catalog, Walton would demonstrate, could not compete with a clean, large, well-stocked store with everyday low prices and smiling, affable greeters at the door. His Arkansas store flourished and the Wal-Mart empire was born. Wal-Mart today employs 1,140,000 people—that's more than the population of Idaho and more than any other company in the world. Wal-Mart is the second largest of the *Fortune* 500 companies, with sales of $166 billion, and has been added to the Dow 30. Meanwhile Sears, which seems to reinvent itself with new strategies every other week, has been in and out of financial intensive care units for a decade now.

Southwest Airlines took on the mighty American Airlines in New York not with gates at the world-class JFK or LaGuardia airports, but at tiny Islip and provincial Albany, New York. Under Herb Kelleher, Southwest has built the most profitable domestic air carrier by ferreting out small airports and short routes that have been over-looked, dismissed or left unprotected by the major airlines.

Saturn, with its no-haggling pricing and amiable salespeople, has carved out a profitable niche by addressing a weakness shared by nearly all auto retailers: customer aversion to the car-buying experience. Today, Wayne Huizenga's AutoNation and several new Internet companies, including CarsDirect.com, are probing the same weakness.

A quarter of a century ago Xerox owned the copier business. So dominant and pervasive was its position that the very word "Xerox" had become a verb referring to copying or replicating. Still to this day one hears, "Pat, please Xerox this for me." In all likelihood, however, Pat is "Xeroxing" on a Canon, not a Xerox, machine. In the mid-1970s, Canon, a modest-size Japanese company known primarily for its cameras, attacked a Xerox weakness at the low end of the market. From that small beginning, Canon has now become the world's leading copier company, even licensing copier technology to other major original equipment manufacturers (OEMs) including Hewlett-Packard. Xerox meanwhile has just fired its latest in a string of CEOs,

Richard Thoman, who had been brought in to turn the company around. He failed as have others before him. In the early years of Xerox dominance of the mid- and high-end of the copier market, Canon could never have successfully attacked its strength. But an attack-weakness strategy at the low end of the market led ultimately to a Canon victory and a crushing Xerox defeat.

> NEWSFLASH! (January 2001) After another quarterly loss, and with its stock at a fifty-two week low, there are rumors that Xerox has become a takeover target. Added to Xerox woes is an SEC probe of alleged financial reporting irregularities.

Only some five years ago, Barnes & Noble, with its hundreds of brightly lit and comfortable stores in excellent locations, stood at the pinnacle of retail book sales. Its only real competitor, Borders, had tried to go head to head with it, attacking its strength, but was failing. Then a congenial unknown thirty-one-year-old named Jeff Bezos spotted a weakness. He and his Amazon.com people wielded a techie-geek weapon called the "Web" against which Barnes & Noble had no immediate defense. While a series of early victories, including the creation of a 23-million-person customer base, have gone to Bezos, Barnes & Noble's chairman Steve Riggio is a tough, smart businessman and will fight back hard. This war isn't over yet, especially because Amazon has—dangerously—lost concentration by moving far beyond selling just books to thousands of disparate products. Nevertheless, Amazon's running start was obtained by a strategy of attacking weakness.

From Sam Walton to Jeff Bezos, attacking a competitor's weakness has been shown to be a winning strategy. That strategy isn't new—it was perfected over 2,000 years ago on battlefields of central and southern China by the warrior-philosopher Sun Tzu. From that long-ago time and that distant place, the strategy has now, quite clearly, come to the business wars.

Strategic Choice: Prevailing Circumstances

The close of the last chapter suggested an apparent paradox: While a strategy of attacking strength can lead to victory—recall Lexus against

Cadillac and Rupert Murdoch against the established TV networks—as just seen, for other companies attacking *weakness* has also been a winning strategy. Attack strength, attack weakness: These are antipodal. How can both be winning strategies? The answer lies in the earlier-noted fact that *strategy depends on prevailing circumstances.* The circumstances for attacking strength are quite different from those for attacking weakness.

The choice of an attack-weakness strategy should be based on several specific prevailing circumstances: One's own resources are limited, the enemy or competitor is powerful but too complacent or distracted to respond to an attack against its weak outposts and one's own people and organization lack experience and must be bloodied to obtain it. Consider each of these in some detail.

The first prevailing circumstance leading to the choice of an attack-weakness strategy is that only limited resources are at hand against an overall very strong competitor. Sam Walton, in his memoirs, wrote that "Part of our initial strategy was really a child of necessity. We had very limited capital available."[2] That may have been an understatement—Walton had only his $5,000 personal savings and family borrowings of another $20,000 to begin his enterprise. Sears at that time was a multibillion-dollar top *Fortune* 500 company.

Second, the competitor is too arrogant, complacent or elephantine to respond to an attack on one of its outlying garrisons. Had the Goliath that was Sears made an effort to monitor Walton's embryonic venture and realized the danger it represented, very little of its resources would have been required to smite the David upstart.

Third, the people in the organization need to undergo a baptism by fire to gain confidence and experience. Indeed, the organization itself must be shaken out to identify and correct problems and resolve bottlenecks. Wal-Mart, in its early days, was not staffed with high-priced Ivy League MBAs imbued with the latest sophisticated marketing and sales methods. Nor were its ranks filled with experienced retailers. To the contrary, the company recruited its employees from the Arkansas countryside and made a practice of promotion from within. Learning and training was on the job, and pricing, promotions, store layout, buying, inventory control, property management and a thousand other matters were tested by trial and error. Over time, from a group of modestly educated but highly motivated people, Wal-Mart produced cadres of fine managers who went on to district, regional, national and even international responsibilities. While Wal-Mart people were developing, so, too, were the company's practices and procedures, including profit sharing, maintaining non-union shops, manufacturer alliances, competitor analysis, a liberal returns policy and zany one-day sales of unusual items—all of which later would become industry benchmarks.

All three of these circumstances also prevailed at the time of Patton's initiative in North Africa. Eleven months after the disaster at Pearl Harbor, America's war production machine was just beginning to reach full capacity. The American military personnel still were, for the most part, green civilian draftees, inexperienced in warfare, inadequately trained and completely lacking the killer instinct. The weaponry was poor—shells fired from American tanks could not penetrate German armored vehicles. Meanwhile, the powerful German army, the *Wehrmacht*, was spread over nearly all of Europe and had never been defeated. Hitler and his generals were dismissive of America's ability and willingness to fight. Indeed, an American attack against a German stronghold could easily have been turned back. Morocco, on the other hand, was deemed by the Nazi high command strategically unimportant and hardly worth defending.

Factors of Success

When prevailing circumstances are highly suggestive of an attack-weakness strategy, what crucial factors are necessary to successfully design and execute it? The factors include satellite snapshot, stealth mode, leadership and mission.

Satellite Snapshot

Once war against Hitler and his Nazis had been declared the Pentagon began to carefully reconnoiter possible enemy targets for its first attack. After much debate, Morocco was chosen as most suitable. Arab spies and Vichy informants provided the American planners with crucial information regarding German fortifications and manpower as well as the local weather and landing conditions at the Port of Oran. All of this comprised a pretty accurate satellite snapshot from which operational plans could be developed.

In the business arena, executing the attack-weakness strategy also calls for assiduous intelligence gathering that falls into separate but related categories. The first, and most important, involves the competitor's products, services, distribution channels, infrastructure, financial strength, alliances, management talent and more. The attack-weakness strategy, like every strategy presented in this book, targets the competition—companies must know everything pertinent about the competitor or competitors in order to shape and execute their strategies.

The second type of satellite snapshot information gathering is directed inward: What are one's own strengths and weaknesses in terms of each of the elements noted above for the competitor—products, services, distribution channels, resources and so on?

Finally, there is the customer. Required here is a detailed analysis of who he or she is and how the product or service is used, bought, paid for, stored and disposed of. A variety of market research methods, including product beta testing of prototypes, usability labs and focus group sessions, contribute yet further insights.

Strategic planners must immerse themselves in all of the information they receive, arguing, questioning, probing and speculating until slowly, or sometimes as an epiphany, the exactly right target for a strategy of attacking an adversary's weakness becomes evident: Morocco for Patton and small-town America for Walton. In summary, then, the attack-weakness strategy depends greatly for success on a highly detailed and accurate pre-attack satellite snapshot.

Stealth Mode

Another factor critical for success with this attack-weakness strategy is to maintain a stealth mode, under, or invisible from, the enemy's radar, for as long as possible. That's what Wal-Mart did. Throughout its early years, Wal-Mart did not trumpet its own achievements or in any way beard Sears' lion. Partly because of that, Sears paid little attention to Wal-Mart until the early 1990s when the latter shifted strategy and began attacking Sears' strength in large cities. By then,

Sears could no longer ignore Wal-Mart—the barbarians were within the gates.

In hindsight, it is easy to see how Sears lost its primacy. Here is an imaginary, but telling, vignette. The time is fall of 1976. The place is Sears' Chicago headquarters, the tallest building in the United States. The structure's dominance of the city skyline is symbolic of half a century of retail industry leadership and perhaps more than a little corporate arrogance. A high-level senior management meeting is under way. The attendees around the large, polished mahogany table are all white males. Most of them are gray-haired. All are identically garbed in dark suits with white shirts and striped ties. All have been with the company for their entire careers. They are conservative, cautious, confident, like-thinking organization men. Several of them are smoking. Seated inconspicuously at the back of the room, a matronly, primly dressed woman stenographer is taking notes. Far down the printed meeting's agenda is an item listed simply as "Wal-Mart." Referring to it, a somewhat nettled meeting chairman unaccustomed to seeing things he was not familiar with gruffly asks, "What's this?"

"Sir," says the youngest among them, "we, uh, have been hearing about a company operating out of Arkansas that perhaps uh, warrants, uh, uh . . . some of our attention."

A few seconds of embarrassing silence envelops the room and then the chairman condescendingly responds, "Red-necked, cowboy-booted Arkansans. Surely you can't be serious?"

There is a smattering of smug, or maybe nervous, laughter around the room as the younger man reddens and retreats into himself. It is not likely that he will anytime soon again rock the self-assured Sears culture. The agenda moves on to the next item. Wal-Mart remained below the Sears radar. Incredibly, it was not until 1992 that Sears began to include Wal-Mart among the competitors it benchmarked against.

Having found and attacked a competitor's weakness a company should make every effort to stay undetected and inconspicuous for as long as possible so as not to be merely swatted away by the stronger adversary. Time is needed to secure a firm beachhead. Sam Walton wrote, "Sears ignored us in the early years and in the end we simply blew right by them."[3]

Leadership

Patton was arguably the most charismatic WWII military leader. He was always to be found at the front lines where enemy fire was the heaviest. With his ivory-handled pistols, profane language, starched uniforms and iron discipline, his men mostly loved him. But whether they loved or hated him, they believed in and followed him; and that was vitally important in North Africa and for later Patton-led victories against the Nazis in Sicily and France. Military leadership is crucial when embarking on a strategy of attacking weakness, especially when the armed forces under the leader's command lack the necessary experience, confidence and esprit. Leadership is also of vital importance in business.

Before anyone had ever heard of Warren Buffett, Bill Gates or the dozens of today's peach-fuzzed Silicon Valley e-billionaires, there was Sam Walton—the wealthiest man then in America. Most people who knew him found it almost impossible to believe that he was a multibillionaire. The grandfatherly, crusty old man led company cheers, drove a battered and mud-spattered ancient pickup truck around town, lived in a relatively modest home and only occasionally took a little time off to go duck hunting with friends. Walton's temperate home lifestyle was in sharp contrast to his near-obsessive passion for the welfare of Wal-Mart and his employees, who he always credited for the company's success—a success that turned hundreds of them into millionaires as a result of a very generous profit-sharing program. Sam Walton, like Patton on the battlefield, imbued his people with the self-assurance that they could compete with, and indeed vanquish, any adversary, no matter how strong. The people of Wal-Mart loved Walton for that. Wal-Mart became almost a Mao-like personality cult that was centered around its grizzled and homespun leader.

With all the treacly New Age talk one hears today of teams and egalitarian business organizations, the unique role of the leader may sometimes be overlooked. It shouldn't be. There could have been no Wal-Mart without Sam Walton. His mind had created what would be a winning strategy and his indefatigable will and perseverance were brought to bear on its execution. It is noteworthy that Wal-Mart stumbled badly in the years after Walton's death. Only recently under a new generation of outstanding leaders has the company found its footing and renewed its advance.

Mission

Finally, critical to the success of the attack-weakness strategy is a painstakingly crafted mission. For Wal-Mart under Walton, the mission included, among other things, employee commitment to the organization, sharing of profits, celebrating achievements, serving the customer with value and friendliness and communicating throughout the company. In the early years, Wal-Mart people lived the mission— that was fundamental to their great success. It is just as crucial for Wal-Mart today to remain true to those mission principles as it slowly introduces strategic shifts into groceries, price clubs and international markets. Indeed, it is crucial to any business executing the attack-weakness strategy. Without the compass of a robust mission, during periods of strife and turmoil, which are certain to come, it is all too easy to lose direction and begin to drift or flail about aimlessly, adopting one nostrum after another. Just as dangerous is overconfidence that flows from a series of battle victories using the attack-weakness strategy—that, too, can lead to straying from the mission upon which the company was founded.

Walton never lost sight of what he wanted Wal-Mart to become. The mission kept that distant objective constantly before him and he in turn kept it constantly before his people. There is a story, apocryphal perhaps, about two veteran Wal-Mart executives, reflecting on the company's great and quite extraordinary success. One of them says, "Here we are at the new millennium and our stock is soaring, we are listed among the Dow 30, our international business is rapidly expanding, Sears has been left in the dust and we are the second largest company in the world employing well over 1 million people." The other executive slowly nods his head and says, "Sam [Walton] has been dead now for almost 10 years. If only he could have seen this."

The first executive pauses and then somberly replies, "He did." What Wal-Mart is today was conceived in Sam Walton's mission.

Not all companies are like Wal-Mart and not all CEOs are like Walton. The consulting arm of PricewaterhouseCoopers, in a recent research exercise, gathered mission statements from some two dozen well-known mid- and large-size companies. The collected missions were later presented to the CEOs of those same companies. Shockingly, half of them were unable to identify their own company's mission. No strategy—not the attack-weakness strategy presented here or any other—can succeed without a clearly articulated, and lived, mission. Indeed, strategic success is measured against the mission. Mission is basic to any strategic plan. Strategies are not ends in themselves, they are means to achieving the mission.

What of those CEOs in the PricewaterhouseCoopers study who were seemingly unaware of their own company's mission, thus rendering corporate strategies meaningless? When their companies fail, as fail they must, the CEOs will likely walk away with multimillion-dollar severance packages while employees, suppliers and investors will be left holding a nearly empty bag. Surely there is a reserved spot in corporate purgatory for such irresponsible and incompetent leadership.

A company without a mission is like an airliner with no meaningful flight plans and no destination. The plane sometimes circles lazily overhead, or suddenly dives and then rapidly climbs, or races at near-Mach speed or slows to a far more leisurely pace. Sometimes it flies north to south and sometimes east to west and then for no discernible reason reverses course. The airliner has no identity, direction or purpose. Sooner or later its fuel tanks will be emptied; the result can only be a disaster that leaves few survivors.

Hadrian's Wall

Many of today's Internet start-ups have exploited the Sun Tzu strategy of attacking a strong competitor's Achilles' heel. One can almost always find some weakness in Microsoft, Cisco, Oracle, AT&T or any other large and powerful company. Sometimes the weakness is to be found at or very near the core of the company. More often it is found at the periphery.

The bigger a company, the more expansive and vulnerable is its frontier. At the zenith of Rome's might, lightly manned, scattered outposts at the far reaches of its empire in North Africa, Western and Eastern Europe and the Mediterranean were largely defenseless against barbarian attack. The outposts were mere shock absorbers at best. The larger the Roman Empire grew, the more susceptible it was to assaults against its most distant borders. By way of example, Rome's farthest reach to the north was Hadrian's Wall, remnants of which still stand to this day. Stretching across northern England from the Irish Sea to the North Sea, it was named after the Roman emperor who ordered its construction. It was intended to suppress raids by the savage Scots who lived farther to the north. It didn't. Rome could not man the walls heavily enough—not when those walls were so very far from home.

The question is not whether a business competitor has a weakness, it does. The question is what the weakness is and how it can best be attacked. Perhaps the weakness is a fatal flaw inherent in the basic business model or perhaps it is a mere chink in some non-core competency. Whatever it might be, it can be isolated and attacked. The likelihood of success is high. At least initial success.

Phase II

After three consecutive strategic successes in attacking German weakness—first at Morocco, then at Sicily and finally at Anzio in Italy—the Allies completely reversed strategies and henceforth attacked strength. At dawn on D-Day, June 6, 1944, some 5,000 American and British ships lay offshore the beaches of Normandy behind which lay Hitler's "Fortress Europe." The assembled vast armada, filling the horizon, was by far the largest the world had ever seen. In the dark of night it had crossed the English Channel's rough waters from southern England to northern France. Just after first light, troop and cargo ships began to disembark some 125,000 troops and to offload tons of equipment. Specific landing areas had been designated—Omaha and Utah for the Americans, Sword and Gold for the British and Juno for the Canadians. Allied airborne forces had landed behind the lines in the predawn hours to disrupt and confuse the Germans. American cruisers, destroyers and battleships prowled the waters off the beaches lobbing a torrent of shells down on German fortifications. In the first twenty-four hours of the attack the Allies flew thousands of air sorties bombing and strafing German targets. All of this was a direct assault against Nazi strength.

The Allies landed in the face of powerful German opposition: mines, barbed wire, machine guns, mortars and 88-mm Krupp cannon housed in concrete bunkers above the beaches. The defenses had been designed by one of Hitler's favorite generals, the famed Desert Fox, Gen. Erwin Rommel. Beyond the beaches, in France alone, the German army numbered some 1.2 million men organized into sixty divisions, many of them bearing the insignia of the elite and much-feared Panzer and SS. The Allies were indeed attacking strength. Across the beaches, through the tangled hedgerows and across France, Belgium, the Netherlands and finally into Germany itself they battled. Some of the planning didn't work out as expected—there was the disaster at Arnhem and the surprise in the Ardennes—but much of it did. When the war's outcome became clear, Hitler committed suicide and the German high command capitulated a few days later, on May 8, 1945, less than a year after the Normandy landings.

The Anglo-American strategy in four years of warfare against Hitler then can be roughly described chronologically, year by year, as attack weakness, attack weakness, attack weakness and then, finally attack strength.

The attack-weakness strategy, if successful, always arrives at a Phase II decision point. At that point, when beachheads have been firmly established and but a few weak enemy positions remain, there are but two basic choices. One is holding and strengthening even further what has been captured and blocking any future enemy offensive initiative—this is essentially the strategy of containment explored later, in chapter 12. The second is to completely alter strategies and attack strength as the Anglo-American forces did against Hitler on those Normandy beaches more than half a century ago.

So, too, with Wal-Mart, which after toiling for some twenty-five years in America's hinterland came to its Phase II strategic shift. Wal-Mart chose to put aside its attack-weakness strategy—which had served it so well—and began to attack Sears' strength in large cities. After this complete reversal of strategy, it took Wal-Mart less than a decade to achieve near-total victory. Sears today, with the exception of some scattered pockets of resistance, does not even pretend to compete with Wal-Mart.

A successful attack-weakness strategy leads at some point to a strategic decision: Either consolidate and strengthen captured positions and accept the status quo, leaving the enemy safely behind his fortress walls, or entirely reverse strategies and attack the strength of those selfsame walls. Often the former is the best strategy even though it is not chosen. After several battles have been won, the organization's blood is up and there is great internal pressure to continue the attack. Wall Street and the investment community, like a rabid crowd of bettors at a Las Vegas heavyweight bout, urge the company on, prodding and cajoling for more aggressive initiatives. Restraining the organization and resisting the abandonment of the attack-weakness strategy may be a leader's greatest challenge.

———————

Depending on circumstances, attacking strength can become a winning strategy—that was seen in chapter 4. For other circumstances, attacking weakness can lead to victory—think Gen. George Patton in Morocco and Sam Walton in Arkansas. Indeed, for start-ups, attacking weakness is the strategy of choice. But what strategy is there for an organization that has known nothing but defeat, has shattered morale and is devoid of resources? Look to Moses.

CHAPTER SIX

Moses' Hebrews in Sinai

Bringing Change to a Failing Company

From the wilderness and this Lebanon as far as the great river [Euphrates], all the land of the Hittites to the Great Sea . . . shall be yours.
        —The Lord to Joshua, Joshua 1:4

There is nothing more difficult, nor dangerous nor doubtful of success than to institute a new order of things.

                    —Machiavelli

The willingness of people to change is limited . . . and inversely correlated to what you pay them.
        —John Reed, CEO, Citigroup[1]

It took a tremendous force of will to get the organization . . . to change.

            —John Roth, CEO, Nortel[2]

"All Fell Before Them"

Afer freeing the wretched and broken Hebrews from Ramses II's cruel bondage in Egypt, Moses was ordered by the Lord to take them into the stark wilderness and deserts of Sinai. There they would await the call for entry into the Promised Land. But before that call came, the Sinai's scorpions, serpents and blazing sun would be set to work stripping away the Hebrews' invisible but very real chains of timidity, defeat and subservience that centuries of slavery had wrought. The older adults among Moses' followers at first were jubilant at their newly found freedom. But shattered in mind, broken in body by Pharaoh's whip and lash and set in their ways, they could not meet the physical and spiritual demands Moses placed on them. Many rebelled, refusing to change. The more recalcitrant among them were killed, and the rest were left largely alone to gradually die away.

Key to the future were the children. It was they who would become the instrument of change. From an early age, they were raised as fearless warriors, recruited into the Lord's service, dedicated to Him and His laws, including ten quite specific commandments. Slowly, year by year, under Moses' leadership, a new nation was being forged in the bleak desert beneath the torrid sun. The stricter and more disciplined the military and religious training, and the greater the privation, the more pride and confidence the people gained. After four decades had passed, a new generation of Hebrews was finally militarily and spiritually ready to fulfill its destiny.

Moses, a centenarian by then, but with "eyes not dimmed nor natural force abated," climbed alone to the peak of Mount Nebo and looked down upon the river Jordan and beyond, yearningly, to the place of milk and honey, of cattle, sheep and abundant crops. For the last time the Lord spoke to him: "This is the land . . . I will give to your descendants. I have caused it to be seen by your eyes but you shall not go over there." Moses then died and for thirty days the people wept and mourned.

The Lord selected Joshua, Moses' longtime lieutenant, to lead the Hebrews into what is now Israel. It was Joshua who took the strong, lean, sun-bronzed Hebrew cadres across the Jordan and moved them quickly against enemy tribes: Ammonites, Amalekites, Jebusites, Canaanites and Moabites. All fell before them. God's *chosen*, a revitalized, proud and fierce people, had conquered the Holy Land. A strategy of change, adhered to over some forty years, had taken an entire people directly from slavery and transformed them into a powerful fighting force and from that into a nation-state. Israel was born and an era of glory, with kings like Saul, David and Solomon, was about to begin. All of this happened a very long time ago in the thirteenth century B.C. The story offers profound lessons for today's world of business.

Strategy of Change

Companies, like armies, and even nations, fall upon hard times and into decline—sometimes quickly after a major defeat, but more generally very slowly, over long periods of time. Over the last two decades Sears, GM, Kmart, USX, J. C. Penney and Kodak are among the companies that have become corporate versions of huge, ponderous, gradually melting icebergs. Periodically, new CEOs are appointed to bring about change, but they immediately encounter resistance from entrenched stakeholders, including union officials, directors of the board, suppliers as well as senior and middle managers. Typically, the just-installed CEO shuffles about some boxes on the organization chart, launches a few new ad campaigns and perhaps goes around the company giving gung-ho speeches and calling for the start of a new era. But people of the organization have heard and seen all that before. The situation declines further as predatorlike competitors, detecting a wounded adversary, become ever more aggressive. Meanwhile, disillusioned investors wring their hands in frustration.

Dainty, incremental, step-on-no-toes changes won't work for these companies. If change is to come, it must be revolutionary, bold and total. The specifics of that will be addressed shortly. But first a more fundamental question must be considered: *When* should a strategy of change be invoked?

Strategic Choice: Prevailing Circumstances

The prevailing circumstances calling for a corporate strategy of change generally are all too evident. They include: the flip-flopping of strategies, the defection of the better employees, a shrinking market share, declining financial statistics, frequent CEO changes or conversely a cobweb-covered CEO who has stayed in place far too long, a dearth of innovation, de facto union extortion, an overpaid senior management riding out the years before retirement, the hiring of no-name auditors, the resignation of a respected chief financial officer (CFO), the selling off of corporate assets, high-profile social responsibility campaigns, acquisition binges, a bottom-dweller stock price, a pliant board of directors and an ineffable, overarching defeatist corporate mood. For such circumstances a strategy of change is long overdue. But things are not always so clear.

A strategy of change may also be called for even if none of the above circumstances are apparent. It may be that the problems are simply hidden while nevertheless looming over the not-too-distant horizon. Consider the example of General Electric.

It is the near-unanimous conventional wisdom that Jack Welch is the nation's most outstanding CEO. His exemplary performance over the last two decades at GE's helm has indeed been unprecedented—in 1999 the company pocketed $10 billion in profit, more than any other company in the world. But of most interest here is the fact that the GE he inherited in 1981 was thought by nearly everyone, both inside and outside the company, to be quite healthy. Welch was not expected to be much more than a mere caretaker. But his greatness is that he saw beyond the immediate to his own inner future scan. There he beheld potentially catastrophic dangers for GE and instituted an aggressive strategy of change to meet them. He did that under the most difficult of circumstances: when the corporate ship was currently navigating through calm seas with cloudless skies overhead and the people of GE were feeling quite secure and had no compulsion to change. Reflecting on those early days now as he nears retirement, Welch says, "I should have acted even quicker and been even more aggressive."[3]

Whether a company has already fallen into a state of near ruin or whether there are indications that it soon will, a strategy of change is called for. Having determined that, what factors will effect its success or failure?

Factors of Success

Machiavelli, an extraordinarily insightful chronicler of human nature, wrote that "There is nothing more difficult, nor dangerous, nor doubtful of success than to institute a new order of things." In any organization, from business unit to army command to entire nation, and in any given circumstances, there are always those who benefit from the status quo—these organizational reactionaries are bitterly opposed to change and will never yield or compromise unless forced to do so and even then only grudgingly. Others, no matter how terrible their situation, will resist change out of fear of the unknown. Still others cannot overcome embedded habits of the past.

To institute a new order of things is indeed very difficult. But it can be done successfully if several crucial factors are addressed. Those factors include removing dissidents, speed, symbols, mission, upward communication and leadership.

Removing Dissidents

Not even the most charismatic new leader can persuade every one of his or her followers to accept revolutionary change. It follows then that once persuasion has clearly failed, the next step must be taken: physically removing heretics from the organization. This has to be done quickly, before the new order can be sabotaged. Moses realized this was so when, just months after the Egyptian exodus, he was confronted by angry apostates who had become afraid of an uncertain future and demanded a return to the land of Pharaoh and its pagan gods. Enraged, Moses intuitively acted correctly. Barely controlling his anger, he gathered all of the Hebrews before him, drew a line in the sand with his walking staff and roared, "Whoever is on the Lord's side, let him come to me." While the great majority did, some 3,000 refused and were immediately put to death. Modern business is not so harsh but, still, revitalization must begin with the removal of dissidents by imposition of sometimes selective, and sometimes widespread, firings, especially at senior levels. A few examples.

Jack Welch, in his first year as GE's CEO, earned the sobriquet "Neutron Jack" for his decimation of management and employee ranks. He disliked his reputation but knew that decisive actions were necessary to implement a strategy of change. Removal was the only way to deal with those who could not, or would not, rally to his call for renaissance. Dissidents, by their passive-aggressiveness and their water-cooler subversive derision, are quite able to undermine a strategy of change. Because of that, those who cannot be won over must be let go. "Even senior people [who are doing great jobs in terms of numbers] have to be removed to support our values,"[4] says Welch.

Ford's new CEO, Jaq Nasser, has recruited dozens of key executives from other companies, including many from outside the automobile industry, to fill a variety of positions. At the same time, old-timers who have openly or covertly impeded Nasser's grand vision of a revitalized company have been nudged out. Behind his back, some have begun to refer to him as "Jaq the Knife."

Upon becoming CEO of the struggling Nortel, John Roth encountered a good deal of internal resistance. Nevertheless, he acted boldly. Roth fired or forced out more than a third of his inherited executive team, ripped away layers of bureaucracy and introduced performance pay. He went on to shut down dozens of the company's plants and outsourced what they had been producing. Roth believes that it is almost an ironclad rule of management that real change, the kind he imposed, can occur only after dissidents have been removed from an organization. The turnaround at Nortel has been extraordinary. In a few short years, under Roth, it has become a leading telecom equipment provider.

Like Roth, Nasser and Welch, the Romans, as they conquered new lands, were known to deal severely with those who challenged their laws, customs and authority. Dissidents were bound hand and foot and stuffed into a weighted sack along with a live chicken and dog. The sack was then tied shut and the whole tossed into a river, where the dissidents ultimately drowned after being clawed and bitten by the crazed animals. Torn, bloated and grotesquely distorted from long hours in the water, the remains were later recovered and hung in the town square as a lesson to others. From early Rome of 2,000 years ago, to the sixteenth century Inquisition to Cambodia's Khmer Rouge of the 1970s to Rwanda today, the lion pit, sword, firing squad, hangman's noose, rack, guillotine, fiery stake, Gulag and burning tire necklace are among the creative means humankind has used to tidy up after a revolution and ensure that its objectives are met. Such measures are indeed extreme but they are historic reality—the means for bringing about significant, revolutionary, nation-state change.

Now return to our relatively benign world of business, where there are no dogs, chickens and weighted sacks but there are pink slips. The extent to which employee, especially executive, ranks are winnowed and people are brought in from outside is the acid test of just how serious a newly appointed manager, preferably also brought in from the outside, is about achieving change. Simply put, a strategy of change is successful in direct proportion to which dissidents are removed and adherents of change are promoted or brought in from the outside.

Speed

Speed is a necessary second factor for bringing about change. Today, Wall Street, the god of Mammon, will not give a just-appointed CEO even two, let alone Moses' two score, years to change the corporate culture and strategic direction of a failing company. Attrition works far too slowly as a mechanism to eradicate the status quo mind-set. Warren Bennis, an expert in leadership at the University of Southern California (USC), has written that for a new leader, speed is crucial. "A just appointed CEO should have his mission, strategy and new team in place within three months."[5]

Robert Lutz had a fine career as CEO at Chrysler. He retired after Daimler acquired his company—perhaps with a nudge from Juergen Schrempp, Daimler's CEO, a fine executive but one who is reluctant to share power. Bored by retirement, in 1999 Lutz became CEO of Exide Corp., a troubled car battery maker. Acting swiftly, within a single year he sold off nonproducing assets, canceled unprofitable contracts, settled lawsuits, replaced nearly all of the senior management and recruited an almost entirely new board of directors. Exide is now poised to grow and likely will.

Another newly appointed CEO is Carly Fiorina of Hewlett-Packard. She, too, believes in rapid change. "I came into Hewlett-Packard believing that, whatever changes we needed to make, we needed to make them quickly. You don't want your people to waste time and be distracted by speculation and wondering."[6] Initially, Fiorina's top executives had told her that a major reorganization would take a year. She ordered it to be done in three months. "We needed to take bold steps to dislodge an entrenched culture,"[7] she said later. Better to act swiftly, make the change and then move on. Fiorina has done that successfully.

In his first month on the job, Kmart's new CEO, thirty-nine-year-old Charles Conaway, has ordered scores of stores closed, fired a dozen top executives and revamped the inventory system. Michael Exstein, a retail industry analyst at First Boston, says, "The message Chuck [Conaway] is trying to make is there's going to be change and there's going to be change fast."[8] For decades, Kmart has focused myopically on the immediate quarter with little attention paid to long-term profitability. The result is a floundering company. Conaway seems to recognize that if there is to be real change, it must come quickly.

"There is no sense in dawdling. I don't believe that it is prudent to follow a dribble out approach."[9] That was Alan McCollough, the new CEO of the struggling Circuit City. The company's earnings have been declining, down 20 percent in the last quarter of 2000, and competitors like Best Buy and Good Guys have been gaining market share. After just two months on the job, McCollough struck swiftly and boldly. He curtailed the sale of home appliances, which had accounted for 15 percent of revenues, ordered a remodeling of every one of the roughly sixty stores in the chain and closed down warehouses by putting merchandise directly on the showroom floors. Top executives not buying in to his changes have been swiftly eliminated.

In another example, the French automaker Renault paid $5.4 billion for a 37 percent stake in the faltering Nissan. With that came operating control. The Brazilian-born Carlos Ghosn was brought in as chief operating officer (COO) to initiate change at Nissan. During his first six months on the job he ordered staff reductions of 21,000, shut down several plants, thereby reducing manufacturing capacity by 30 percent, and cut the number of suppliers in half. "The restructuring plan is on a *very* fast track,"[10] emphasizes Ghosn. This kind of rapid change is without precedent in Japan; perhaps it could have been carried out only by a foreigner. Expect more of this kind of thing in tradition-bound Asia and Europe, where change is even more difficult to accept than in America.

Quick and bold action to bring about change is needed because the organization offers the new CEO or manager only a very short window of opportunity to make his or her influence felt. A tidal wave of change must be unleashed that sweeps over the organization as a fait accompli. Some research indicates that people will accept change more willingly if they are involved in the process even if their suggestions in the end are not accepted. That may be so, but old-style town hall meetings with much discussion and debate take time. Meanwhile the company's external problems worsen and opponents of change within the company strengthen their position. It is certainly appropriate, even desirable, for senior management to talk with employees, starkly depicting for them the current situation, quelling unfounded rumors and painting in large strokes the company's mission. But beyond that the management focus should be on actions, not rhetoric.

"If it were done when 'tis done, then 'twere well / It were done quickly," wrote Shakespeare. He was referring to unpleasant, but necessary, actions that in today's world of business would include layoffs, plant closings, consolidating product lines, severing ineffective alliances and ending fruitless R&D. Unless the CEO or senior manager acts quickly, the organization will, like some sci-fi blob, surround, stifle, paralyze and in the end consume him or her. That's what happened to Durk Jager.

"You have to create a revolution here,"[11] said Procter & Gamble's new CEO, Durk Jager, in 1999. It was needed. The hidebound Cincinnati-based company had a Byzantine multilayer management structure. It had more than 300 brands, some good, some bad, some overlapping, and all were being challenged by tough competitors in a stagnant consumer product marketplace. In addition to that, while the Internet was revolutionizing most of the retailing industry, it had not yet penetrated the insular and impervious ranks of P&G management. And finally, the investment community was railing about lackluster financial performance. Jager, a twenty-year company veteran, looked forward to the challenge. He began issuing orders methodically, step by step. Although accused by detractors of acting too quickly, Jager did not act quickly or decisively enough. His directives calling for change disappeared into the vast quagmire of P&G bureaucracy. Complaints from people throughout the organization who had been nudged out of their comfort zones filtered upward to a sympathetic board of directors. Criticism grew louder and in the end became shrill. An acquisition attempt went bad, quarterly earnings were down and the stock took a huge hit. Jager was forced to resign. Score: Jager 0, Organization 1. Several analysts, including Andrew Shore of Deutsche Banc, believe that stockholders also lost. Alan Lafley, who replaced Jager, has been with the company for three decades; he is no revolutionary.

Symbols

Symbols are also important factors in achieving a strategy of change. The move of Lincoln-Mercury's headquarters from Michigan to California signaled a new beginning. So did the decisions by Bernie Ebbers, WorldCom's new CEO, to sell off company cars and his predecessor's beloved $40 million Gulfstream jet and to order that executives traveling overnight henceforth stay at modest-price hotels—no more neatly turned bed covers or chocolate mints neatly placed atop a fluffy snow-white pillow. To symbolize crossing the chasm into the new Internet world, Charles Schwab's co-CEO, David Pottruck, hiked his top 100 executives across Golden Gate Bridge. Then there is Thomas Ryder, the new CEO of *Reader's Digest*, who has ordered the sale of $100 million of corporate art. "It is a trapping we no longer can afford,"[12] he says.

New ventures can be useful as symbols of change. Ford's Nasser has put together task forces to work with Sprint and Qualcomm to see if any intercompany synergies can be found. These task forces convey to the several hundred thousand men and women of Ford that change and innovative thinking have come to the company. Acts such as this are symbolic of the CEO's willingness to try new ideas and reshuffle the deck of corporate culture. They become the stuff of much coffee-break and company grapevine discussion and have a considerable positive impact on a jaded and skeptical workforce.

Mission

A company in a failing state likely has a mission that is simply outdated and wrong for the times or has a mission that is basically sound but that senior management has chosen not to heed. In the latter situation, the company can be turned around by returning to the wisdom of the mission. If the problem is the former, an entirely new mission is called for. Such an extreme step means essentially the demise of the former company and the birth of a new one. A new company name may even be appropriate. In this regard the story of Westinghouse is classic.

The eponymous company was founded late in the nineteenth century by George Westinghouse as a manufacturer of air brakes for the nation's burgeoning railroads. Over the years, the company expanded into various new businesses. By the 1950s, Westinghouse was manufacturing automobile parts, nuclear reactors and even consumer electronics and appliances. In the early 1990s it added the CBS television and radio network to its patchwork of businesses. At that point, Westinghouse had lost all sense of mission and was performing poorly in the diverse markets where it had a presence. Finally, the company moved to sell off all but its entertainment business, renamed itself CBS and adopted a completely new mission. In late 1999 CBS was acquired by Viacom, the entertainment giant, and disappeared as a stand-alone company. The CBS mission will have to be revised once again to fit the demands of its new parent. The creation of George Westinghouse is no more.

Certainly, with a new mission will likely come new strategic building blocks. But even an unchanged, or merely dusted off, mission will likely elicit revised, or brand-new, strategic building blocks. Jack Welch, immediately upon becoming GE's CEO, brought back to the fore the company's largely disregarded mission, made some modest revisions and then raised it to a place of prominence. That was followed by the development of some half a dozen new strategic building blocks designed to fulfill the mission's objectives. Specifically, Welch ordered that every one of the GE business units must be either first or second in their markets or be sold. He instituted a brutal winnowing process to maintain only the best employees. GE Capital, the financial division, was strengthened; it now accounts for half of GE's net income. An aggressive move into services was begun several years ago—GE not only produces jet engines but is in the high-margin business of servicing them. And more recently six-sigma quality control, globalization and Internet strategies have been put into place. GE's strategy, the sum of its strategic building blocks, today is barely recognizable compared to what it was when Welch took control.

Moses saw his mission as preparing the Hebrews in mind, body and soul for the rigors of coming battles and nationhood. That meant, among other things, living by God's law and the Ten Commandments. Change becomes far easier to achieve when a mission like that given to Moses is both so noble and at the same time so clearly articulated. Such a mission becomes an ever-present guiding force for strategic initiatives.

Upward Communication

It is crucial for a midlevel manager brought in to change a department or a CEO tasked to turn around an entire company to communicate upward effectively. To do this, midlevel managers trying to bring about change need to co-opt and win over senior management; CEOs must do the same with their board members and investors. Part of that process involves not overpromising, but, indeed, doing the reverse by emphasizing difficulties.

Without higher-level support, change is impossible to achieve. An organization will obstruct, delay, roadblock, sabotage, complain and ambush as means to counter an agent of change. Higher authority must help clear away obstacles, provide the necessary resources and remain resolute during the transition period when all is chaos and no progress is apparent. An organization's grapevine will quickly pick up on even the most subtle hint of a chairman and board withdrawing support for the CEO. The result of such withdrawal will be the CEO's undoing—he or she will be left twisting in the wind, already dead. "I stand fully behind Rick Thoman,"[13] said Paul Allaire, Xerox's chairman, of his CEO in December of 1999. No he didn't, and the fractious Xerox organization knew it. Thoman, who had been brought in to change the organization, was fired four months later.

Gen. Patton knew how to flatter and gain the support of superiors. He was a prolific note writer, recipients were his superiors and various political and other influential people who could be of future help to him. The notes, sometimes accompanied by thoughtful gifts, kept Patton in the minds of friends and supporters even when he was stationed in remote commands. Patton, independently wealthy, lavishly entertained people of importance always with an eye to his own benefit. It all proved effective; indeed, on at least two occasions, friends in high places saved his career: There was the politically incorrect slapping of a cowardly soldier in Sicily and then the quite public pronouncements of the threat and evils of Communism at a time when Russia was still an American ally.

Without intervention by Chief of Staff Gen. George Marshall and a number of top-ranking congressmen, Patton would have been cashiered and many of his great contributions to the war against Hitler unrealized.

Patton was a brilliant field commander. He was arguably at his very best when turning around a demoralized and poorly performing unit. Patton took command of the shattered II Corps in North Africa, which under Gen. Lloyd Fredendall had been routed by Germany's famed Desert Fox, Gen. Erwin Rommel, and his Afrika Korps at Kasserine Pass in Tunisia. Americans there suffered over 3,000 casualties and the loss of hundreds of tanks, trucks and artillery pieces. Seldom in American history have units performed so poorly—some 4,000 barely engaged GIs surrendered and were taken prisoner. Both friend and foe began to question American fighting ability. Yet within only a few months, Patton, taking over for the disgraced Fredendall, whipped the demoralized remnants of Kasserine into the confident victors of El Guettar, where it was the Germans who were sent fleeing. Those same GIs went on to become the core of America's renowned Third Army—among WWII's best fighting units and the most feared by the Nazis. None of that would have happened had Patton failed to maintain his upward communications and been relieved from duty.

Moses had a singularly demanding higher authority to whom he had to report. It should be easier for the rest of us. Still, the reader will need to work at diligently maintaining upward communication if he or she is to be an agent of change.

Leadership

Change cannot come without leadership. It was not a committee that faced down Pharaoh and brought the Hebrews out of Egypt. It was not a task force that served as the Lord's hand to chisel out of stone ten great commandments that would become the plinth upon which an entire nation would be built. It was not a council to whom those same Hebrews looked during forty years of wandering in the arid deserts of Sinai with all of the attendant vicissitudes, trials and tribulations. And it was not a board of directors that forged the Hebrews into a powerful fighting force. It was a single man. Moses. A leader.

Gen. Patton made a point of taking a new command with much pageantry to say nothing of considerable noise. With sirens wailing, accompanied by a motorcycle escort, there was Patton, his chest covered in ribbons and medals, standing ramrod straight beside his driver in a half-track, roaring into the headquarters' compound in a swirl of dust. This was pure spectacle. No humble, one-of-the-guys modesty here. This was in-your-face leadership—but leadership still.

In the biggest financial merger ever, Travelers Insurance and Citibank came together in early 1999 to form Citigroup. Vast organizational change was needed to meld the disparate corporate cultures of the buttoned-up Citibank and the free-wheeling Travelers. Co-CEOs led the company, Sandy Weill from Travelers and John Reed from Citibank. Predictably, one of them would be forced out. It was Reed who stepped down in April 2000, leaving Weill alone at the top. It is always one man or woman of enormous will and ability who is needed to lead a change.

Thomas Carlyle, the great Scottish writer of the nineteenth century, once observed that "History is the essence of innumerable biographies." It is individuals who guide the destiny of nations, empires and business enterprises. Almost always, only one individual is identified with the founding of America's great companies: John D. Rockefeller and Standard Oil, Andrew Carnegie and United States Steel, Henry Ford and Ford Motor, Alfred Sloan and General Motors, Thomas Watson and IBM; more recently, Sam Walton and Wal-Mart, Ray Kroc and McDonald's, Herb Kelleher and Southwest; more recently still, Bill Gates and Microsoft, John Chambers and Cisco, Andy Grove and Intel, Steve Case and AOL, Larry Ellison and Oracle—and so it goes.

Founders put their indelible stamp on a company, as do those who turn a company around after it has fallen into a tailspin. The Disney corporation is a classic example. The company has had many CEOs. None are remembered save two: the first, Walt Disney, who founded and built the company, and the last, Michael Eisner, who, twenty years after Walt's death, saved the company from the precipice of bankruptcy and turned it into an entertainment powerhouse.

Disney Corp. could not have reached maturity without the leadership and vision of Walt Disney nor could a strategy of change have been implemented, nearly half a century later, without the leadership of Michael Eisner.

Companies often founder after the loss of a great leader. Disney is but one example. Others come quickly to mind: Coca-Cola is still struggling a decade after the death of Roberto Goizueta. So, too, is Toys"R"Us with the loss of Robert Lazarus, ditto for Sears without Robert Wood. Those companies, and dozens like them, search for their Michael Eisners. It is, and will be, a most difficult search.

Corporate failures at attempted strategies of change tell as much about the importance of leadership as do the successes. Consider Xerox, introduced earlier. Richard Thoman was fired from his CEO position after little more than a year on the job. He had been brought in from GE to turn around a sclerotic firm whose days of glory had passed. Thoman did make some marginal changes, but during the last financial quarter of his tenure, sales were soft, income was down and the stock had declined 60 percent. He succumbed to powerful internal factions of the status quo that had rebelled against his restructuring plan. Paul Allaire, the chairman, has himself replaced Thoman as CEO and promoted twenty-four-year company veteran Anne Mulcahy to president. Among her first pronouncements was "I promise to do a lot of listening."[14] No, no, no, no no! Leaders do not use touchy-feely phrases like that. What is there new for her to listen to after being with the same organization for nearly a quarter of a century? Douglas MacArthur, among the greatest of American military leaders, once wrote, "Councils of war breed timidity and defeatism." MacArthur looked within himself for direction. Leadership can be summed up in two words: "Follow me." Which brings us back to Xerox under Mulcahy—unless she looks to herself for direction, expect little change and the company to remain beleaguered.

NEWSFLASH! (January, 2001) Xerox has slashed its dividend by 75 percent following the report of another financial quarter of losses and a credit down-rating by Moody's.

In nearly every one of the ten strategies presented in this book, leadership is among the factors needed for successful execution. In no other situation is a leader more important than in the design and execution of a strategy of change. Indeed, robust leadership is an absolute necessity for overcoming the oppressive inertia of the status quo and bringing about substantive change.

"The Cadillac of the Sky"

Several business examples help to highlight aspects of the factors of success associated with a strategy of change. The cases of Chrysler, Sunbeam, Gateway, *Harper's Bazaar* and Cadillac offer particular insights. Consider first the turnaround at Chrysler, which is perhaps business history's best known.

Iacocca

In 1978, the flamboyant Lee Iacocca took control of a nearly bankrupt Chrysler. To accept the job, he had to come out of retirement after spending decades at Ford, where he had been credited with the highly successful Mustang. His wife and friends pleaded with him not to take on the disaster that was Chrysler: negative net worth, 200 days of unsold inventory, a rabid union, dealers in insurrection, banks demanding loan repayment and intracompany feudal empires. Iacocca set to work managing and negotiating his way out of the morass. He maintained an outwardly optimistic and calm facade in the face of the fear, chaos and ambiguity around him. Iacocca was a tough man and a strong leader. Those who stood in his way were eliminated. The federal government helped with an unprecedented, and never since repeated, multibillion-dollar loan.

Iacocca and the men and women of Chrysler worked hard. Within a decade, helped by the advent of the minivan, Chrysler's turnaround was complete—an unquestioned personal triumph for Iacocca. Yet after stabilizing the company, Iacocca's leadership results were modest at best. It took a board coup to dynamite him from his CEO and chairman position. His successors went on to grow the company until its recent acquisition by Daimler.

Chainsaw Al Dunlap

In the late 1980s and early 1990s, Albert J. Dunlap had earned a reputation as a turnaround artist. He had indeed reversed the disastrous state of some half a dozen companies. His formula for treatment was simple and hardly subtle. He moved quickly to close down factories, consolidate product lines and fire employees—up to 80 percent of them in one case. Within a year or so, when the hemorrhaging of red ink had been stanched and even a modest profit obtained, he moved on. He would leave behind a company with a few solid products and a cost structure cut to, no, make that beyond, the bone. Proudly he accepted the nickname "Chainsaw."

Dunlap's callousness was an asset. Not everyone savors intimidating others and enjoys firing people. Indeed, many cannot do it at all. Things were going Dunlap's way, his reputation reaching new heights. But, how does that saying go?, "Whom the gods will destroy they first make arrogant." Dunlap wrote a cloying, self-aggrandizing book trumpeting his achievements and self-proclaimed management skills. His glowering, drill-sergeant face adorned covers of business magazines. He became a popular speaker at top business schools around the country where young Gen-X students, never before much taken by authority figures, suddenly decided they wanted to be just like Chainsaw. Dunlap was at the top of his game. Then came Sunbeam.

Dunlap was brought in to reverse the fortunes of the floundering Sunbeam and immediately set about applying his usual prescription of plant closings and consolidations, paring of product line and mass firings. At first, it seemed to work. The company's stock doubled, then tripled. A spectacular turnaround had been achieved. The media gushed. Investors swooned with delight. But Dunlap made a great mistake; he decided to stick around and build the company. Too bad. To a manager whose only tool is a chainsaw, everything looks like a tree to be cut down. The company began to struggle and within two years again verged on bankruptcy. The once-swaggering Dunlap was forced out. He hasn't written any more books.

The Germans have a wonderful word, *schadenfreude,* referring to the great satisfaction or pleasure one takes from seeing a nemesis, or one heartily disliked, fall from grace or upon rough times. Thousands whom

Dunlap had run roughshod over during his career must have felt some of that and savored the delicious news of his decline. But, in retrospect, his skills and ability were outstanding, just limited. Change requires killing the old and building the new. Dunlap was adept only at the former.

NEWSFLASH! (February 6, 2001) Some three years after Dunlap's departure, Sunbeam—unable to recover—seeks Chapter 11 protection.

Gateway

In mid-1998 Gateway, while a volume-leading PC manufacturer, saw its profits disappear and its stock descend to new lows. The management was bloated and the company was being overtaken by a swifter and leaner Dell. The company attempted to reinvent itself using several of the factors of success discussed here. Most important, a new CEO, Jeff Weitzen, was hired. Headquarters was moved from South Dakota to San Diego. Alliances were struck with AOL, OfficeMax and Sun Microsystems. A strategic move was made into consumer PC services and training. Top executives were replaced. The company was reorganized into several business units: systems, software, peripherals, Internet access, service and training. All of that was to the good.

There is, however, a wildcard in this recasting of Gateway: Ted Waitt, the previous CEO and a major stockholder, kicked himself upstairs to chairman. He is the higher authority to whom Weitzen must report, but he is the same man who put Gateway into its precarious position to begin with. This story of change is still unfolding, it will be worth watching.

NEWSFLASH! (January 11, 2001) After the fourth quarter of 2000 loss of $94 million, Gateway announced the dismissal of some 3,000 more employees. "I don't see it getting a lot easier in the course of the next year,"[15] Weitzen lamented.

Harper's Bazaar

Kate Betts only recently was made editor of the venerable, 137-year-old *Harper's Bazaar*—venerable but arthritic and problem plagued.

For years, advertising revenues and paid subscriptions had been declining, and the readers, at least those who were still loyal, were rapidly aging. Betts swept in and launched mass firings, changed the masthead, used new fonts and dramatically shifted story lines to appeal to younger readers.

One immediate result of the changes was a near insurrection among the magazine's staff. The situation was exacerbated by the untimely death from cancer of the much-loved, and long-serving, previous editor. Betts faces the magazine's internecine battles with the putative support of her boss, Cathleen Black, the president of Hearst Magazines. Ms. Black says, "I believe that Kate has the vision to take *Harper's* into the next century."[16] We will see.

Cadillac

Steven Spielberg is arguably the greatest of today's filmmakers. Among his best, but less well known, works is *Empire of the Sun*. Set in WWII, most of the action takes place in a Japanese prison camp outside of Shanghai where hundreds of British civilians have been interned. The film's star is a twelve- or thirteen-year-old English lad who had been separated from his parents at the war's onset and imprisoned ever since. In a scene toward the film's end, a Japanese landing field next to the prison camp is being strafed by American aircraft. The boy, who had for years dreamed of flying, and is something of an expert on Japanese, German, British and American combat planes, races to a rooftop in the camp to better watch the attack. Overcome with excitement and emotion, he begins to wave wildly and jump up and down, as he screams, "It's the P-51 Mustang, the Cadillac of the sky!"[17] You got that? *Cadillac* of the sky. This is an English boy. In Shanghai. Fifty years ago.

Cadillac, at the close of WWII, was *the* worldwide recognized symbol of unparalleled excellence. The factories of German luxury car manufacturers were mere rubble. No Japanese luxury, or any other, automobile plants had survived the incessant fire bombing by American B-29s. Cadillac, with Lincoln a distant second, owned the world's luxury car market.

Time went by and year by year Cadillac's leadership diminished. Today, Cadillac struggles in the United States against Lexus, Mercedes, BMW, Infiniti and Ford's collection of marquee luxury brands: Lincoln, Aston Martin, Volvo, Land Rover and Jaguar. Cadillac's presence in Europe and Asia is negligible. Worldwide, Mercedes, BMW, Audi and Lexus outsell Cadillac—Mercedes by five to one. Whatever preeminence Cadillac had half a century ago, it assuredly does not have now. This is not to say that Cadillac isn't trying. A very exciting luxury roadster, the Imaj, and a new SUV are coming in to dealer showrooms; they should do very well. In addition, there are a few interesting new marketing concepts on the horizon. But all of that is probably mere futile incrementalism, tactical tinkering at the edges. Merrill Lynch analyst John Casesa says, "Cadillac is now an outsider fighting its way back to a market it created."

For Cadillac, the seeds of a renaissance, if there is to be one, could be found in these past few pages. Change requires bold moves. How bold? Spin off the Cadillac Division from GM in an initial public offering or tracking stock. Move the headquarters out of Michigan and to Southern California, or better yet, replace the headquarters with a triquarters located in Frankfurt, Tokyo and Beverly Hills. Move all manufacturing to nonunion Tennessee, Kentucky or Mississippi. Fire nearly the whole senior management and much of middle management. Bring in a new young CEO, maybe a GE alumni, from the outside and surround him or her with very tough, car-loving, really smart people. Sweat blood in clearly defining the Cadillac mission of the twenty-first century. Develop a Dell-like build-to-order manufacturing system. Completely alter manufacturer-dealer relations. Strike unimagined alliances. Turn the vehicles into consumer electronic and telecom platforms. Invade Lexus' home market of Japan. Assault Germany, the home of BMW and Mercedes. Make daring acquisitions that shake the industry. And more.

It is unlikely that any of these things will happen—the people of General Motors and its Cadillac Division will voice a hundred, a thousand reasons and excuses why it cannot be done. The most trenchant argument against change likely to be heard is "Look, we are still doing OK." It is not clear but Cadillac might be practicing some variation of a strategy of containment as discussed in chapter 12—contain the competition and hold on to what we have. It remains to be seen whether change, real change, will come. But it may—GM's CEO, G. Richard Wagoner, has urged his people to shake off complacency, caution and tradition and begin to take more risk. There is rumor that Wagoner may shut down the Oldsmobile Division—a bold move.

Cadillac is just one of a long list of American, and for that matter European and Japanese, companies in vital need of a strategy of change—a strategy upon which the very long-term survival of the company depends.

———————

When Joshua crossed the Jordan, he immediately deployed all of his forces against tribal enemies in the Holy Land's central region. Victorious there, he then concentrated and coordinated his forces against enemies in the south. Victorious once again, he then moved against hostile northern tribes, again with his own army concentrated and coordinated at the point of attack. Concentration and coordination of forces is the most fundamental of military, and by extension business, strategies. Gen. Schwarzkopf's Desert Storm did exactly that against Saddam Hussein in the Gulf War.

CHAPTER SEVEN

Desert Storm

Concentration of Forces

There is no higher, or more basic, military strategy than keeping one's forces concentrated at the point of attack.
— Carl von Clausewitz

Desert Storm was intended to . . . pulverize the [Iraqi] enemy with overwhelming force.
— Gen. Barry McCaffrey[1]

We built our company by focusing upon a pretty simple, but focused premise of Quality, Service, Cleanliness and Value.
— Ray Kroc, founder, McDonald's

We probably didn't run our everyday business as well as we should have.
— David Glass, CEO, Wal-Mart[2]

We will concentrate on fewer things.
— Geraldine Laybourne, CEO, Oxygen[3]

It was a strategic error to diversify out of our core brands.
— Robert Eckert, CEO, Mattel[4]

Feeding Frenzy

Norman Schwarzkopf, the Gulf War's United Nations' Commander, insisted that his forces attacking Saddam Hussein's elite Republican Guard in occupied Kuwait must first be concentrated and coordinated to bring overwhelming power to bear against the enemy. This was done—it took six months to assemble the necessary troops and massive materiel stockpiles during which time coordinated training among infantry, mechanized, artillery and air units was ongoing. The world waited for the clash that was sure to come. On one side was Iraq with the fourth-largest army in the world. Opposing the Iraqis would be UN forces, composed of nearly 1 million men drawn from thirty-one nations including America. The battle began on January 6, 1991 with concentrated round-the-clock air strikes pounding Iraqi targets. Two weeks of that followed. Then came the concentrated and coordinated ground attack. It was spearheaded by massed armor and infantry assaults with a rolling artillery barrage leading the way and air-cover overhead. The impact of this concentrated blitzkrieg on the Iraqis was devastating. Typical was Medina Ridge, where Gen. Barry McCaffrey's 24th Mechanized Division deployed its M1A1 tanks and Apache helicopters to destroy sixty-six Iraqi tanks without suffering a single casualty of its own.

Then came the endgame as the panicked Iraqi soldiers began to flee, ripping off their uniforms as they ran to show they were unarmed. The single highway leading from Kuwait City back to Baghdad became clogged with Iraqi men and vehicles. Spotting the rich target, American fighter pilots, in a joyful feeding frenzy, began repeated strafing and carpet-bombing. The "Highway of Death," as the Iraqis came to call it, was littered with the twisted and smoldering wreckage of transport and armored vehicles. Carried by the desert winds, the stench of the sun-bloated dead could be detected miles away. Iraq's abortive Mideast power grab ended in the mauling of its infantry and near-total destruction of its weaponry: the UN captured or destroyed 363 Iraqi tanks, 314 artillery pieces, 207 antiaircraft guns, 1,278 trucks and 25 warplanes. The ground attack, aptly code-named Desert Storm, ended after just 100 hours. The Gulf War was won. Kuwait was liberated, Saddam was hamstrung and Persian Gulf oil once again flowed unencumbered to the industrial world. Gen. Schwarzkopf's strategy of concentrated and coordinated force was crucial to victory. Carl von Clausewitz should have gotten some posthumous credit.

While a West Point cadet, Schwarzkopf had studied Clausewitz, the great Prussian military scholar and practitioner, who first went to war in 1793 as a twelve-year-old lance corporal. One of the most enduring of Clausewitz' contributions to the art and science of warfare is the strategic principle of concentrating and coordinating forces at a single point of attack. Clausewitz came to this from his own experiences on the battlefield as well as an analysis of earlier wars, including Caesar's that were fought in Gaul, roughly today's France, almost 2,000 years ago. Caesar was always victorious even when overall he was vastly outnumbered. By hard marches and ingenious signal systems he was able to concentrate his entire army against one selected enemy position. Clausewitz also studied Genghis Khan, the great Mongol leader, who, like Caesar, used overwhelming force in sudden attacks to defeat his enemies piecemeal.

Perhaps no strategy is more fundamental than this in military warfare: Concentrate and coordinate your forces at the point of attack so that even a small force can rout a much larger one. Nor is there a strategy more basic in the business wars. Companies disregard this strategy at their great peril.

ITT, Espresso, Mach 3s and Big Macs

Failing to apply this fundamental military strategy in business almost always has led to failure. Younger readers may not have lived through the era of the conglomerates during the 1950s and early 1960s. The conglomerates were collections of disparate businesses having no relationship to one another, the very converse of concentration. They were managed and directed from central headquarters by the numbers: sundry quantitative measures and financial ratios that could be used no matter the specific businesses. For a while, even though there was not even a pretense of synergy between the multifarious business units comprising the conglomerate, it seemed to work. The new corporate model was proclaimed to have achieved the ultimate in corporate efficiency and profitability. Investors became infatuated and drove conglomerates' stock prices to stratospheric highs. The haughty faces of LTV's Jimmy Ling and ITT's Harold Geneen were splashed across the covers of business magazines The two epitomized the flinty-eyed, number-crunching new conglomerate CEOs. Then, in the mid-1960s, came the rather sudden and precipitous collapses and bankruptcies. In retrospect, the conglomerates were simply variations on the old-fashioned holding companies with central headquarters dispersing or withholding capital without really understanding the diverse underlying businesses. The lack of concentration made failure inevitable. Get a cup of espresso and consider another case—this one of focus once had, but lost.

Few business models have been more successful than Starbucks' with its coffee houses offering expensive and exotic brews in a relaxed ambiance. But dissatisfied with growth rates, Starbucks began in the late 1990s to expand into coffee ice cream, iced drinks, airport coffee-dispensing kiosks, packaged coffee sold in markets, cafes serving full meals and liquor, an Internet capital fund, a magazine and . . . the sale of high-priced luxury home pasta makers. Concentration and coordination, once fundamental to the company, is slipping away. The result: Competitors are attacking and same store sales are stagnant.

Warren Buffett rarely makes mistakes, but one company in his portfolio of a dozen or so stocks is Gillette, of which he owns 11 percent—and Gillette has lost both concentration and, in a bull market, about half its market cap. The company produces the finest shaving system ever made, the Mach 3. It is a global leader in men's shaving needs with 64 percent of the market. Schick runs a poor second. Gillette's mission, going back a century, was built around shaving. King Camp Gillette—his real name—invented the disposable steel razor blade and concentrated all of his efforts on improving it and building the company he founded. That concentration was as it should be. Growth was explosive: in 1903 Gillette sold 168 blades and in 1904 more than 12 million. But somewhere along the way, years after the founder's death, the company began to drift. First, Gillette picked up the Braun line of kitchen devices, hair dryers and healthcare instruments. Later it added a battery business and then still more encumbering baggage with a stationery unit that included Parker, Waterman and Paper Mate pens. All of these businesses are doing poorly. Gillette looks like a messy garage filled with years of indiscriminate acquisitions bought for reasons now long forgotten. The company's recent financial performance has been disappointing. Senior management blames global economic turbulence and foreign currency woes. A more accurate assessment places the blame on management itself for losing sight of the Clausewitz strategy of concentration.

NEWSFLASH! (December 29, 2000) Gillette has announced the sale of its stationery unit to Newell Rubbermaid. Good. Perhaps Gillette's CEO Michael Hawley has begun to read Clausewitz.

NEWSFLASH UPDATE! Only weeks after the stationery unit sale, Gillette has reported another bad quarter and Warren Buffett has engineered the firing of Hawley. Maybe he did not read Clausewitz after all.

One final example of the importance of concentration. Ray Kroc founded and built one of the twentieth century's most successful companies with a simple and highly focused business plan: hamburgers, fries and malts sold with Quality, Cleanliness, Service and Value. Kroc's first McDonald's opened in southern California in the 1950s. The hamburgers cost 20 cents, the fries were crisp and the malts refreshing. The outlet was white-tiled, sparkling clean and featured fast service provided by smiling and friendly attendants. Over the next thirty years the company thrived and served up not only billions of hamburgers but billions more of dollars of return to investors. But since Kroc's death, and especially during the 1990s, McDonald's has been grappling with sluggish sales growth. A newly appointed vice president of corporate strategy, Mats Lederhausen, has been appointed to generate some fresh ideas. That he assuredly has done with the dubious result that McDonald's has bought the bankrupt Boston Chicken chain as well as a Mexican food and pizza chain. Each addition has made McDonald's strategically less focused.

But there is even more diffusion of concentration at McDonald's. Watch for the retailing of McKids clothing and shoes as well as McD books and videos for kids. There is more. There are plans for grocery stores to feature McDonald's ketchup, snacks, ice cream and baked goods. "There is an enormous opportunity to find new streams of income,"[5] says CEO Jack Greenberg. No, there isn't. Take the McDonald's ketchup initiative as only one example. H. J. Heinz, with 54 percent of the U.S. ketchup market and selling 650 million bottles a year worldwide, has been making, marketing and distributing this all-American condiment for over 100 years. How is a McDonald's management steeped in the fast-food restaurant business going to compete with that? This is a classic example of chasing incremental sales and synergy and walking into a waiting ambush.

Greenberg, who did not come up through restaurant ranks, has been lauded by some analysts for a willingness to try new ideas. But there is a danger of losing core restaurant business focus. If history is a guide, McDonald's will have at best modest success in these new ventures and lessened attention will further weaken the existing restaurant business. There are signs of trouble even now with McDonald's failing to meet analyst expectations over the last few quarters. A company spokesman says, "We had problems with unusually hot weather, televised soccer and waning enthusiasm for Beanie Babies."[6] Oh. Today, the restaurant of choice for nearly any three-year-old in the country is McDonald's. For corporate management to take steps that cause a loss of concentration and put at risk that kind of invaluable brand loyalty, caught at such an early age, borders on the irresponsible.

One wishes that the late Ray Kroc, a good man but an earthy-tongued tyrant when it came to operating details and focused concentration on his business strategy, could spend just one hour with the company's current management. "Look," he would likely say, "It's not that complicated: 'hamburgers, fries and malts with Quality, Cleanliness, Service and Value,' and not !@#$% ketchup, or kid videos and books." We can only guess what else the self-educated, impatient and cantankerous Kroc would say to the young MBAs who, although never having worked behind a counter, nevertheless dreamed up the sundry "brand extensions."

Strategic Choice: Prevailing Circumstances

The circumstances that signal a concentration and coordination business strategy are based on fairly evident signs of corporate pathology: noncore acquisitions, a CEO intent on mindless growth for its own sake, a weed-filled and nonmarket-leading product mix, much talk of synergy and incremental sales, a vaguely articulated and largely disregarded mission, poor financial performance and a continuous wailing lament that "Investment analysts just don't understand us."

It is not just Starbucks, Gillette and McDonald's that are adrift. Sears, Kmart and GM are among a hundred and more companies that have lost concentration in their markets and their capital allocations. Conversely, other companies excel precisely because they adhere to Clausewitz's strategic principle of concentration, companies like Nike, Nordstrom, Southwest Airlines, Home Depot, Nokia and FedEx.

To balance the strategy-of-concentration argument, there have been a few occasions in military history where concentration of forces has *not* been adhered to and success was nevertheless obtained. Robert E. Lee sometimes split off Stonewall Jackson and his men to flank the enemy while Lee held the enemy's front. The daring Gen. George Patton also liked to use this approach occasionally. He described it as "Hold them by the nose and kick them in the pants." And then there was MacArthur's splitting of his forces to achieve a successful flanking attack at Inchon in the Korean War. But in each case a unique set of circumstances suggested a departure from principle; even then the actions were very dangerous and filled with risk.

How dangerous and risky is challenging this principle of concentration? Lt. Col. George Custer, with his blond walrus mustache and long flowing hair, had sought the spotlight throughout his career. His daring had always worked beginning with the Civil War when he had been a boy hero. In the summer of 1876, in a major campaign against the Sioux, he chose once again to defy military principle. Believing his luck would hold, he divided his regiment into three units just hours before attacking Sitting Bull, Crazy Horse and what turned out to be some 5,000 Sioux warriors at the Little Big Horn in Montana. Custer ordered Captains Benteen and Reno to take their respective commands on a wide flanking double envelopment of the Sioux village while he attacked from the front. But Benteen and Reno never really got into the fight. In a battle that lasted less than an hour, the unit headed by Custer was wiped out. Every single man, including Custer, his two brothers, his brother-in-law, a nephew and 242 others, lost their lives. In war and business, and under almost all prevailing circumstances, forces should be strategically concentrated and coordinated at the point of attack. In the case of Custer's last stand, they were neither.

Factors of Success

To achieve success with the strategy of concentration and coordination requires addressing a number of factors including mission, attention to detail, outsourcing, Scylla and Charybdis, leadership and communication. Begin with the mission.

Mission

Earlier reference was made to Microsoft's mission: "Empower people through great software, any time, any place and on any device." That's very good, except now comes news that Microsoft will soon launch its Xbox game player in direct competition with Sony, Nintendo and Sega. This hardware initiative does not fit at all within the stated mission. The initiative may have been undertaken as a retaliation against Sony, which refused Microsoft's offer to write software for the former's enormously successful PlayStation. Nevertheless, this is exactly the kind of diffusion of resources and management attention that insidiously leads companies into treacherous waters. In the case of Starbucks, Gillette and McDonald's the original mission apparently has been lost sight of, shelved or conveniently reinterpreted. That may now be happening with Microsoft as well.

Napoleon once raged at his generals, "When you start to take Vienna, take Vienna!" When the mission is Vienna, no strategy that weakens the concentration and coordination of forces needed to capture it is acceptable. The mission must be constantly kept in mind's eye. Every strategy must be tested against it for consistency, and every strategy should have the intent of bringing the mission one step closer to fruition. When McDonald's mission is Quality, Cleanliness, Service and Value, it should not capriciously decide to become a retailer of ketchup and children's videos. By no stretch of the English language can such diversions be shoehorned into consistency with the mission that Kroc first articulated some forty years ago.

NEWSFLASH! (November 17, 2000) McDonald's has just announced the construction of two hotels in Switzerland, repeat: two hotels in Switzerland. At a recent press conference, CEO Jack Greenberg defends the action by saying "Our passion for making customers smile extends very naturally to the hotel sector."[7] It does?

In the midst of the e-commerce boom in the late 1990s—and to much trumpeting—Geraldine Laybourne launched her e-business venture called Oxygen. Beyond some muttered words about selling to women, there was no clear mission. "We thought we had an enormous, limitless canvas [to paint on]," CEO Laybourne later said. "Oh God, why did we think that we could do 19 different websites?"[8] The company is now languishing badly from lack of concentration. Laybourne had earlier success at Disney and earlier still had achieved well-deserved prominence in the cable TV industry. But at Oxygen she gave far too much free rein to her talented and spirited people. Without an overarching mission to constrain it, the organization lost concentration and spun out of control. A more tightly drawn mission would have saved Oxygen. For any company, mission is a crucial factor of success in the execution of strategic concentration and coordination of resources.

Attention to Detail

Often, out of intellectual and psychological laziness, companies get into trouble, straying from a strategy of focused concentration. It is really hard to take an already fine product like Gillette's shaving system of the mid-1990s and refine it to today's state-of-the-art Mach 3. Gillette's development costs were $245 million, with commensurate hours of struggle and frustration, but the finished product has been a great market hit. The work was tedious, painstaking and demanding, but that didn't matter because the involved engineering and design people experienced the great satisfaction that comes from resolving the finest and smallest of details.

In contrast, it was quite easy for Gillette to acquire the Parker Pen company. Consider a typical scenario in which one company acquires another. One phone call to an investment banker is all it takes to get things started. After that there are meetings for the CEO to sit through with bankers, lawyers and accountants close at hand. Spreadsheets, with ersatz numbers camouflaging the guesswork involved, are stared at and, truth be known, not completely or always understood. Outside, high-priced, advisors are listened to raptly and a few high-level negotiation decisions have to be made. There is nothing too difficult about any of this. Nevertheless, the CEO and the select few senior managers who are putting the deal together are treated, during the negotiations, by all involved like visiting foreign dignitaries. They are flown about in private jets to various locations and driven from here to there in stretch limousines with blackened windows. Their every personal request is responded to with a "Yes, sir" or "Yes, Ma'am." Sycophants and little people are all about. Faced with such VIP treatment, members of the CEO-led negotiation team begin to feel rather self-important. They are movers and shakers—indeed empire builders. It is illusion. The reality is that going through the mechanics of acquiring a new business different from one's own is hardly much of an achievement. On the other hand, growing, concentrating and coordinating one's own business, down to the most minute detail, is hard, very hard, but it is a winning strategy.

General Motors is an example of a company that seemingly has difficulty concentrating on detail. The company has been troubled for decades, falling ever further behind Ford and Chrysler as well as the Japanese and European automakers. CEOs come and go trying the same tired and old marketing nostrums. But GM still refuses, or is unable, to focus on the simplest of details: the meticulous, painstaking, nitty-gritty of manufacturing quality cars. Its labor costs per car are 16 percent higher than Ford's, and still Gabe Shenhar, the senior auto testing engineer at *Consumer Reports*, observes that "GM is at the bottom of the charts."[9] The company has been there for a quarter of a century.

Durk Jager, upon becoming CEO of Procter & Gamble late in 1998, attempted to increase revenues by acquisitions into noncore pharmaceutics; he made a bid for American Home Products. P&G investors were apoplectic at what they thought to be a senseless initiative that was inconsistent with a strategy of concentration and proceeded to pound the stock. One-third of the company's market value vanished in a single day of trading, an unprecedented drop.

P&G still has some 300 brands, including Pampers, Old Spice, Crisco and Crest, many of which are struggling. Colgate and Unilever, major competitors, are becoming ever more aggressive and nimble while P&G lumbers forward with far too many brands and redundant levels of management. An example of the right direction for P&G is its revitalized information technology and Web initiative. A new chief information officer (CIO) was hired to report directly to the CEO. It is expected that new software will provide valuable product tracking and distribution information. Detail-oriented actions like that, multiplied a thousandfold, are the essence of a winning concentration and coordination strategy. Unfortunately for Jager, as noted in the last chapter, he will not be around to see victory, if indeed there is to be one. Jager has been replaced by Alan Lafley, who talks about taking the company back to basics.

In 1997, Jill Barad, Mattel's new CEO, made as one of her first decisions the $3.5 billion purchase of the Learning Co., a developer of children's education-oriented CD-ROMs that were distributed to Kmart and Target. This was a business that neither Barad nor Mattel had much experience with. The acquisition proved to be a financial disaster and cost Barad her job. From the beginning, the CD-ROM sales were very disappointing and losses were a drag on the rest of the company. After missing several quarters of promised earnings, Barad was fired. This might have been predicted. Acquisitions that deviate from the acquirers' core businesses fail far more often than succeed.

Ironically, Barad rose to the CEO position in the company as a result of her great success with the Barbie line for which Mattel was best known. Had she built on that, along with the popular Hot Wheels matchbox-size toy cars, she would still be in the CEO's office. Worrying the details of red, as opposed to orange, flame decals on a matchbox car, or the color of Barbie's new hiking backpack, perhaps lacks the glamour of engineering a multibillion-dollar acquisition, but the former leads to profitability and the latter has led to a financial debacle. Barad's replacement, the newly appointed CEO Robert Eckert, says, "Ms. Barad's bid to fashion Mattel as a diversified family consumer-products company was 'a strategic error.'"[10] Eckert vows to bring concentration to Mattel by refocusing on its main brands.

There are two telling addendums to this Mattel story. First, the company's board of directors lavished upon Barad a $47 million severance package even though under her brief reign investors saw their individual shares plummet from $46 to $10. "It's horrifying,"[11] says Nell Minow, a shareholder activist referring to the severance package. Second, in late 2000, Mattel sold the albatross Learning Co. to Gores Technology, a buyout firm, for no cash and a maximum of $300 million from future earnings should there be any. Don't count on much of that $300 million finding its way back to Mattel—the folks at Gores Technology have too sharp of an accounting pencil. Nearly $3.5 billion is gone, making the original Mattel acquisition arguably the worst in business history. A strategy of concentration and attention to detail would have avoided the entire fiasco.

A return to attention to detail is also key to McDonald's future. In the fast-food industry over the last few years, the drive-through segment of the business has been the fastest growing. There is stiff competition among the major players—McDonald's, Burger King and Wendy's—to shave time off of the customer's entire transaction; even a few seconds matter. In this regard, McDonald's has spent heavily in the detailed engineering of a new device that cooks up a fresh batch of fries in only 65 seconds. To an outsider, there is not much allure in the mundane operating details, but the engineers of that frying system are the company's heroes and heroines as well as its salvation. Vince Lombardi once wrote, "Discard the immaterial and perfect the few things you do best."[12] That is good counsel for McDonald's.

One day, in the midst of WWII, a young tank officer found his machine mired in mud at a crucial river crossing. He tried everything that he knew but could not extricate the tank. Suddenly he heard pounding on the turret above him and a high-pitched American voice shrieking a consummately creative stream of profanities. Opening the hatch, the tanker looked up into the florid face of Third Army's sixty-year-old, three star commander, Gen. George Patton. "!@#$% son, move over," shouted Patton as he took the tank's controls and, with some deft shifting of gears and maneuvering, quickly freed the monster machine. Patton made a point of knowing, to the smallest detail, every weapon and vehicle used by his men. Patton's Third Army reminds one of Wal-Mart and Gen. Patton reminds one of Wal-Mart's CEO, David Glass.

Wal-Mart has always practiced a strategy of concentration and coordination with its attendant attention to detail. David Glass recently gave a forty-minute speech to his store managers arguing the merits of stocking Halloween candy early so that customers will buy it, thoughtlessly eat it themselves and then have to come back for more. Now David Glass is the senior man at the second-largest company on the *Fortune* 500 with 1,140,000 people reporting to him. Still, he finds time to pay attention to Halloween sweets. "Retail is detail,"[13] he says. He is right, but more accurately: "Business is detail." This kind of attention to detail is a crucial factor for the success of this chapter's strategy of concentration and coordination.

Outsourcing

The term "outsourcing" entered the business lexicon in the early 1990s and has rapidly become basic to business. "We outsource all of our maintenance and various operational stuff. I don't care, they're not strategic."[14] That was Sun's CEO, Scott McNealy, talking about outsourcing—one of the most important means to positively affect a strategy of concentration and coordination. Sun of course is not alone in this regard.

Hewlett-Packard has ten contract electronic manufacturers (CEMs) that it outsources to. IBM has eight and Cisco, nine. By taking on manufacturing, the CEMs leave companies like HP, IBM and Cisco to concentrate on their R&D and marketing. The most nimble and profitable of the CEMs are Flextronics, Celestica, Selectronics and Jabil.

Qualcomm is renowned for its outsourcing. Unlike Intel and Texas Instruments, Qualcomm outsources all of its chip manufacturing, rendering it the world's largest so-called fabless semiconductor company.

Motorola and Flextronics have just signed the biggest outsourcing deal ever between a name-brand company and a contract manufacturer. The deal will extend over five years and involves some $30 billion. Flextronics will manufacture cellular phones, pagers, TV set-top boxes and electronic components for Motorola.

Saturn outsources all of its logistics to Ryder, United Air Lines outsources engine maintenance to GE, AOL outsources Web design to Inktomi, Cisco outsources shipping to FedEx, Nike outsources manufacturing to dozens of Third World contractors and Exxon outsources oil exploration to Schlumberger. In a very short period of time, outsourcing has become pervasive, indeed matter-of-fact.

Outsourcing is a wonderful thing, allowing companies to concentrate their efforts only on mission-critical issues. But outsourcing does come with warnings, the most important of which is to never outsource activities that are critical to the mission—more about that in chapter 8. Another cautionary note is that outsourcing does not mean abdicating responsibility. A company must carefully monitor its outsourcing efforts if it is to avoid some very unpleasant surprises. Nike has been hit with some terrible public relations (PR) because the Third World manufacturers it outsourced to allegedly paid below-minimum wages and were guilty of various other labor abuses. In a second example, in late 2000 Ford announced a massive recall of defective tires that had been part of the original equipment on new Explorers. The tires, outsourced for manufacturing to Bridgestone with its Firestone brand, allegedly blew under certain road conditions causing vehicles to spin and flip out of control. It is claimed that over 100 fatalities have resulted. By the time this mess is over, Ford will have lost hundreds of millions of dollars in litigation and sales. Ford did not monitor Bridgestone diligently enough and is now paying an enormous price. Nike and Ford, two fine companies, were blindsided as a result of their outsourcing. They offer a free lesson for everyone else: Outsource but monitor and verify.

Scylla and Charybdis

In Greek mythology, Ulysses found himself navigating his ship through the Strait of Messina. On one side was the sea monster Scylla, part woman and part fish with dog heads growing from her waist, who had a nasty habit of eating sailors that ventured too close. Ulysses lost six of his men to her. Across from Scylla was the terrible whirlpool Charybdis that trapped ships and took them, and their men, to the ocean's bottom and a watery grave. In business today, the sea monster is the illusion of incremental sales and the whirlpool is the chimera of synergy. Even the best companies have a difficult time navigating these treacherous waters. The pull toward disaster, in either direction, is both strong and insidious. Many fall prey. Nike, Home Depot, Southwest Airlines, The Gap and Crate & Barrel are examples of outstanding and highly concentrated companies. Yet even they are being tempted.

Nike, known for its athletic shoes, is launching a brand extension campaign. Soon the Nike swoosh will be seen on ergonomic watches, digital audio players for joggers, heart-rate monitoring devices and high-tech walkie-talkies. This may make some sense, in that the products are all related to athletic activity, but Nike will be bumping up against established industry leading companies like Sony and Panasonic. Nike will not venture too far afield; it will outsource the manufacturing of these products although the design will be its own. Nevertheless, Nike now has footwear, clothing and its fledgling electronics division. Phil Knight is an Olympics-quality, gold medal-winning CEO, but he may have extended himself too far here, falling prey to Scylla's seductive call.

Line extensions are always dangerous but sometimes can be achieved. Introducing a new name brand can be helpful. The Gap did that with its initially highly successful Old Navy stores that featured comparatively lower prices and lesser-quality items, but Old Navy recently has had problems. The use of subbrands can sometimes also be effective. The upscale Marriott hotel chain, for example, built Courtyard by Marriott for business travelers and price-conscious families as a way to move downscale. But even here there is a danger of cannibalization or simply trading one set of customers for another.

Home Depot has been one of America's most successful companies. Founded in the 1970s by Bernie Marcus and Arthur Blank, two disgruntled hardware salesman, it has revolutionized the retail hardware and home improvement business with its clean, well-stocked, category-killer stores. Home Depot has some 32 percent market share today with Loew's running a distant second. The company's concentration in serving home improvement aficionados and their professional counterparts is near total. Even outside members of its board of directors are required to visit a score of stores every year to make certain they understand the business. All of that is as it should be—but Home Depot has announced it is beginning to sell home appliances in their stores. Even though there is a perceived synergy here, Home Depot is moving into terra incognita with this white-goods foray. Danger and high likelihood of failure awaits. It is astonishing to see a successful and superbly managed company like Home Depot drift into the treacherous arms of Scylla or the black death of Charybdis.

Another example concerns Southwest, arguably the best airline in the country. Southwest's past success came from its concentration on short routes, use of small airports, excellent customer service and a blanketing of readily available flights in its eponymous geographic region. It attacked competitor weaknesses and has thrived. But again Scylla and Charybdis call. Southwest is now expanding into the highly congested central and eastern regions of the United States. This will bring a whole new set of problems the company has never before seen. Another worry is that Southwest's charismatic CEO, Herb Kelleher, is about to retire. A loss of concentration could be a disaster for Southwest. We now have an airline called Southwest that flies in the *Northeast* . . . hmmmm. There is more than a naming problem here.

A final case. CB2 is to Crate & Barrel, the trendy upscale home furnishing company, what Old Navy is to The Gap. While CB2 sells $240 white laminate dining room tables, Crate & Barrel sells $2,000 mahogany tables. The downscale reach succeeded reasonably well for The Gap. It may or may not succeed for Crate & Barrel. Crate & Barrel management can't seem to resist what it perceives to be all that money left for the grabbing if it just extends its brand downward. But that management might recall the words of Andy Grove, Intel's Chairman, "So often, when . . . companies try to move from one area of dominance to another, they fail."[15] Ulysses' fate may well be waiting.

Leadership

Success or failure of this strategy of concentration depends largely on leadership. Leadership is guardian and steward of the mission. Companies that lose their focus do so either because leadership has inadvertently allowed it or because leadership itself has intentionally, for whatever reason, strayed from basics. Outstanding CEOs understand the importance of concentration.

Taizo Nishimuro, Toshiba's president, says, "Our new strategy should return us to profitability by next year."[16] The strategy of which he speaks is one of concentration and coordination—investing $3 billion on core growth areas of computers, wireless communications, networking and semiconductors while spinning off power systems, medical equipment and various other businesses. This kind of dramatic change is difficult to achieve in Japanese companies where multidivision operations in diverse businesses are common. Nishimuro's leadership will be key to their success.

Hewlett-Packard, under Carly Fiorina's strong leadership, has spun off its electronic component and measuring device businesses into a new company called Agilent Technologies. HP now is entirely focused on its computer, printer and Internet-related businesses. The number of business units within those areas have been consolidated from eighty-three to twelve.

Nokia overtook Motorola as the world's largest provider of mobile phones only after its new CEO, Jorma Ollila, brought focus and concentration to the Finnish company. Ollila, upon assuming a leadership role in the early 1990s, quickly moved to sell off television, diaper, rubber boot, computer and paper businesses. He prevailed over enormous internal opposition. The story of Nokia, from a struggling conglomerate of failing businesses to the world leader in mobile phones with 27 percent market share, is one of the most extraordinary in business history. With $26 billion in sales and $3.8 billion in net income in 2000, it is a classic example of concentration as a winning strategy and the crucial role of leadership in executing it.

Communication

Clausewitz wrote not only of concentration of forces at the point of attack but of concentration *and* coordination. Both are vital. Coordination relies on communication. The economist Ronald Coase demonstrated that the boundaries of a corporation are set by the cost of exchanging information. Thus the lower the cost of information, the more far-reaching those boundaries can be, and those costs have been plummeting.

Like being at the tranquil eye of a hurricane, people in the midst of a revolution are often unaware of what is going on around them.

The extraordinary technological breakthroughs in telecommunications of the last few years have created such a revolution for all of us. The reality is that a CEO with a laptop computer, cellular phone, Palm Pilot and a few other devices, along with a Gulfstream jet for occasional face-to-face conclaves, can readily, and quite literally, direct an immense global operation.

Information exchange and instant communication are vital if a strategy of concentration and coordination is to succeed. General Electric is a firm to be benchmarked against in terms of its excellent internal coordination and communication. Early in January of every year, GE gathers its top 600 executives at Boca Raton, Florida, to review current and projected strategic initiatives. That is the first of nine scheduled annual strategic planning meetings of its top people. Those meetings underscore the importance of face-to-face gatherings to augment everyday e-mail, phone, pager and fax communications between managers.

The flatter the organizational structure of a company the better its internal communication. Nokia, noted above, is probably the least hierarchical large company in the world. In the United States, old-economy companies with a dozen and more management levels still exist. CEOs and senior vice presidents of those companies are largely isolated in top-floor aeries of skyscrapers that serve as corporate headquarters. That won't do. Intel serves as a better model—its chairman, Andy Grove, has a small, messy cubicle not much different from anyone else's in the company.

Office architecture also is a factor in internal communication and coordination. Rather than a multistory corporate high-rise, a single-level campuslike structure is suggested with the CEO's office at the center of the building surrounded by concentric rings of the organization's people. Transparent glass walls contribute further to openness and communication. So, too, do comfortable gathering points in hallways and food courts. Whiteboards and meeting areas should be ubiquitous.

Concentration and coordination can be achieved only with effective means of communication. Accurate and timely communication, then, achieved by a mix of managerial practices and high-tech hardware, is a key factor of success for the execution of this strategy.

Keiretsus *and Jack Welch*

There are two seeming paradoxes in this chapter that need to be addressed. The first deals with Japan's *keiretsu* and the second with GE's Jack Welch.

Since the mid-nineteenth century, Japan has had its *keiretsu*. They are bank-centered, cross-shareholding conglomerates that are involved in disparate businesses, from steel making to shipping to electronics. Historically, the companies have tried to keep as much business within the family as possible. Among the largest of the *keiretsu* are Mitsui, Sumitomo and Mitsubishi. The Koreans have something similar with their *chaebols*, the most important of which are Samsung, Daewoo and Hyundai. Other countries of the Far East, including Indonesia and Thailand, have similar structures.

Why did these families of companies, the antithesis of concentrated enterprises, evolve if they were not efficient? A business Darwinism should have eliminated them. The answer is a historic lack of business infrastructure and a problematic legal system in the countries in question. Until recently, in the Far East, one did not have the luxury of opening a comprehensive phone directory to locate a dependable steel maker, lending firm or shipping company. Even if such companies could be found, the legal system could not be depended on to assure contract fulfillment. The result was that firms, of necessity, developed their own in-house capabilities. *This* is the factor that explains the *keiretsu*. But that was yesterday. Today the forces of globalization are breaking down the barriers between these companies and the outside world. The Japanese *keiretsu* have been among the first to go. They are beginning to collapse as this is being written.

The second seeming paradox is General Electric. The company has assuredly not followed a strategy of concentration. Few, if any, companies in the United States are more diversified. Not only does GE make jet engines, light bulbs, plastics, medical scanning devices, gas turbine power systems, television sets, refrigerators and semiconductors, but it also owns NBC and the financial powerhouse GE Capital. By all that has been said in this chapter it should be failing, but it isn't. To the contrary, profits for the last quarter of 2000 were a world-breaking record $3.4 billion. The explanation for GE's counterintuitive success can be summed up in two words: Jack Welch. So valuable has he been, and so unique a role has he played, that General Electric has seemingly defied the strategic verity of concentration of forces.

There is only room and time here to touch on a few aspects of Welch's leadership. First, he has demanded that each of the GE businesses, whatever they may be, must be either first or second in their industry or be shut down. Second, he has stayed focused on only half a dozen or so strategic initiatives over the last two decades—six-sigma quality, globalization and the Internet being the latest. Third, Welch has emphasized close communication across diverse businesses to assure best practices are being adopted throughout the company. Finally, and perhaps most important, GE with its in-house university and winnowing out of what the company calls C employees, while keeping only the As and Bs, has probably the best cadre of middle and senior managers in the country.

Jack Welch is scheduled to step down from the GE helm late in 2001 after his recent $40 billion acquisition of Honeywell has been digested. The company won't implode immediately. Its individual businesses are too strong and it has too many good people. But it won't have Jack Welch to hold it all together as in the past. GE's long-term future, at least in its current organizational form, is problematic.

Welch and General Electric have proven to be the exception to the strategic rule, indeed almost principle, of concentration and coordination at a single point of attack. The Japanese companies Hitachi and Matsushita are structured similarly to GE but are doing relatively poorly. Jack Welch is the difference. But he is sui generis—one of a kind. Jack Welch will move on, leaving behind an unparalleled career that successfully challenged the concentration and coordination principle. It is unlikely there will soon be another like him.

Only the alliance between the United States, England and Russia could overcome the strength of Nazi Germany during WWII. Alliances have now come to the world of business. So sophisticated and complex has the global economy become over the last ten years that it is all but impossible to compete alone. Strategic alliances for a company have become vital.

CHAPTER EIGHT

United States– England–Russia

Forging a Strategic Alliance

Churchill is an incompetent alcoholic demagogue, Roosevelt suffers from syphilitic paralysis and the Russians are weak, poorly organized barbarians; we will smash these so-called Allies.

—Adolf Hitler

We have no eternal allies and no perpetual enemies . . . Our interests are eternal and perpetual.

—Lord Palmerston, British foreign minister

[Coke] can grow faster by forming alliances that give it access to research and other expertise.

—Douglas Daft, chairman, Coca-Cola[1]

We believe in the network of alliances. We believe it works for us.

—John F. Smith, chairman, GM[2]

The computer industry is all about alliances. And that is something that we do very well.

—Michael Capellas, CEO, Compaq[3]

Their Finest Hour

In the desperate days of 1940-1941, England stood alone against the apparently invincible Nazi Germany. Nothing but the Royal Air Force shielded the country from invasion. Nothing, that is, except the courage of its people. Amid the heaviest of the German bombing raids on London, the blitz they called it, Winston Churchill, the almost mythic wartime leader, in an inspiring radio address to his nation sonorously intoned, "We must so bear ourselves that if the British Empire and its Commonwealth last for a thousand years, men will say this was their finest hour." Bear themselves indeed . . . the English fought on.

History often genuflects to such courage. It did so here as events transpired to bring the United States and Russia also into the war against Hitler. The English were no longer alone; the newly formed triumvirate came to be called simply the Allies. While Hitler initially scoffed, the balance of power gradually began to shift as coordinated attacks on Germany were launched on all fronts: Russia from the east, England and the United States from the north, west and south. Four years of savage warfare ensued. Millions perished and much of Europe, and especially Germany, lay in ruins, but finally WWII came to an end. The once-vaunted Third Reich took its last gasping breath as Hitler, in his besieged Berlin bunker, put a Luger to his head and pulled the trigger. The three-power alliance had proven to be the cornerstone of a winning strategy. Without it, the war's outcome assuredly would have been quite different.

Military alliances are not new. With few exceptions, since the beginning of recorded time, where there has been war, alliances have been forged among the combatants. Individuals, clans, tribes and, today, entire nations join together to wage war on other individuals, clans, tribes and nations. As it has been in war, so it is becoming in business.

The reality of the just-dawning twenty-first century global economy is that where there will be business, there will be business alliances. Indeed, the alliance is already an important strategic building block for a growing number of companies large and small. And there is this: History's strategic military alliances, including the one among the United States, England and Russia noted above, offer profound lessons for designing and managing current and future *business* alliances. Those lessons are the essence of this chapter.

The Strategic Alliance

The strategic business alliance was an exception as late as the beginning of the 1990s. Yet now, just a step beyond the threshold of a new millennium, it is becoming the rule. Few companies today are self-contained, vertically integrated entities that face the competitive world dependent on no one but themselves. With markets reaching to every corner of the globe and R&D, plant and equipment costs ever increasing, alliances have become near necessities. At the same time, greatly improved efficiencies among air, highway, sea and rail carriers combined with today's superb telecommunications technology have made alliances pragmatically workable. A quick survey of the auto, retail, entertainment, airline, high-tech and telecom industries suggests just how pervasive strategic alliances are today.

Autos

In the 1970s, Toyota was the first auto company to recognize the benefits obtained from close strategic alliances with suppliers. Now the practice has become common throughout the car and truck manufacturing industry. DaimlerChrysler outsources three-fourths of its vehicle parts to a relatively small number of long-time allied suppliers. GM has spun off its parts division, Delphi, in order to rely more on outside suppliers. Ford is doing the same with its Visteon Division.

Auto part suppliers Delphi, Allied Signal, Dana, Litton, Visteon, Denso and Bosch are fabricating ever-larger modular units: entire brake systems, steering mechanisms, drive trains and cockpits with preinstalled airbags, radios, air-conditioning, CD players, navigation units and steering columns. Alliances between these suppliers and the major manufacturers are marked by close cooperation that makes possible just-in-time inventory and lean production methods. Cost reductions and efficiency improvements have resulted. This is a good thing, but the major manufacturers will have to proceed with caution to avoid becoming mere assemblers with control, and profit, passing to the suppliers. People buy any brand of personal computer if it is labeled "Intel Inside." That's been profitable for Intel with its leading-edge semiconductors—but it has been much less profitable for the PC makers Compaq, Dell, HP, IBM, Gateway and the rest. Will buyers someday purchase any brand of car if it is labeled "Delphi Inside"? For the auto manufacturer, or for any company no matter the industry, there is real risk in allowing a high-margin, mission-critical, strategic need to be outsourced or provided by a joint-venture ally. Already, Toyota has raised vocal concerns with Denso about the latter's selling key components to Nissan, Ford and GM. Turning over a responsibility to an ally is one of the critical factors, discussed later, in executing a successful strategic alliance. Aside from that caveat, the auto industry's supplier–manufacturer alliances are now firmly established and indeed growing stronger. But the auto industry alliances go much beyond those between suppliers and manufacturers.

The auto companies, while remaining fierce marketplace competitors, have allied with one another in various R&D projects. Hundreds of engineers from Toyota and General Motors, for example, are working together to develop vehicles powered by alternative fuel. Ford and DaimlerChrysler have allied for the same reason. GM, with the most tangled web of alliances of all the automakers, has a joint manufacturing facility with Toyota in Fremont, California, that produces Corollas and Geo Prizms. GM, on its own, had made little progress selling cars in Japan until, through its equity alliances with Isuzu, Suzuki and Subaru, it managed to capture a respectable 18 percent of the market. In Europe, GM has a $2.4 billion stake in Fiat. GM, Ford and DaimlerChrysler have allied to launch a new Internet-based auto parts–buying company that will soon be spun off with an IPO and an expected $4 billion market cap. In Europe, Toyota and Volkswagen are developing a number of identical parts to be used by both companies. DaimlerChrysler has bought 34 percent of Mitsubishi, hoping that the alliance will give it an advantage in the small car sector, which is still growing outside of the United States. In another newly formed alliance, Honda has begun to build V-6 engines and transmissions for GM-branded cars. It gets more complicated still.

Isuzu, aligned with GM, builds SUVs for Honda. These are just a few of the many auto industry alliances. The future will bring still more.

Retailing

For decades now, manufacturers have been waging a rearguard battle against retailers as the locus of power has slowly transferred from the former to the latter, especially to the big-box category killers like Home Depot, Office Max and Circuit City. Once cavalier and haughty manufacturers now must grovel for a retailer's limited shelf space. Adding to the indignity, retailers are larding those same shelves with their own private brands.

But out of the turmoil, strategic alliances are beginning to transform the retailing landscape. Procter & Gamble (P&G) and Wal-Mart have now formed a nearly seamless vertically integrated alliance. Their inventory, pricing, delivery and billing systems have been made largely compatible. It is sometimes difficult to know where P&G, the manufacturer, ends and Wal-Mart, the retailer, begins; some 250 P&G people, responsible for the Wal-Mart alliance, are based just minutes from Wal-Mart's headquarters in Arkansas. Look for Kimberly-Clark, a P&G rival, to set up a similar kind of alliance with Costco. Retailers, including Kmart, Target and J. C. Penney, can be expected to search out similar manufacturer alliances.

In another example, the long-struggling Radio Shack, with its hundreds of underperforming retail stores across the nation, is basing its turnaround effort on an alliance strategy. It has allied with RCA to sell only the latter's TVs, VCRs and camcorders. Radio Shack has struck similar alliance deals with Compaq, Sprint and Microsoft to sell only their computers, wireless phones and Internet access service respectively. The strategic alliance building block is key to Radio Shack's future success.

Gateway has allied with OfficeMax to become the latter's exclusive provider of PCs, Internet access and computer training. Gateway is building 1,000-square-foot centers within OfficeMax stores manned by their own employees.

Fingerhut, long known for its catalogs and now a unit of Federated Stores, in 1998 allied with eToys to handle all the latter's Internet orders. FedEx and UPS have similar alliances with other retailers.

Microsoft is playing in the same arena—it is allied with Ford in developing a system that would allow Web users to customize and then order their vehicles factory-direct. GM and AOL have a broad working alliance to accomplish a near-identical end, ditto IBM and Nissan.

Pepsi's Frito-Lay Division is in an alliance with the fast-food retailer 7-Eleven to develop new "dashboard dinners" presumably to be eaten while, or just before, driving. After nearly two years of effort, a team of food specialists from the two companies has come up with their first creative offering: Frito pie. Sold exclusively at 7-Elevens, for $1.99 the customer receives a plastic tray containing a serving of Fritos corn chips and then, for free, all the chili and yellowish cheese sauce that can be splashed on top from available dispensers. Martha Stewart somehow missed this visually and gastronomically pleasing delight.

"Clicks-and-bricks" retail alliances are proliferating. Home Depot, concerned that its suppliers will circumvent it with their own Web sites, has strategically moved to ally with Amazon.com. That Internet portal will serve as Home Depot's cyberspace storefront. Kmart and Yahoo are putting finishing touches on a similarly structured alliance. Microsoft invested $200 million into a wide-ranging alliance with Best Buy that will, among other things, promote and sell MSN Internet service.

These are but a few of an ever-increasing number of creatively structured retailer, manufacturer and distributor alliances that have begun to appear in only the last few years. They provide a glimpse of tomorrow.

Entertainment

The ground roars and convulses beneath us. Thunderous explosions rock the area. We raise crossed arms to shield our eyes from flying debris and struggle to evade the grasping mandible of an evil, grotesque robot. A fiery inferno lashes out to consume all in its path. A bedlam of sound assaults our ears. The smell of cordite fills the air. Death is about to engulf us. There is no hope.

But then, miraculously, a heavily armed Arnold Schwarzenegger steps forward to contest on our behalf. After the mayhem of a brief, gore-filled battle, Arnold, our paladin, with his flame-throwers and missile launchers, emerges victorious. The day is saved. There is a collective sigh of great relief as the shaken, but now smiling, crowd erupts with spontaneous applause. It is the climax of the really quite extraordinary *Terminator II: 3-D* show at Universal Studios in Hollywood, California.

The show is only one small aspect of a mutually beneficial strategic alliance between Japan's Matsushita and France's Vivendi-Universal. Matsushita, with its Panasonic brand, brings to the alliance its cutting-edge high-tech expertise and a cornucopia of digitized home-entertainment hardware devices: DVD players, HDTVs, cameras, VCRs, camcorders. At the same time, Edgar Bronfman, head of the Vivendi entertainment division, provides a dowry of content: music, film, TV programming and theme parks. The two are allied with one another in pursuit of the Holy Grail of synergy. They are making some progress. On the other hand . . .

Japan's Sony in 1989 had the same idea as Matsushita: to complement its manufactured electronic hardware with entertainment content. A provider of the latter was needed. Sony chose an acquisition, simply an alliance taken to the extreme, by buying Columbia Pictures for some $6 billion. The story of Sony's venture into the film industry has an important business moral pertinent here. First the story, with highlights from Nancy Griffin's book *Hit and Run: How Jon Peters and Peter Guber Took Sony for a Ride in Hollywood.*

The duo of smooth-talking, self-promoting and film-star good-looking Jon Peters and Peter Guber convinced Sony to let them run the latter's just-purchased Columbia Pictures. The two Americans insisted on, and were given, carte blanche—there would be no Japanese interference. The engineer-trained Sony people back in Japan day-dreamed of both their future tuxedo-clad appearances at Academy Award ceremonies and the Hollywood gold that would surely flow into their corporate coffers. Six months and then a year passed, but there were no Oscar acceptance speeches and the flow of money, a tsunami of it, was in the wrong direction: eastward, from Japan *to* Hollywood.

With an overhead twice that of the industry average and some terribly embarrassing high-budget box-office flops, the studio operation, from the very beginning of Sony's ownership, lost money. That did not deter Peters and Guber from maintaining a lavish corporate lifestyle—cavernous and sumptuously appointed offices, stretch limousines, jet aircraft, beautiful starlets, yachts, rumored sinecures for relatives and friends, to say nothing of multimillion-dollar salaries. Hollywood moguls have been known to live high; Peters and Guber operated in the best of that tradition. The frugal and austere Japanese watched from afar with ever-growing horror as Columbia hemorrhaged money. Sony was forced to take a $3.2 billion write-off. The allure of Hollywood had become a nightmare. Hollywood insiders snickered at the hapless and naive Japanese management. Belatedly, Sony acted: After two years it handsomely paid Peters and later Guber to go away. Little hardware-content synergy had been achieved. Sony's initial foray into Hollywood was a disaster.

There is a rather plaintive postscript here. Akio Morita, Sony's founder and CEO, who had so brilliantly built his company into one of the world's most admired and who had been instrumental in hiring Peters and Guber, suffered a debilitating stroke at the height of the Columbia Pictures debacle. Too late, Morita realized his mistake of not directly involving himself in the management of Sony's Hollywood venture. It was a humiliating coda to an otherwise extraordinary business career—a real-world Greek tragedy played out amid the artifice and glitter of Hollywood.

The moral of the story and then a post-postscript: Neither alliances nor acquisitions should be managed as passively as Sony managed Columbia Pictures during the Peters-Guber era. This is particularly so when the ally or acquirer knows so little of the other business as assuredly was the case with Sony. A new Sony CEO, the cerebral Nobuyuki Idei, after taking control, purged nearly everyone of rank at the studio and installed new management reporting directly to him. Idei's style was hands-on. The situation has improved. Sony Pictures, as the movie operation is now called, is doing better although still losing money. But the Sony Cineplex in New York City is the highest grossing of its kind in the country and Sony's Loews theater chain netted $1 billion in 1999 profits. Sony's TV programming unit that includes *Wheel of Fortune* and *Jeopardy* is profitable and Sony music has a strong position in the charts. Most important, state-of-the-art Sony electronic audio and video hardware is playing a modest, but growing, role in all the above, indeed, Sony's new PlayStation is the quintessential convergence of electronic hardware and quality content.

Meanwhile, other electronic hardware manufacturers continue to look for allies able to provide content. The content providers are much in demand and can play the coquette because television networks, cable and Internet companies are also frantically courting them.

NEWSFLASH! (January 13, 2001) AOL, in a move that has shaken Wall Street, has finalized its acquisition of content-laden Time Warner. There will be many other alliances and acquisitions in the entertainment world. Among the future guileless outsiders entering into Hollywood alliances will likely be more than a few who will be unaware of, or choose to ignore, the lesson of Sony's early experience. Their travails will be fascinating to watch, train wrecks always are.

Airlines

Delta is seeking a global reach with its recent Air France strategic alliance. This is not an industry anomaly. United Airlines, Lufthansa, Air Canada, Scandinavian Air, Thai Airways, Varig, Singapore Airlines, All Nippon Airways and Air New Zealand have joined together, calling themselves the Star Alliance. They in turn are being challenged by the American Airlines, Cathay Pacific, Canadian Airways, Finnair, Iberia and Qantas alliance. WWII, with its various alliances, ended in 1945. That great military conflict was global in extent. So, with its complex alliances, are the airline wars of 2001.

The airlines are moving rapidly toward a future of intra-alliance cooperative ticketing, advertising, reservations, baggage handling, aircraft maintenance and more. The alliances also pose a negotiating threat to the duopoly power of Boeing and Air Industrie that together dominate commercial aircraft manufacturing in the world—Bombardier of Canada and Embraer of Brazil run a very distant third and fourth place. Over the last few years the alliance has become one of the crucial strategic building blocks for global passenger and cargo airline carriers. Its importance will grow commensurate with globalization. Indeed, airline strategic alliances are both a cause and effect of globalization.

High-Tech and Telecom

SAP, a German company founded by several IBM veterans, is the world leader in enterprise resource planning (ERP) software. The complex system software allows the same data to be used in real time throughout a company by its disparate finance, human resources, manufacturing, marketing, purchasing and other functional units. To help develop the software, SAP has allied with numerous small firms that provide specialized features. SAP peremptorily drops those providers that, in its judgment, become too greedy and attempt to strike their own deals directly with the end user. SAP's truculent chairman, Hasso Plattner, threatens, "If our partners cross us, we will crush them into dust."[4] This rather iron-fisted approach in the use of alliances has worked for SAP— until recently. More about this in a few pages.

AT&T is building its global network using the strategic alliance. In 1998, AT&T formed a joint venture with its once-hated nemesis, British Telecom. There will be no single headquarters for the joint venture, and management leadership will be drawn from the two parents. The alliance has since expanded to include Japan Telecom and several major Canadian wireless providers. You can see the global strategy of AT&T's chairman, Michael Armstrong, unfolding before your eyes. Watch for a major South American telecom company to be brought into the alliance next.

Microsoft is another AT&T ally, providing Ma Bell with software for TV-top cable boxes. This is only a minuscule part of Microsoft's strategy of alliances; few other companies implement the strategy better or use it so extensively. A recent $100 million investment with Teléfonos de Mexico will yield the world's largest Spanish-language Internet portal. The Gates reach extends farther south to Brazil with an 11 percent interest in, and alliance with, Globo Cabo, that country's largest cable-TV operator. And north of the U.S. border, a $400 million investment in Rogers Communications, a Canadian company, will position Microsoft in interactive services. Microsoft, Softbank and Tokyo Electric have formed an alliance to develop wireless technology to link Japanese PC users to the Internet. Microsoft has hundreds of these alliances, both domestic and international, usually cemented with an equity stake ranging from a few to hundreds of millions of dollars. The alliance allows Microsoft to wage simultaneous battles across a rainbow of high-tech specialties. No matter what direction technology may take in the years to come, Microsoft will have at least a foothold either directly or indirectly through one of its alliances.

In another telecom example, there is the alliance called Symbian composed of Motorola, Nokia, Matsushita, Psion and Ericsson. It has a dominant position in the rapidly growing wireless telephony industry—there are already 65 million cellular phone users in the United States alone. Symbian provides the operating system, dubbed Pearl, that serves as a standard for 85 percent of the world's portable phone manufacturers. It is battling another alliance, one between Microsoft and Nextel. Microsoft aims to ensure that its Windows-based Stinger System will become the industry standard.

It would take 1,000 pages, probably more, to compile all of the existing alliances in high-tech and telecommunications. Indeed, with covert alliances, constant formation of new alliances and terminations of old alliances, it may be impossible to do at all. The denizens of San Jose's Silicon Valley, Boston's Route 128, North Carolina's Research Triangle, New York's Silicon Alley and the dozen or so other high-tech centers around the world are forming a nearly incomprehensible web of ever-changing alliances.

Strategic Choice: Prevailing Circumstances

The strategy of alliances is one of the few presented in this book that is fitting and appropriate essentially for every company, no matter its size or the industry within which it operates. What makes this so are the near-universal prevailing circumstances of global markets and the complexity and cost of doing business, even only domestically. Reasons for entering a business alliance may take many forms: market access, technology acquisition, risk reduction, core competence concentration, competitor preemption, delaying action, leveraging an asset, shoring up a weakness and more. Whatever the reason, in a relatively short span of years, the alliance has been elevated from a near anomaly to strategic importance for nearly every business—quite likely including the reader's own.

Factors of Success

Over the course of the 1990s, business strategic alliances have become pervasive, not just for the five industries noted above, but for essentially every industry. Interestingly, the proliferation of business alliances has occurred *in spite of* the considerable difficulty in managing them. Partly because alliances are new to business and not well understood and partly because of unavoidable conflicts of interest, they have failed far more than they have succeeded. Enormous obstacles have kept their full potential from being achieved.

Dwight Eisenhower, chief of Allied forces in Western Europe during WWII, was held in disdain by fighting field generals who viewed him as being little more than an affable bureaucrat. The American general, George Patton, and the British supreme commander, Bernard Montgomery, in particular held Eisenhower in low regard. Indeed, Eisenhower, the future president, was far removed from the battlefront and seldom in harm's way—but directly facing enemy fire was not his role. At command headquarters, he *did* have to deal with conflicting strategic issues, dated and inaccurate battlefield information, vast uncertainties about enemy plans and a panoply of prima donnas with oversized egos: Churchill, Roosevelt, de Gaulle, Marshall to say nothing of Patton and Montgomery. While the Allies shared the overall objective of victory over Germany, they were rarely in agreement as to the means of achieving it. In addition, differences in national culture and tradition led to serious misunderstandings. The Free French, Polish, Czech, Dutch and Belgian forces under Eisenhower's command, while limited in numbers and fighting capacity, nevertheless had their own special interests and demands that had to be addressed. On several occasions arguments became so bitter that the alliance's very survival was threatened. Somehow Eisenhower was able to placate all parties and keep the alliance intact—an unappreciated but crucial accomplishment. Managing a wartime alliance is an extremely arduous task. Managing a large-scale business alliance is no less Herculean.

The Sprint, Deutsche Telekom and French Telecom alliance has disintegrated after months of brawling over forging a cohesive strategy and integration of disparate operating systems. The Toys "R" Us and Benchmark Capital alliance has foundered over Web strategy disagreements. The AMR and British Air alliance has collapsed over reciprocal airport landing rights disputes. Sun and Intel are loudly and publicly feuding: "Sun's effort was never in good faith,"[5] grumbles an Intel senior vice president. "Neither was theirs,"[6] counters a Sun spokeswoman. Ford and Firestone have been allied since 1906, but the relationship has come to an end with reciprocal finger-pointing over the very serious matter of defective tires on new Explorer vehicles. These are but five examples among today's thousands of troubled or recently dissolved alliances. An identifiable set of nine factors provides the key to successful military, and by extension, business strategic alliances. They are equity stake, self-interest, consistency, specific objectives, CEO responsibility, scorpion's embrace, integrity, mercenaries and command structure.

Equity Stake

Benjamin Disraeli, one of England's most renowned prime ministers, once noted that "Peace has been preserved, not by statesmen, but by capitalists." Rather than hold alliances together by multipage treaties with their minutiae of codicils or with the dazzling rhetoric, personal persuasion and brilliant maneuvering of a Machiavelli, Metternich or Kissinger, peace between nations can better be maintained, it is argued, by cross-border private investments. Certainly that was the case for Disraeli's nineteenth-century United Kingdom. It is also the case for today's business alliances.

Microsoft, as noted earlier, has refined the art of strategically using alliances to fill gaps in either its in-house technology or market penetration and to position itself ideally for whatever the future might bring. For the most part, Microsoft has strengthened its alliance relationships with an equity stake, preferably a mutual one. Microsoft's $15 billion cash reserves and its nearly $350 billion market cap make that possible, and the stake assures Gates and his people a voice in the allied firm's management and access to its technology. Greg Maffei, while Microsoft's CFO, engineered many alliance deals specifically with an eye to building strategic relationships. Maffei has recently left Microsoft to start his own company. Gates and Co. will miss him.

The earlier-referenced British Telecom and AT&T alliance was financed with a $5 billion cash infusion equally funded by the two companies. That alliance, in turn, acting as a single independent entity, paid $1.9 billion for a 30 percent interest in Japan Telecom and another $1 billion for leading Canadian wireless providers to bring them into the alliance. AT&T apparently recognizes the benefit of equity positions in strengthening an alliance.

In today's litigious environment, domestically and especially internationally, the term "binding contract" is little more than an oxymoron. A legal document, no matter how painstakingly drawn, cannot assure fulfillment of contract obligations among members of an alliance. Equally important, legions of lawyers poring over a contract have a stifling effect on a pending alliance before it has even begun. Alliances that depend on a legal contract are fragile at best.

At the other extreme, dependence on good intentions, friendship and trust is more than a bit naive in our contemporary world of commerce. Several Asian nations, China especially among them, have their own interpretation of reciprocal obligations. American companies have rushed lemminglike with investment dollars into China seeking alliances. Often they have teamed up with princelings, sons of the Communist ruling elite, who provide a measure of *quanxi*, that is contacts or connections, to help cut through the maze of entangling government controls. That can be quite beneficial. But rarely do the Chinese put up equity. Rarer still are those American companies that are profiting in China; indeed, many have recently packed up and walked away from their investments. This contrasts with Japan's and Taiwan's relatively straight forward and transparent mode of business—they are Asian exceptions. Microsoft and Japan's NTT, for example, have just put up 50-50 funding for their new smart-phone alliance dubbed NTT Mobile. GM and Fuji Heavy Industries have formalized a jointly funded alliance to develop small-car technology. In Taiwan, Microsoft has a 9 percent stake in GigaMedia, a high-tech leader in broadband services. Microsoft's initial $35 million investment in that Taiwanese company is now valued at some $300 million.

The equity stake then serves as a highly effective Super Glue to hold an alliance together.

Self-Interest

Military alliances are not forever. Granted, some do last decades, a very few for centuries. Most, however, survive only a few years or even a shorter period of time. In 1699, Russia's Peter the Great ordered an attack on Sweden's Charles XII *three days* after signing a nonaggression and mutual support pact with him.

Almost immediately following WWII, America's erstwhile ally, Russia, became a fierce Cold War antagonist, while [West] Germany, the once-despised and feared jack-booted enemy, became a steadfast friend.

The United States joined forces with China throughout WWII to fight the aggression of Japan. The fighting was intense, savage and brutal. Hatred toward the adversary ran deep. But by 1948 the geo-political deck had been shuffled. The United States and Japan were allied in warm friendship against China and its Communist leader Mao Zedong.

Military alliances in medieval Japan were even more transient. Before the first shogun, Nobunaga, unified the country, it was not uncommon, during the centuries of civil wars, for allies to change sides in the very midst of a battle.

The common factor, and underlying explanation, in each of these military examples is self-interest. Lord Palmerston, the British foreign minister of the nineteenth century, wrote: "We have no eternal allies and no perpetual enemies . . . Our interests are eternal and perpetual." That is the essence of it: self-interest. Nations ultimately form, or break, alliances depending on what is in their perceived self-interest. Businesses do the same.

For over a decade, Hewlett-Packard had been allied with EMC, the leading memory device manufacturer. HP installed the latter's memory into its servers. Yet recently HP announced that it was dropping EMC in favor of a Hitachi alliance. For several years, HP's continued complaints to EMC about high prices had fallen on deaf ears. Seeking higher profitability, it was in HP's self-interest to switch suppliers and begin marketing the Hitachi-made memory devices under its own label. Meanwhile, the jilted EMC has lost its most important customer accounting for 20 percent of its revenues.

Whatever the benefits may be for one party in an alliance, there must be a commensurate benefit for the other as well if the alliance is to sustain itself. Thus, in the long run, it is self-defeating to put onerous burdens on an ally, as EMC did with HP or as SAP, mentioned earlier, apparently did with its small software company allies. Today, *Fortune* reports that those allies are rebelling and that

SAP revenues, earnings and stock prices are all down. SAP's clients are caterwauling over high costs, delays and snafus in installation, and competitors like Ariba, Oracle, Siebel Systems and Commerce One are pirating away key employees. In still another example, no small part of Coca-Cola's current problems stem from past rather cavalier dealings with its bottler allies. The company's new CEO, Donald Daft, has vowed to redress that problem.

For a successful alliance, partners must be ever aware not only of their own but of other members' self-interest. If a company's self-interest is not being satisfied from an alliance, sooner or later, it will find an alternative.

Consistency

In the mid- and late-1930s, the U.S. strategy relating to Japan was ambivalent at best. It was not clear whether Japan was to be treated as an ally, an enemy or somewhere in between. At issue was geopolitical control of the Far East. Guam, Wake Island and the Philippines were among the U.S. protectorates in the region. Matters were further complicated by America's tacit alliances of friendship with England, France and the Netherlands, three countries that had extensive colonial holdings in India, Malaysia, Indonesia, Singapore, Hong Kong and Vietnam. The Japanese themselves coveted these resource-rich lands, calling for a "Greater East-Asia Co-Prosperity Sphere" under their hegemony and free from European and American influence. The resulting broad U.S. strategy toward an ever more militant Japan was a near-incoherent mix of threat, cajolery, pleas, buying of time and even hope. A reflection of that confused strategy was the controversial selling of scrap metal and petroleum products to Japan. The U.S. Department of Commerce encouraged it, arguing the benefit for business and emphasizing that the country was still in the throes of the Great Depression. The U.S. military, however, was bitterly opposed. Admirals and generals believed the Japanese would use the purchased raw materials to feed their war machine. An intragovernment compromise was reached: The sales would go forward but at reduced levels. It took Pearl Harbor to bring an end to the debate. There, on December 7, 1941, scrap metal from America was returned having been transformed into bombs and torpedoes, while refined West Texas crude oil fueled

Japanese aircraft carriers. America's lack of a unified and consistent alliance strategy contributed to the brutal Pacific War of 1941-1945. Equivalent scenarios play out in today's business world.

IBM recently signed a ten-year, $16 billion strategic alliance with Dell to supply it with electronic computer parts. Dell, a competitor in final products, including PCs, enjoys a comfortable profit margin. In contrast, the IBM PC Division lost nearly $1 billion in 1998. IBM both competes and is allied with Dell: *Coopetition*, it is called. This lack of a consistent IBM approach vis-à-vis Dell may be expedient, and hence in the short run justifiable, but it is not tenable in the long run. Something will have to change. The IBM Parts Division currently suffers because other PC manufacturers are reluctant to buy from it knowing that their final product competes with IBM's PC Division—only Dell with its market power has no such concern. On the other hand, IBM's PC Division must go head to head against Dell, the latter benefiting from the technology of IBM's Parts Division. Alliances can indeed serve as one of a company's strategic building blocks. But to do so, they must be consistent with a unified overall strategy. That is not now the case for IBM's Dell alliance.

Another example involving Dell goes back some fifteen years when Michael Dell assembled and then sold his first PC out of his University of Texas dorm room directly to a fellow student. That customer-direct and build-to-order sales strategy is unchanged today and has made Michael the wealthiest man in America under forty years of age. A competitor, the problem-plagued Compaq, has been eyeing Dell's highly successful direct sales strategy. However, not willing to completely eliminate its long-established reseller base, Compaq has chosen to sell only some 15 percent of its product direct to consumers while aiming for 25 percent over the longer term. The result of even this toe-tipping, mincing approach has been a not-surprising insurrection among Compaq's resellers. Alliances that have been nurtured with them over the years are now threatened. Compaq, with its self-created channel conflict, does not have a consistent sales distribution strategy that can be sustained.

Sometimes hedging bets is appropriate. "Someday a freight train will come roaring through here [General Electric headquarters] and smash everything in its path. I just don't know when that day will be or where the train will come from."[7] That was GE's chairman Jack

Welch reflecting on future business uncertainties. Nowhere is the uncertainty greater than in the operating environment of high-tech where change occurs at Mach speed. To deal with that change, it may be appropriate in some circumstances to hedge positions temporarily. IBM, for example, depending on how the future unfolds, is positioned to be either a PC parts supplier or a manufacturer, and Compaq, again for example, can choose to sell either direct or through resellers. It might be argued then that IBM and Compaq are pursuing clever contingency strategies—simply keeping their options open. It might also be that they are brilliantly disguising their true underlying strategies with mere feints to confuse competitors. Perhaps they have thought through and rationalized their actions. It is more likely that both firms simply don't know what to do and so are drifting with hybrid, inconsistent strategies that must fail in the long run. Recall chapter 7's fundamental strategy of maintaining a consistent concentration and coordination of forces. Strategy is about deciding—that includes deciding *not* to do certain things. More often than not, companies that boldly focus on a single unified strategy, even if that strategy is somewhat flawed, are able to force the future to their will. This is especially so if the strategy's execution is methodical, aggressive and unstinting.

America's uncertain and inconsistent Japanese strategy in the 1930s led to the devastating Pacific War that began on December 7, 1941. In the business arena, companies, be they IBM, Compaq, or the reader's own, must consider whether any proposed or existing strategic alliance is consistent with the larger corporate strategy and mission. If it is not they must plan and then act decisively to make it so. The long-term success of an alliance depends on this.

Specific Objectives

During the worst of the WWII European fighting, the Allies gave little thought to post-war issues. The only agreed-on specific objective was Hitler's unconditional surrender. Thus as the war was drawing to a close, there was no framework for dealing with once-occupied, but now-liberated, Nazi territory. Into much of that vast area goose-stepped the Russian army: Poland, Czechoslovakia, Romania, Bulgaria, Hungary, Latvia, Estonia, Lithuania as well as the eastern portion of Germany itself were peremptorily seized by the Communists. The Americans and British huffed and puffed and bitterly protested to Stalin, but to no avail. The United States–England–Russia alliance that had so successfully worked to defeat Hitler was shattered. An "Iron Curtain," as Churchill called it, had descended over Eastern Europe. The seeds of the coming fifty-year Cold War, pitting Communism against the Free World, were sown. Yet the Cold War might have been averted, or diminished in intensity, had specific objectives been more clearly articulated at the outset of the alliance. The same principle holds for business alliances.

Research indicates that alliances, in all their various forms, are more likely to be successful if the responsibilities and objectives of each party are clearly specified beforehand. It is the gray areas that ultimately cause dissension. In a rush to make the alliance official, too often, partners agree to put off contentious issues hoping that at some future date they will somehow be amicably resolved. Doing this is almost always a mistake. Patent ownership, reporting authority, objectives, executive compensation, budgets, confidential information exchange, product or service pricing and availability, profit sharing, timing of product launches, alliance headquarters location and other issues metastasize and become alliance breakers.

In 1999, the Toys"R"Us and Benchmark alliance sundered as a result of many of the unresolved issues just noted. Interestingly, Benchmark, the Internet portal and Web site provider, has just struck another alliance with another retailer, Nordstrom. This time, after some tough negotiations, all crucial matters have been agreed on in advance. That approach should generally be used if alliances in the end are to be successful.

CEO Responsibility

FDR, Churchill and Stalin, the leaders of the Allies, met four times during WWII, at Yalta, Cairo, Potsdam and Tehran—meetings they called summits. Only the highest-level and most important issues of the alliance were discussed: prioritizing the European over the Pacific campaign, the timing of the cross-channel D-Day landing, Russia's entry into the war against Japan, dealing with France's nettlesome Charles de Gaulle and China's imperious Chiang Kai-shek, and providing U.S.-made war materiel to the Russians through the northern port of Archangel and from the south through Iran.

Today's CEOs must play a similar role to that of WWII's Allied leaders. With the recent advent of business alliances, this is a new CEO responsibility, but one of ever-growing importance. Lower-level managers should be given considerable autonomy in carrying out their day-to-day alliance duties, but strategic issues remain the province of the CEO. Scheduled periodic, or emergency, summits held with major alliance partners are becoming part of already-crowded CEO calendars. Compaq's newly appointed CEO, Michael Capellas, is but one example. He has made strengthening the Intel alliance one of his top priorities.

Microsoft provides another example of this CEO responsibility for alliances. Steve Ballmer, who has just taken the chief executive reins from Bill Gates, has announced his intent of personally shoring up the existing Radio Shack and Best Buy alliances noted earlier.

All of a company's strategic building blocks, whether they are as few as two or three or as many as ten, are the ultimate responsibility of the most senior management. That holds especially for strategic alliances. The CEO must not only constantly monitor alliance issues but also maintain personal communication and rapport with counterparts among the allied companies. Responsibility for the strategic alliance cannot be delegated—recall Sony's CEO Akio Morita and his grave error of not aggressively managing the Columbia Pictures acquisition.

Here, then, is one more crucial factor in the success of a strategic alliance: the CEO's direct involvement and assumption of responsibility.

Scorpion's Embrace

In the years leading up to WWII, Italy's fascist dictator Benito Mussolini, or *il Duce* (the leader) as he demanded to be called, allied with a powerful Hitler. Mussolini, believing that the Nazis were invincible, wanted to be on the winning side and share in the future spoils of war. But for all of Mussolini's pompous posturing, the Italian military was poorly equipped, inadequately trained and had no zest for battle. The Ethiopians, armed with little more than spears, fought the Italian army to a near standoff in East Africa, and entire Italian divisions surrendered to Anglo-English forces in Sicily and North Africa without firing a shot. Mussolini quickly became little more than a Nazi stooge trapped in Hitler's web. By 1943, the war had come to Italy itself, leaving in its wake millions of refugees and a wasteland of rubble-strewn cities and towns. Mussolini's fate was perhaps fitting: Captured by antiwar partisans in Milan, *il Duce* was stripped naked, garroted and ignominiously suspended upside down from a lamppost in front of a rundown garage. Beside him, equally dead, naked and inverted, hung his once quite beautiful mistress, Clara Vitachi. The townspeople were encouraged to spit on and poke at the corpses, which they cheerfully did.

Early in the sixteenth century, in what later became Mexico, dozens of native tribes that had been suppressed and all but enslaved by Montezuma and his Aztec warriors enthusiastically rallied to the flag of the invading Spaniard, Hernando Cortés. They allied out of their own weakness, hoping for release from the despotic Montezuma. The Aztecs fought bravely against the Spaniards but had never before encountered armored men on horseback or faced cannon fire. Cortés was victorious. The freed tribes rejoiced and prayed to their gods in fervent thanksgiving; their joy was short-lived as they quickly fell under the even more repressive yoke of the Spanish conquistadors.

History is replete with similar examples in which the weak ally with the strong, seeking either windfall gains or protection from an adversary. With few exceptions, this strategy becomes, for the weak, a deadly scorpion's embrace. There is a flip side to this. A predator nation can feign sympathy for an attractive but weaker nation, ally with it proclaiming a noble altruism and then devour it when convenient. Business is no different.

In early 1995, tiny Netscape, with its Navigator Web Browser, was far ahead of Microsoft in recognizing the Internet's potential. A giddy Netscape suddenly found itself courted by Microsoft, but chose to reject the evidently wealthy but perceived arrogant and brutish suitor. It saw itself rising on its own to become a dominant *Fortune* 500 powerhouse. However, when denied Netscape affections, an indignantly spurned Microsoft became bellicose and began bringing its own massive resources to the Internet wars. Netscape was being hammered. Looking for protection, Netscape sought out alliances with strong partners. Yahoo, AOL, Sun Microsystems and several others provided support. But in little over a year, Netscape was acquired by mighty AOL and has now all but disappeared as a stand-alone entity. It has become a mere asterisk in the history of the still-unfolding maelstrom of high-tech industry warfare.

There were no real white knights in Camelot to protect the poor and weak, indeed, there was no Camelot. Nor are these chivalrous white knights to be found in business today. All parties to an alliance must have and contribute their own strengths. There must be quid pro quo. To seek an alliance out of weakness is to exchange one bad situation for what likely will become a worse one.

Integrity

One evening during the Cairo Summit of WWII, President Roosevelt entered Winston Churchill's private quarters unannounced. Roosevelt, meaning to discuss an important confidential matter, called out but received no reply. FDR pushed open the bathroom door and was dismayed to see Churchill blissfully drowsing in a large bathtub. Suddenly awakened, the orotund, hairy-chested Churchill slowly rose, majestically stepped from the tub, raised his arms from his sides, and solemnly declared, "The British Prime Minister has nothing to hide from the President of the United States."

Alas, not all alliances are so open and trusting. Indeed, the United States and England, while working closely together on the Manhattan Project, were not forthcoming about atomic weaponry development with their Russian ally. But the Russians knew anyway, as spies kept them informed.

No matter the nature of the alliance, even under the best of circumstances conflicts of interest arise. Individuals working for an alliance organization find their allegiance torn between their own parent on one hand and the allied partner on the other. These conflicts are inherent in any relationship between disparate partners and make mutual complete candor about such matters as proprietary technology, for example, very difficult to realize. Still, every effort should be made to honor agreements, be as candid as possible, maintain integrity and provide sincere after-the-fact apologies and explanations for unavoidable dissembling in word or action. Doing so is good business.

Many American and, to a greater extent, European and Japanese companies have been in business for over a century. To achieve that longevity, a reputation for business integrity is indispensable. Companies work mightily to maintain a strong brand in the eyes of the consuming public. That is all to the good but, equally important, no company can afford a reputation for deceit and mendacity in its business-to-business alliances. Ultimately, a duplicitous company becomes an isolated pariah and is destroyed. A few examples.

Oracle, now a leader in database, network and e-business software, in its early years had such a poor reputation, resulting from heavy-handed and sharp business practices, that some companies were reportedly reluctant to do business with it. Even the narcoleptic SEC took notice and imposed a fine. But with time, Oracle and its driven CEO, Larry Ellison, matured and are now recognized as quite reliable and trustworthy.

Cisco, the Internet blue chip, has always had a sterling reputation for integrity. Its CEO, John Chambers, has built the company with fifty-one strategic acquisitions over the last seven years. The acquisitions, or extreme alliances, have been at the core of Cisco's strategy. Silicon Valley is too intimate and interpersonally connected for Chambers to have executed this strategy and negotiated those acquisitions seriatim if he lacked the requisite integrity.

Disney presents a warm, friendly, benevolent front to the public. But Mickey Mouse, in fact, is an iron-jawed corporate tough guy when dealing with suppliers and alliance partners. Disney recently clashed with Time Warner, demanding programming carriage on the latter's cable systems. The dispute became public, with Time Warner loudly complaining of Disney's hard-nosed negotiating style. Time Warner, hardly known as a pushover, capitulated. Disney is indeed tough. It negotiates hard and is infinitely demanding of suppliers. But tough is not dishonest, conniving or deceitful. Disney cannot be accused of lacking integrity, and that is what we are talking about here. Integrity, then, is a requisite factor of success in any alliance.

Mercenaries

Late in the eighteenth century, England was almost fully engaged against France in a protracted European war and so was caught short in manpower when its American colonists, with exquisite timing, chose to become obstreperous—indeed, revolutionary. The English moved quickly to augment their limited forces in America by hiring mercenaries—literally leasing soldiers from the Crown Prince of Hesse. The German-speaking Hessians were shipped across the Atlantic, placed under the command of English officers and marched into battle to face the guns of George Washington's Continental Army.

The Hessians, however, far from home, meagerly paid and more than a little sympathetic to the Yankee cause against which they were fighting, sensed a better opportunity. Rather than complete their tour of duty and return to Germany, many chose to desert and build for themselves a new life in the vast and free land of America. George Washington's first important victory in the Revolutionary War came at Trenton against the Hessians, where some 900 of them were captured without having put up much resistance. In other battles, many of the Hessians joined the rebels or quietly slipped away, headed west and settled in Pennsylvania and what is now Ohio and Indiana. Mercenaries will do that. They will fight, sometimes quite well, so long as they are adequately paid and no better opportunity presents itself elsewhere. However, as allies they cannot, and never should be, trusted with critical missions. King George III's army in 1776 allied with mercenaries. Today's corporations are involved in a modern-day equivalent—outsourcing alliances.

The major auto manufacturers, as noted earlier, have turned ever more responsibility over to their suppliers. In the short run, the supplier alliances have been beneficial to the manufacturers. In the long run, their empires, like George III's, may be lost. Toyota, for one, is openly sensitive about this—"We are manufacturers, not mere assemblers,"[8] defensively postures Toyota plant manager Tetsuo Taniguchi, who perhaps doth protest too much.

A second business example is offered by eToys. With a business plan based on selling toys and games exclusively on the Internet, its market cap within one year of its IPO was greater than Toys"R"Us with its hundreds of stores. But eToys had a serious problem. After twenty-first century technology had allowed Grandma and Grandpa to order birthday or Christmas presents via their PC, a second, much-antiquated, mid-twentieth century technology took over that was labor-intensive, error-prone and quite inefficient. Pooh bears, Poké-mon, Chutes & Ladders, Barbies and Power Rangers were among the cornucopia drawn physically from warehouse shelves, packaged, labeled and shipped to the grandkids: all of this performed by un-motivated, semiskilled workers earning only a few dollars over mini-mum wage. Not deigning to deal with this nastiness, eToys turned to an outsourcing alliance with Fingerhut, which had decades of expe-rience in this kind of activity as a result of its catalog business. eToys had delegated a mission-critical responsibility to a mercenary ally. With low barriers to entry for potential competitors having similar Internet business plans and near-identical browser software, eToys' position has become tenuous. The company reported multimillion-dollar losses in 1999 and 2000. Its Nasdaq-traded stock is down over 99 percent from its high of $84—its opening IPO price was $20. The Vulture Capitalists, or short sellers, are circling overhead greedily eyeing what they perceive to be a fatally wounded company. Still, eToys has just announced a strategic change, phasing out Fingerhut and bringing warehousing and distribution centers back in-house. The company's CEO, Toby Lenk, says, "Now we are in complete control of our destiny. We expect to be profitable by 2002."[9] Some analysts agree, but *Fortune* reports rumors that the company may not survive. At this writing the stock is trading at 16 cents. Nasdaq delists companies that remain under $1 for an extended period.

In contrast to eToys, alliances that deal with *non*–mission-critical issues are to be much encouraged. Nike, as noted earlier, outsources all of its manufacturing through business alliances in developing countries. Nike assures that quality controls are in place and that logistics are well coordinated. The company continues to focus on its shoe design, sports celebrity marketing and other mission-critical strategic building blocks.

BP Amoco, in an unprecedented move, has outsourced the entirety of its financial and accounting operations to Pricewater-houseCoopers in a ten-year, $1 billion alliance. It has struck another alliance, this one extending over five years and also valued at $1 billion, with a California start-up called Exalt. That company will handle BP Amoco's global payroll, benefits and related administra-tive work. The oil giant can divest itself of all this responsibility without any threat to its underlying mission. Its chairman, Sir John

Browne, has said, "These alliances free us to focus on our core [energy] business."[10]

The closely held National Airlines has taken the alliance to untested limits by outsourcing its information technology, engine overhaul, baggage handling, reservations, catering and other services. The company believes none of these to be mission-critical. So far the Las Vegas–based carrier, with its fifteen planes, cushy cabins and top-of-the-line service, is thriving. This is a story worth watching.

Ryder, once known only for its truck rental business, has moved aggressively into the field of logistics. Saturn has formed an alliance with Ryder that will give the latter full responsibility for handling Saturn's automotive parts, inventory and finished product shipments. Saturn can do this and then concentrate on the car business because logistics, while important to this GM car division, is not mission-critical. With careful tracking of Ryder's performance, Saturn can confidently outsource to this quite able business mercenary.

Alliances, then, struck with mercenaries can indeed be success-ful, but only if they deal with non–mission-critical matters, are carefully structured and are diligently monitored.

Command Structure

Warren Bennis, the leadership expert at USC, writes, "A company, like an army, needs a commander."[11] Alliances also need a com-mander as well as an effective command structure if they are to be successful. As noted earlier, WWII Allied forces in Western Europe were comprised predominantly of Americans and British, along with much smaller, almost nominal contingents of Free French, Dutch, Belgians, Poles, Danes, Norwegians and Czechs. Supreme Headquar-ters Allied Expedition Forces (SHAEF) stood at the apex of the military alliance command structure. SHAEF's Supreme Commander was the congenial American Gen. Dwight Eisenhower. Eisenhower purposely appointed a disproportionate number of British officers to SHAEF to signal his sympathies for an ecumenical command. Some Americans thought he went too far. "Ike is the best damn general the British have got," Patton once growled. Still, the British, American and other Allied officers did work side by side reasonably well. SHAEF in turn was under the civilian supervision of Roosevelt and

Churchill as well as the less important, but still vocal, Allied political leaders exiled in England. Roosevelt and Churchill were the final decision arbiters, although as the war progressed and the American presence increased, Churchill tended to yield to Roosevelt.

Several characteristics of SHAEF's military command structure lend themselves to business alliances. First, there was unity of command in the person of Eisenhower. Reporting to him at the most senior levels were officers drawn from the various Allied partners. Second, the chain of command down through the organization was reasonably well defined. Finally, SHAEF headquarters was both physically and organizationally distanced from the civilian leadership that held ultimate power. This avoided political meddling while still keeping open a channel for final arbitration of issues that could not otherwise be resolved.

The AT&T and British Telecom alliance, mentioned earlier, fits this pattern in many respects. Michael Armstrong, AT&T's chairman, plays the role of FDR. Without a viable command structure, the AT&T and British Telecom, or any other, alliance will become paralyzed with internecine political bickering and ultimately will self-destruct. A perfect example of that was Iridium, described in chapter 4, where the multiple partners each had veto power and the CEO had limited authority. Command structure then is another factor in determining an alliance's success or failure.

Croesus and Lydia

An organization's overall strategy should be comprised of only a relatively small number of strategic building blocks. Today, for most companies, the strategic alliance is, or probably should be, one of them. Clearly it is so for the many companies identified in this chapter: AT&T, United Airlines, Microsoft, Cisco, American Airlines, Toyota, Sony, P&G, GM and IBM among them. Within the next few years it will also be so for nearly all of the *Fortune* Global 500 and for countless smaller firms as well. Still, manifold difficulties in managing alliances will remain—difficulties that trace back at least some 2,500 years.

In the year 550 B.C., the kingdom of Lydia, with its immense riches and military strength, dominated Asia Minor. To add to his wealth, Lydia's king, Croesus, contemplated attacking and plundering Persia, another great empire to the east. Before ordering a military offensive, he called upon the oracle at Delphi to foretell the outcome of such an undertaking. The terse Delphic response was "If Croesus can find a strong ally and then makes war against Persia, a great empire will indeed be destroyed." Much encouraged and confident, Croesus quickly struck an alliance with Sparta, renowned for its fighting prowess, and launched his intended conquest of Persia. The Spartans, however, were very late to the battlefield. By the time they arrived, the Lydians, overmatched and fighting alone, had been routed by the Persians. With its army lost, Lydia was forced to forfeit much of its accumulated treasures and power. Croesus was driven from his throne. Later, a preternaturally old and broken Croesus rebuked the oracle for the false prophesy. "Ah," responded the soothsayer, "you did not ask *which* empire would be destroyed." Obfuscated advice like that added to avarice and, most important as it relates to this chapter, a flawed alliance with Sparta were the downfall of Croesus and Lydia.

A modern-day business corporation, division or department, including the reader's own, can avoid such a downfall by using the factors of success checklist presented here to identify and resolve alliance management problems. These factors must be addressed if the alliance is to play the role of an effective strategic building block. Achieving that, the reader need not call on any oracle—now called a consultant—to ask what the future will bring, he or she can sculpt their own tomorrow.

Sometimes when an enemy is blundering, it is prudent not to attack but rather to patiently wait for his or her self-destruction. Patience and time can become a winning strategy. The Russians used such a strategy in their war against France and its emperor Napoleon in 1812.

CHAPTER NINE

Napoleon's Russian Invasion

Patience and Time

*The great commander knows when to attack and when
to stand down. Never fight a battle when nothing is
gained by winning.*
> —Gen. George S. Patton

When the foe is desperate do not exceedingly press him.
> —Sun Tzu

*The strongest of all warriors are these two—Time and
Patience.*
> —Leo Nikolaevich Tolstoy

*Not territorial or economic gain, but destruction of the
enemy is the objective.*
> —Carl von Clausewitz

"Now I Will Face Him"

In June 1812, Napoleon crossed the river Niemen from Poland into
Russia with a 450,000-man invading army intent on driving Tsar

Alexander out of the multicountry alliance united against France. Mikhail Hilarionovich Kutuzov, the phlegmatic sixty-year-old supreme Russian commander, in spite of intense political pressure from the government and many of his own staff, ordered the army to retreat before the advancing French. "Patience and time, time and patience," he counseled. Napoleon was drawn deeper and deeper into the Russian heartland; his thinly guarded communication and supply lines stretched well over 1,000 miles. All the while, Russian peasants in the vicinity of Napoleon's approaching army torched their own fields and slaughtered their own livestock rather than have food fall into the despised enemy's hands.

By October, the still largely uncontested French had reached an evacuated Moscow—the city's citizens had fled eastward taking with them foodstuffs and as much of their personal belongings as they could carry. Napoleon set up his command post in a Kremlin palace and awaited Kutuzov's attack. It never came. Weeks passed. With the onset of winter and running low on supplies, a now-dismayed Napoleon was left with no option but to retreat. He issued an order to do so. When news of this reached Kutuzov, he fell to his knees in thanksgiving. Tears of joy splashed from the old man's eyes and down his grizzled cheeks. "Russia is saved and *now* I will face him [Napoleon]." Napoleon's withdrawal quickly turned into chaotic flight as Kutuzov ended his strategy of patience and turned loose his infantry, artillery and horse-mounted Cossacks. The Russians fell upon the long, straggling mob of Frenchmen that had once been the proud and highly disciplined *grande armée* of Napoleon.

French forces disintegrated. Of the nearly half a million men who had confidently marched into Russia, only some 20,000 staggered out. Napoleon had led his army along a narrow corridor of Russia's vast territory and even captured the nation's capital, Moscow. But those military achievements were Pyrrhic; Napoleon had weakened his own army and put it in a precarious position while leaving the enemy largely unscathed. Carl von Clausewitz, who, at the time, was a foreign officer observer on Kutuzov's staff, realized Napoleon's mistake and wrote, "Not territorial or economic gain, but destruction of the enemy is the objective." In the war's aftermath, Napoleon was forced to abdicate his throne and accept exile at Elba. French dominance of Europe came to an end. Kutuzov retired a national hero. His strategy of patience and buying of time had achieved one of history's greatest military victories. That strategy translates directly to today's world of business.

Strategic Choice: Prevailing Circumstances

This strategy of patience is called for when it is perceived that the competitor has launched a flawed marketing, acquisition, R&D, financial or other business initiative. It is assumed that one's losses, as a result of the competitor's initiative, can be held to a minimum even as the competitor is continuously and grievously weakened as a result of his own misguided offensive. Under these circumstances, rather than battle on the attacker's terms by replicating his actions, a company instead stands down and executes a strategy of patience while the competitor self-destructs. Meanwhile, the company prepares to go on its own offensive at a time and place, and in a form, of its own choosing.

To help underscore these points, here are some business examples of companies that have attacked with automation, R&D, line extension or acquisition initiatives while their competitors responded with a strategy of patience.

Capital Spending

Back in the 1980s, General Motors' CEO Roger Smith became enamored with the purported benefits of factory automation. A massive multi-billion dollar capital spending program was launched. But it was all to no avail; after years of heavy spending, GM productivity remained largely unchanged. When Smith retired near the end of the decade, the legacy of his tenure was the loss of double-digit market share points, an alienated and more aggressive unionized labor force and an undistinguished line of vehicles having the industry's lowest quality ratings. Company layoffs were ordered. Smith was lampooned in the popular film *Roger and Me*, which portrayed him as aloof, callous and out of touch. In hindsight, by one estimate, the billions spent on the automation folly could, alternatively, have been used to buy Toyota Motor Corporation, lock, stock and barrel.

Meanwhile Ford stood back and watched GM's failing automation effort. The company instead relied on W. Edwards Deming's quality control methods and the lean manufacturing techniques just then coming into vogue. Today, Ford's plant just outside of Atlanta is the most productive in North America. Overall, Ford has more than a $1,000 per car advantage over GM in reduced labor costs. Rather than being baited by GM to launch a problematic matching factory automation spending program, Ford's strategy of patience has led to victory.

BP Amoco has recently announced a significant capital spending initiative that will carry through 2003. High-return oil and gas projects are targeted in Trinidad, Russia, the Gulf of Mexico and the North Sea. The company's two major competitors, Exxon and Shell, are staying focused on cost reduction and not following BP Amoco's lead with capital spending campaigns of their own. They are practicing a strategy of patience. The future will tell how this unfolds.

R&D

The world now has but two commercial aircraft manufacturers: Boeing and the French, British, Spanish and German consortium dubbed Airbus Industrie. The Airbus' future scan shows global air traffic doubling over the next fifteen years. To meet that demand, the company is betting $12 billion of R&D on a new 650-seat, four-engine jumbo jet—the A380. It is designed to fly between major airport hubs with operating costs some 20 percent less than Boeing's current 747, which seats but 425 passengers. Even though it is constructed using large amounts of high tech plastics, carbon based materials and the latest in lightweight alloys, the A380 will still weigh in at some 265 tons. On the ground, the behemoth, with a nearly 100-yard wing span, will need a parking area the size of a football field. As an added touch, wide spiral staircases, fore and aft, will connect twin decks. Massage, sauna and game rooms may be featured. The new Airbus, available in 2005, will sell for roughly $230 million. It will fly to and from major hubs in Asia, Europe and the Americas. "The airlines are requesting more productive planes with more volume and range," says Phillipe Jarry, marketing vice president at Airbus. "It is our job to show them the possibilities."[1]

Meanwhile, Seattle's Boeing plays the role of Kutuzov. Believing that smaller planes flying direct routes will be the wave of the future, it practices a strategy of patience and time. Boeing is only incrementally upgrading its current offerings. The outcome of this great commercial air battle will not be known for several years. It is a battle not so much between two companies as much as between two quite different strategies.

NEWSFLASH! (January, 2001) Emirate Airlines, Air France, Qantas and Singapore Airlines have just placed orders for forty-four of the A380s at a combined price-tag of about $10 billion.

Market Share

The strategy of patience is probably most appropriate when dealing with competitor market share offensives. Like precious crown jewels, companies jealously guard their market share percentage point figures, including them among the most important of their performance targets. Too often such companies respond to a competitor's flawed market share increasing initiative with a suicidal identical strategy. Zero-sum game price wars or ad campaigns may be the result—witness the e-tailer start-ups and their frenzied, and profligate, throwing of nearly all their cash into 1999 Christmas and 2000 Super Bowl television ads. For several years now the majority of Internet companies have disregarded sound business principles and obsessively chased market share at the expense of profits. A few sat out the madness and practiced a strategy of patience. That was the right thing to do, as evidenced by the growing number of dot-com bankruptcies among the more profligate companies. The twenty-five worst-performing Internet stocks are down 95.7 percent from their highs—$114 billion in market value has been erased. Marc Andreesen, cofounder of Netscape, observes that "A return to profit objectives would be a return to rationality."[2]

Rather than match a cigarette industry competitor's price cuts in the pursuit of market share, contrarian R. J. Reynolds has aimed to strengthen its bottom line. To do that, several steps have been taken: More tobacco has been added to each cigarette; international operations have been sold to Japan Tobacco for $7.8 billion; dividends have been increased; prices have been raised; a $125 million stock buyback has been launched; and heavy investment has been made in four core brands, Camel, Winston, Doral and Salem, with new packaging, advertising and promotions. The company's focus is not on market share but rather profitability.

Back to the auto industry: General Motors CEO G. Richard Wagoner recently declared, "We have a stretch goal of increasing market share from 29.2 percent to 32 percent. We have to run like crazy and sell everything that would lead to some upside in share."[3] GM's board has made market share a critical criterion of management effectiveness. Ford, on the other hand, with several points less market share, is practicing patience rather than confronting GM with, say, matching rebates. As a result it is far more profitable—in 2000, Ford profits were greater than any other car company in the world. In addition, Ford has put together a stable of high-profit marquee brands—Jaguar, Volvo, Lincoln, Land Rover and Aston Martin—to form the Premier Auto Group. Profit margins are lush. "Profits, not volume, define industry leadership,"[4] says a company executive. Ford has opted to return $10 billion to stockholders rather than waste the money on nonproductive acquisitions or join GM in a race for market share that no one would win. Honda, the maverick of Japan's auto industry, shares Ford's strategy of patience when it comes to market share; the company's president, Hiroyuki Yoshino, says, "We believe that success in the future has little to do with size."[5]

Here's one more example. Dell's vice chairman, Kevin Rollins, explains, "Additional revenue streams are marginally important to us, but what's really interesting are additional *profit* streams."[6] Dell has always shown patience rather than join competitors in price cuts to grow or sustain market share. Dell works instead to continually hone its customer direct distribution, inventory and manufacturing systems while constantly improving and expanding its product offerings.

Cigarettes, cars, computers . . . no matter the product or service, a strategy of patience when a competitor has embarked upon a price war, or any other unsound initiative, to gain market share may be, as it was for Kutuzov, a winning strategy.

Acquisitions

Another category of competitor initiative that might call for a counterstrategy of patience deals with acquisitions.

Beginning in the 1990s there was much consolidation in the banking industry. Big is better has been the mantra. Bank One, First Union and NationsBank have been among the most aggressive of the acquirers. But it is becoming evident that size does not necessarily translate into profitability or higher stock prices—in 2000, both are down for these banks by some 50 percent from the previous year. Perhaps synergies have not been realized, excess costs not wrung from redundant operations, disparate corporate cultures not assimilated—or perhaps consumers have found that with the Internet's convenience, there is no great advantage in one-stop financial shopping.

Whatever the reason, banks that have resisted the acquisition fervor and executed a strategy of patience while perfecting their own operations have profited. Indeed, Charles Schwab, after breaking away from Bank of America, has thrived by launching a series of innovative initiatives in discount securities services, online trading and mutual fund supermarkets.

Chicago-based Northern Trust is also successfully using a strategy of patience in the banking industry. The bank concentrates on financial services for the wealthy and has shown five years of 14 percent annual earnings growth. "We clearly were the beneficiaries of the dissatisfaction of some of the clients of these merged institutions,"[7] says CEO William Osborn. Northern Trust stays close to its roots of relationship banking. Osborn adds, "We have a great growth engine the way we are—mergers are not necessary."[8] Osborn has invested $600 million in improving the bank's customer service and makes a point of personally visiting hundreds of clients and prospects every year.

Supporting the patience strategy of Schwab and Northern Trust is Harvard's professor emeritus Samuel Hayes. He writes that "These huge merged banks will become muscle-bound gorillas unable to quickly react. Smaller, mosquito-like, banks will fly in and bite them."[9] Better to adopt a strategy of patience and time than race headlong into the self-destructive acquisition madness.

In another example of a flawed acquisition initiative, WorldCom withdrew its bid for Sprint in 2000 because of Federal Trade Commission (FTC) antitrust concerns. The Feds did Bernie Ebbers, WorldCom's CEO, a favor: The acquisition was a terrible idea. WorldCom's investors rejoiced over the news of the derailed acquisition and pushed the stock upward. The market has concluded that Ebbers' plan to be a major player across the board in long distance, local, wireless and the Internet is a mistake. It appears that Ebbers dodged a bullet of his own making. For years, telecom people have seized on bundling as the wave of the future. A company, it has been argued, should bundle together a full array of services and present a single bill to the customer. That conventional wisdom was no doubt on Ebbers' mind. But bundling, as WorldCom conceived it, may *not* be the wave of the future.

Telecom consumers certainly want simplicity in billing and service, but that does not mean that one company must own the infrastructure that provides the service. An alternative business model comes quickly to mind. Home Depot meets every imaginable home improvement and building need. Customers wander the aisles, make their choices of products and are presented with a single bill at the checkout counter. But Home Depot is a retailer. It has not acquired the power tool, water heater, lumber, plumbing fixture or patio furniture manufacturers whose products it sells. Exactly the same business model can apply to telecommunications.

A new company, call it TCOM, opens its doors to the public, offers a full spectrum of telecom services and provides a single itemized bill to the customer. But the hypothetical TCOM has not acquired telecom service-providing companies. Rather, it is an intermediary that is simply selling long-distance, local, pager, Internet access or wireless service that is provided by other companies—a telecom service retailer, as it were. The customer does not necessarily know that and doesn't care. Even AT&T's chairman, Michael Armstrong, who has made acquisitions valued at tens of billions of dollars, seems to be reluctantly coming to this conclusion. In a sharp reversal of strategy, Michael Armstrong announced the planned breakup of the units he spent billions of dollars acquiring over the last several years. AT&T stock is now trading at a near fifty-two-week low. Badly burned investors can only wish that Armstrong had read *War and Peace* in college and learned a little about Napoleon, Kutuzov and, of course, patience and time. Was that AT&T announcement by Armstrong equivalent to Napoleon's order to withdraw from Moscow? The point here, as in the preceding banking example, is that there are viable alternatives to growth by acquisition, and a strategy of patience may be most appropriate.

In another example, there is Yahoo. "Do I know how to operate a cable system?"[10] That was Jerry Yang, Yahoo's CEO, referring, sarcastically to AOL's acquisition of Time Warner. Better, Yang believes, to focus on expanding his business slowly into broadband and build his already popular site—63 percent of the Internet population visits Yahoo at least once a month. Yang will execute a strategy of patience when it comes to AOL and acquisitions.

Nestlé has not followed the food industry's giants in a rabid bidding war for smaller companies: Kraft just acquired Nabisco for $15 billion, General Mills has purchased Diageo's Pillsbury unit and Unilever has acquired Best Foods. Rather, Nestlé is choosing to focus on its existing brands. The approach is working. Profits are excellent at $6.8 billion on $45.9 billion in sales.

We are witnessing consolidations in a host of industries—banking, telecom, food, airlines, music, autos and more. For a company in such an industry, rather than rush lemminglike to acquire or merge, a more thoughtful approach that recalls Kutuzov's strategy of patience might be a better alternative.

Line Extensions

Cadillac introduced the Cimarron in the early 1980s as a way to extend its product line downward and increase revenues. The vehicle sold for some $10,000 less than the low-end Cadillacs then available. The Cimarron was built on a Chevrolet platform and rumored to have an Oldsmobile engine. The vehicle was an abysmal flop in the marketplace and was withdrawn within two years after terribly tarnishing the Cadillac brand. The Cimarron debacle also set into motion the eventual entry of the Japanese into the luxury car market with the Lexus and Infiniti. Lincoln, BMW and Daimler did not follow Cadillac downscale—they stood back, patiently watching Cadillac damage itself.

To bring complete balance to the argument, note that line extensions sometimes *can* be successful if adequately disguised. It is a delicate matter. Disney creates and distributes child-friendly pictures—*Mulan, 101 Dalmatians, Pocahantas* and the rest—that delight little folks. But children are maturing more quickly nowadays, and Disney product offerings are more rapidly losing appeal to them and to their parents who still control the wallet. So adult fare, with its now pretty boring and predictable violence, sex and profanity, also is coming out of Disney studios, concealed under the Touchstone Pictures label. The Touchstone gambit is a dangerous move for Disney, because parents implicitly trust the Disney name. To taint the Disney brand, in any way, is far too high a price to pay to achieve some modest measure of line extension. Disney had better keep a pretty thick firewall between itself and Touchstone.

The Gap has rather successfully hidden its downward line extension with its Old Navy stores, and upscale Marriott has successfully introduced the downscale Courtyard by Marriott. But both undertakings were, and are, risky. Better for competitors to leave line extensions to others and to practice a winning strategy of patience and time.

Factors of Success

Now, what are the factors of success for a company that has opted for a strategy of patience when the competitor is attacking with an evidently flawed initiative? There are four: future scan, leadership, mission and taking the offensive. Begin with the future scan.

Future Scan

Kutuzov stood atop a high mountain peak with his senior officers gathered about him. The hot July sun of 1812 hung directly above in the Russian sky. In the distant plains below was the grand spectacle of the great French army on the move. Spread over a score and more miles it came—the most powerful killing machine on earth. It was comprised of nearly half a million men, some 200,000 horses and roughly 20,000 wheeled carts, wagons and artillery caissons. Clearly visible were the infantry regiments, veterans of a dozen battles, with their colorful uniforms and unit guidons waving in the light breeze. Riding alongside of them were the famed and heroic generals, Murat, Ney and Davout, mounted on magnificent steeds. Napoleon's Old Guard rode by—every member of which was at least six feet tall, wore huge sideburns, had served for ten years or more and had been wounded in battle at least once. A seemingly endless baggage train followed. Leading it all was the man no one had yet defeated on the battlefield: Napoleon himself. Not since the armies of Alexander the Great or Caesar had the world seen a fighting force as formidable as this.

Kutuzov turned away from the breathtaking sight below and seemed to look far over the horizon. Momentarily shutting out the world, the old general saw not hot, dusty roads filled with the enemy's quickly advancing men, horses and wagons but rather a silent snow-filled panorama where movement would be painful and slow. He saw gaunt Frenchmen, many of them wounded, terribly ill or suffering miserably from frostbite of the feet, hands, ears, nose and mouth. They were, in his mind's eye, stumbling back in full retreat to their own border, frequently pausing to rest and build pathetic little campfires in a futile effort to protect them from biting winds and subzero temperatures. Kutuzov saw more than the coming Russian winter, six months hence, in his mental future scan. He visualized also the intervening months during which the proud and attack-oriented Napoleon would aggressively pursue a retreating Russian army in a vain attempt to bring it to battle.

In setting strategy, not only must the future scan detect all aspects of the operating environment, it must also discern how the enemy will respond to that environment. Kutuzov knew his own men, the Russian terrain and the Russian winter. As important, he knew his enemy. Kutuzov built his strategy of patience upon what he— correctly as it turned out—believed Napoleon would do. In the business arena, this is equivalent to detailed and comprehensive competitor intelligence gathering and analysis.

Boeing, as noted earlier, has opted for a policy of patience rather than confront Airbus with its own jumbo jet. Key to Boeing's decision is its future scan, which shows more direct flights between major cities rather than expanded use of existing giant hubs. That translates into a future need for smaller, not larger, planes. Boeing is also quite aware of the awkward organizational structure of Airbus involving a multicountry consortium. The consortium is probably a bad thing for Airbus in terms of effective decision making, but it may be a good thing in terms of chauvinist government support or subsidy—already Air France has announced it will purchase the A380. Boeing certainly must have expended enormous resources in developing its future scan—it had better have done so, because this is a bet-the-company matter.

The essence of the strategy of patience is to stand by defensively while a competitor is destroying himself by untoward actions. But what if those actions in fact are proper? Hollywood's first "talkie" was *The Jazz Singer* produced by MGM. Dozens of film companies stood by believing talking pictures to be a passing fad. They adopted a strategy of patience. It proved fatal for them. Their mistake was a defective future scan that failed to detect improved technology and the public's more sophisticated entertainment demands.

Any strategy that is set today plays itself out in an uncertain tomorrow. With strategies projected to hold for years or even decades, the ability to accurately see that future is crucial—this is especially so for a strategy of patience and time.

Leadership

Russia, in 1812, would have been lost to Napoleon without Kutuzov's leadership. Napoleon's brilliant field tactics coupled with his experienced and well-trained men would have overwhelmed the Russians had they challenged the French early in the campaign. Kutuzov knew that. However, the very thought of Napoleon occupying their land drove the great majority of passionately nationalistic Russians to a frenzy. For them, Kutuzov's strategy was almost treasonous. The farther Napoleon moved into Russia, especially as he approached the gates of Moscow, the greater were the demands on Kutuzov to stand and fight. Only Tsar Alexander and a handful of subordinates stood with Kutuzov, the rest demanded his dismissal. But Kutuzov held to his strategy of patience and history turned.

Time and again in this book, leadership has been identified as one of the key factors of success in the design and execution of strategy. Whether on the battlefield of war or amid the intense competition of global business, a strategy, whatever it might be, must have a champion if it is to succeed. Military and business history verify that this is so. Organization dissenters are everywhere. Other strategies suggest themselves. Setbacks occur. Committees, councils, task forces, boards, commissions don't stay the course. Leaders do.

To be able to stand in the face of near-total opposition and still hold dear one's principles and beliefs, without compromise, is what leadership is about. It is a magnificent thing, whether on the battlefield or in the boardroom. Leadership is a vital factor in the success of any strategy including this one of patience.

Mission

Kutuzov never lost sight of his underlying mission: to save Mother Russia. He could not afford to risk losing his army in battle against a powerful French force. If temporarily giving up control of some roadways—indeed, if temporarily giving up Moscow itself—was needed to achieve that mission, then so be it. Kutuzov's strategy of patience and time was a logical extension of his perceived mission.

During times of crisis, a company may overreact to a competitor's assault. Companies that rush pell-mell in untoward response to a competitor's offensive move do so because of a blurred or disregarded mission. At the moment of crisis, when the mission is most needed, it is simply forgotten. It is perhaps excusable, or at least understandable, for children to yield to peer pressure and impulsively become involved in inappropriate behavior. They lack a developed self-identity or a self-mission. It is not excusable, however, for corporations run by adults to behave that way. The corporate or business unit mission is a crucial safeguard against such behavior.

Taking the Offensive

Kutuzov delayed attacking Napoleon for some six months after the latter had invaded Russia. Nearly every Russian general opposed

Kutuzov's strategy of patience. Driven by patriotism, pride, civilian urging and the fervor of war itself, they themselves would have immediately attacked the hated invader. Napoleon, at full strength in those early months, would surely have prevailed and destroyed the Russian army. History would have been much changed—a descendant of Napoleon might well be sitting on a French throne this very day as part of a parliamentary government not unlike England's. Fortunately for Russia, Kutuzov's will prevailed, as did his strategy of patience and time. But there was an important addendum to that strategy.

When Napoleon's army marched out of Moscow and headed for home, it was certainly greatly weakened by sickness, inadequate food and the terrible cold to which it was so unaccustomed. Nevertheless, unhindered, much of the army could have made its way safely back to France. After six months of rest and hearty French fare it would have been fully recuperated and wiser from its recent experience. Once again Napoleon likely would have threatened Russia.

But that was not to be. Few in history have understood human nature better than Machiavelli, who wrote, "Men avenge slight injuries but not grave ones." Kutuzov understood that and knew that if he was to avoid French vengeance, he would have to inflict a grave injury upon Napoleon. This he set out to do. Immediately upon getting word that the French were retreating from Moscow, he finally unchained his army—an army well fed, well armed, more than comfortable fighting in freezing weather and filled with pent-up fury. It was this offensive phase of Kutuzov's strategy that led to the French coup de grace. The Russians plagued and harried every step of the now-panicked French forces throughout the entirety of their long, terrible trek home. The highly mobile horse-mounted Russian Cossacks maneuvered to the front and rear of the French and constantly fired on them. Russian infantry and artillery raced forward to position themselves in waiting ambush of the nearly exhausted Frenchmen. Russian musket balls, grape and canister tore into the French ranks. The dead and wounded were left where they lay, some 200,000 of them. Another 190,000 were made prisoner; most did not survive captivity. When the fighting was over, less than one of every ten in Napoleon's invading army made it back home. The rest of them sleep to this day somewhere along that line of retreat from Moscow to the Polish border.

Patience and time, yes. But then at some point there comes the unsheathing of the long-restrained offensive to decimate the weakened and helpless foe. In war, in business, this second phase of the patience strategy is crucial for final victory. Warren Buffett, the preeminent investor of our time, understands this. Standing aloof from the mania of e-commerce investment of the last few years that propelled price-earnings ratios to unprecedented highs, Buffett patiently watched the fortunes of others swept away. Finally, with the 50 percent decline in Nasdaq in late 2000, he has acted, launching his long-delayed offensive with, among other things, the purchase of mundane—but high-profit earning—Shaw Industries, the largest carpet manufacturer in the world. He got it at a bargain price.

"Peace for Our Time"

This chapter's focus has been the intentionally designed defensive, rearguard strategy of patience when an enemy is overextending himself. Rather than meet that enemy on his terms, this is a strategy of waiting until the enemy is so weakened, by his own mistakes, that a deadly strike becomes possible. That strategy is clear enough. But sometimes what appears to be the wisdom of patience is in fact a mere rationale for cowardly vacillation. A military and then some business examples make the point.

Throughout the mid- to late-1930s, Hitler continued to expand his Third Reich by seizing ever more *lebensraum* (living space) from neighboring nation-states: Alsace-Lorraine, then Austria and then Czechoslovakia. Through all of that brazen German imperialism, French and English leaders did nothing except wring their collective hands and occasionally make some threatening, but not too threatening, speeches. The do-nothing strategy of appeasement was *not* based on a belief that Hitler was overextending and weakening himself, as Napoleon had done in 1812 against the Russians. To the contrary, with each territorial addition, Hitler became stronger, and the British and French knew it.

When Hitler made his move against Czechoslovakia, the British prime minister, Neville Chamberlain, hurriedly flew to Munich to confer with the führer. At the meeting, Hitler promised this would be his very last land grab: "The last territorial claim I have to make in Europe." He would be content. Czech President Eduard Benes pleaded with Chamberlain for help. But Chamberlain turned a deaf ear and signed away Czech sovereignty in what became the Munich Accord. Upon his return from Germany, Chamberlain, looking terribly tired and haggard, descended the steps from his plane and walked to a bank of waiting microphones. There, under a London drizzle, he pulled from his pocket the paper he and Hitler had just signed. Chamberlain waved it above his head and declared, "[I have] returned from Germany bringing peace with honor. I believe it is peace for our time." But there was no honor here, only shame. Nor was it peace for our time—a few months later Hitler struck again, invading Poland, and WWII was on. A lack of courage kept the French and the British from acting while there was still time. Now they had their backs to the wall and were at a great disadvantage. "[The god of war] hates those who hesitate," wrote Euripides. The hesitance and reluctance to act against Hitler cost France defeat, Nazi occupation and an indelible stain on French honor. England paid perhaps an even higher price: five years of terrible warfare, a lost empire and the snuffing out of the lives of scores of thousands of the nation's finest young men.

Business leaders often respond to overwhelming external threat just as Chamberlain did. They fail to act decisively. They fret, procrastinate and refuse to face reality. They have no strategy beyond hoping and praying that the situation will somehow improve. The results are almost always disastrous. There are any number of examples. Here are two.

One, most to the point, was highlighted in an earlier chapter dealing with the experiences of Encyclopaedia Britannica's dithering and near paralysis in the face of Microsoft's Encarta attack.

A second business example, of this failure to act, is the woeful tale of Smith Corona—perhaps not woeful as much as reprehensible. The Wang word processors began to make inroads into the typewriter market in the 1970s. Other word processors and then Macs and PCs followed. Smith Corona, the leading typewriter manufacturer, did nothing in response. For some three decades, year after year, sales and income declined and the company failed to act. That Smith Corona's senior management could stand idly by watching a new technology that they themselves could have easily obtained destroy the company is no different in essence from Chamberlain's shameful Munich Accord and his "Peace for our time."

Military and business history is replete with examples like these. They demonstrate the clear distinction between two strategies. One, as presented here, is the well-thought-out, rearguard strategy of patience and time, to be followed by one's own offensive at a time and place of one's own choosing—think Kutuzov and Warren Buffett. The second is the craven and irresponsible head-in-the-sand strategy of hoping that things will somehow improve—think Chamberlain and Smith Corona.

——————

The Spartans, unlike the Russians in 1812, chose to act decisively against an invading Persian army. Act they did, seizing control of a narrow pass in northern Greece called Thermopylae. The Greek historian Herodotus wrote that at that geographic choke point, 300 of them contested an enemy of 400,000—and met their destiny.

CHAPTER TEN

Spartans at Thermopylae

Control the Choke Point

What manner of men are these Spartans?
—Xerxes, king of Persia

People will remember for a thousand years what we do here today.
—Leonidas, king of Sparta

We have a once-in-a-lifetime opportunity to establish a [choke point] for the next 100 years.
—Jeffrey Skilling, CEO, Enron[1]

"Come and Get Them"

It was the summer of 480 B.C. Like a vast swarm of locusts, a massive Persian army, numbering some 400,000 men, descended on the thirty-one fledgling democratic states of Greece that together comprised the Hellenic League. That invading army, under command of King Xerxes, was supported and protected on its eastern seaward flank by a large Persian fleet. The Greeks were caught unprepared. They needed time to recruit, train and arm their own forces in order to defend themselves against the aggressor.

Only Sparta, the most warlike of the Greek states, was able to meet the Persian threat immediately. Its king, Leonidas, selected 300 of his best men and rapidly set forth northward to block and delay the Persian advance, thus providing their fellow Greeks with a needed breathing spell during which they could prepare defenses. The Spartans chose an ideal location at which to challenge the Persians— the narrow, fifty-foot-wide pass at Thermopylae. It was a choke point—the only possible invasion route from northern Greece to Athens and the other Greek city-states to the south.

The Spartans arrived at Thermopylae late in the afternoon of a sweltering summer day. Without resting, they quickly established a makeshift defensive barricade and prepared for the assault that was sure to come. The Spartans were few in number but nevertheless formidable. From an early age each had been disciplined in the rigors and skills of war—swimming in icy rivers, sleeping on rocky ground, pushing themselves on exhausting forced marches, learning the secrets of hand-to-hand combat and the use of a variety of weapons. The Spartans were arguably the best-trained and conditioned warriors of their time. Their officers were among the finest of Greek athletes, many of them Olympic Game winners in running, wrestling and javelin throwing. Stoic in the face of pain, Spartans looked on death in battle as the supreme virtue. When a young Spartan, that first day at Thermopylae, spoke of rumors he had heard that the Persian bowmen were so numerous that their arrows would block out the very sun, the veteran Dienekes clapped the youngster on the back and cheerfully shouted so that all could hear: "Good, we will be able to fight in the shade." The men laughed heartily, went about their tasks and waited for the enemy with a confident eagerness.

The following dawn, with trumpets blaring, drums beating and much shouting, the Persian army arrived at the northern end of the pass. Xerxes immediately ordered the deployment of his cavalry, light infantry and archers. But the Persians were faced with a craggy, mountainous terrain in the shape of a lengthy funnel with themselves at the large end and the Spartans at Thermopylae, the small end, blocking the way. Xerxes had little room to maneuver. His only option was to feed his men small unit by small unit, one after another, into the battle in a frontal assault against the Spartan redoubt. This he did.

SPARTANS AT THERMOPYLAE 165

Pierced by Spartan spears, swords and arrows and bludgeoned by Spartan clubs, the Persian dead piled on top of one another: 100, 500, then 1,000 and more. Never before had Xerxes encountered an enemy of such bravery, determination and fighting ability. Counting his ever-growing casualties, Xerxes, late in the afternoon, ordered a halt to his attack and sent one of his generals to Leonidas to offer him and his men freedom if they would just deliver up their arms. "*Molon labe*," Leonidas tersely replied—"Come and take them [if you can]." The Persian attack resumed.

After days of ceaseless battle, finally overcome by sheer numbers and their own exhaustion, the Spartans began to fall. Nearly every one of those still standing had suffered grievous wounds. At a moment of brief respite, Leonidas gathered his remaining men around him and told them, "People will remember for a thousand years what we do here today." The men rallied.

Again Xerxes attacked. Now it was primitive butchery with axes, daggers, stones, teeth and fists. Finally it came to an end. Silence lay over the battlefield. The Spartan 300, including their king, lay dead. Some 15,000 of Xerxes' men who had perished in the fighting lay beside and among them. Walking over the now-quiet battlefield, Xerxes was struck by the Spartan display of military valor and professionalism that he had witnessed. He wondered aloud, "What manner of men are these Spartans?" They were indeed extraordinary. Leonidas' prophecy to his men that they would be long remembered has been realized. We do remember.

Thermopylae changed the course of world history. The Spartans had stood their ground for a precious seven days, giving their Greek brethren time to raise land and sea forces that would be able to challenge the Persians. As important, when word spread of the Spartan courage, all of the Greek people took heart. In contrast, the Persians were dispirited and made fearful by the Spartan bravery and fighting prowess. Although not yet evident, the tide of war had turned. Thermopylae had physically and psychologically blunted the Persian attack. It had been a great Spartan victory. Only a few months later the Greeks would utterly defeat the forces of Xerxes on the ground at Plataea and at sea in the Straits of Salamis.

The seedlings of Western democracy that the Greeks had cultivated were saved in no small part because of the martial spirit of 300 Spartans and their inspirational leader, Leonidas. But something more was key to the Spartan victory: Leonidas' choke-point strategy and choice of Thermopylae as the ideal location to stand and execute it. No matter their great valor and combat abilities, the Spartans would have been simply overrun, and quickly dispatched, had they met Xerxes' forces on an open plain. Strategy made the difference.

Viagra and Bill Gates

AOL, with its 26 million-person service base in the United States, is by far the most popular Internet portal for electronic messaging—Yahoo and Microsoft combined run a poor second. The AOL portal, with the crucial choke point it provides, serves as an almost perfect metaphor for Thermopylae. In front of a PC's monitor, or the readout window of any one of a myriad of electronic access devices, is the consumer. On the other side is the wondrous, Promethean world of the Internet. Deployed across the divide, at the choke point, is AOL. If a competitor is to win the consumer, he must either smash through the choke point or go around—either way at enormous cost. Steve Case, AOL's chairman, achieved his position by being a first mover to the choke point where he then rapidly strengthened his defenses. Those defenses are stout—to little avail, in 2000, competitors threw $1 million thirty-second Super Bowl ads against AOL, much as Xerxes threw thousands of his men at the Spartan redoubt.

Patents and licenses are another form of choke point. Pfizer's Viagra has generated enormous revenues for the company and will continue to do so until the drug's patent expires. After that, typically within a few months, Viagra, like any other patented drug, will give up 50 percent of its market to generics; after one year, that figure reaches 80 percent. But so long as the patent is in place—seven years is the rule—it serves as a formidable strategic choke point.

In another example of a patent as a choke point, there is Qualcomm. Along the walls of its San Diego headquarters' lobby there are 327 plaques, each denoting a patent protecting some aspect of the company's leading-edge Code Division Multiple Access (CDMA) wireless phone technology. Those patents, and another 846 pending, stand guard at Qualcomm's cyberspace choke point. The company's treasury is enriched by an average of about $10 in licensing fees for every wireless phone sold in America today; competitors must pay this tribute to pass through the choke point.

A discussion of business choke points is not complete without mention of Microsoft and its dominant PC operating system (OS). The choke-point strategy is fundamental to Microsoft's enormous success. It has also made it the target of Justice Department nannies—more about that in a few pages.

It is not a coincidence that the preceding examples of choke points all involve intellectual property rights. Today's business choke points are more likely to be intellectual than physical. This is a change from decades ago, when control of *physical* assets or resources provided the choke point. John D. Rockefeller, for example, controlled refining capacity and so was able to wield great power over independent oil producers. Cornelius Vanderbilt's railroads, with their laid track, locomotives and rolling stock, served as choke points in the regions where they operated—there was no other equally efficient means of passenger and cargo transportation. For well over a century, De Beers controlled the worldwide diamond industry through its choke point of South African mine ownership. Krupp dominated the European steel and arms industry for nearly 200 years with its vast mining and factory complex in and around Essen in Germany. Even today, while physical choke points are less in evidence than intellectual ones, they still exist. Global Crossing is building a choke point in the form of an undersea telecom fiber network linking Europe, Asia and the Americas, and AT&T has been buying up cable companies with their in-place underground cables and home connects to serve as broadband choke points.

The brilliantly conceived and courageously executed choke-point strategy at the blood soaked battlefield of Thermopylae resulted in the Spartans achieving their military objective and in the process winning immortality for themselves and ultimate victory for the Greek states. That same history-changing strategy has come to the boardrooms of the great business enterprises of the world: AOL, Pfizer, Microsoft, Qualcomm, Global Crossing and AT&T among them. From battlefield to boardroom the choke point has been a winning strategy.

Strategic Choice: Prevailing Circumstances

This choke-point strategy is most effective when a war is in its early phase, when scouts are still reconnoitering the terrain, when skirmishers are still probing enemy positions and when the armies themselves are still on the move and battle lines have not yet been drawn. Thus it was that the Spartans seized control of the pass at Thermopylae while the great Persian army was still on the march.

Equivalent prevailing circumstances in American industrial history, when many competitors were in the field and no one had yet staked out a strong position, come readily to mind. In the latter half of the nineteenth century, that was the case for railroads, steel and oil. In the first decade of the twentieth century, there were the auto and film industries, followed by air travel in the 1920s, radio in the 1930s, TV in the 1950s, shopping malls in the 1960s, category killer retailers in the 1980s, PCs in the early 1990s, deregulated utilities in the mid-1990s and the Internet in 2001.

When markets are still in flux, technologies unproven, customer interest uncertain and when competitors are pursuing trial-and-error approaches and jousting for position—indeed, when the field is up for grabs—it is then, under those circumstances, that a choke-point strategy is called for.

Factors of Success

Having chosen a specific strategy, what are the factors key to its success? Three will be discussed here. The first is the satellite snapshot that assures an awareness and knowledge of rapidly unfolding events. The second deals with racing to the recognized choke point before the competitor arrives, that is, to be a first mover. Finally, there is dealing with inevitable antitrust implications. Consider each of these in some detail.

Satellite Snapshot

If it were not for runners bringing advanced news of Xerxes' movements, the Spartans would not have had time to respond. Even as things were, it took a forced march to bring them to the pass at Thermopylae only hours before the Persians arrived. Today, using all the means of competitor intelligence available, the satellite snapshot must be maintained in real time, 24-7-365, to discern any competitor movement, or outside event, that threatens to alter the status quo. Anything that the satellite snapshot discloses that might serve as an early warning to a competitor's future action is of great value.

The satellite snapshot does something more than signal the urgent need for a choke point. It also provides necessary information to help identify just where the choke point should be located and what form it should take—Thermopylae for the Spartans and CDMA for the people at Qualcomm. Finally, it tracks competitor efforts to breach or flank the choke point once the battle has been joined.

There is a measure of the future scan at work here as well. Not only must the current situation be clearly understood and monitored, but enlightened speculation about the competitor's future movements is also important. During, or in preparation for, a war, military strategists should be constantly speculating about the future with the intent of predicting enemy movements, strength and offensives—war gaming, it is called. Business, too, must future scan to foresee, or speculate on, competitor efforts at flanking or attacking a held choke point.

First Mover

Had Xerxes arrived at Thermopylae before the Spartans, the battle's outcome—and history, for that matter—would have been entirely different. Indeed, had the Spartans seen that the Persians controlled the pass, likely they would have withdrawn and sought another strategy that would limit or neutralize the Persian advantage of overwhelmingly large numbers. They may, or may not, have found such a strategy. But the Spartans *did* get to Thermopylae before the Persians. They were what today in the world of business have come to be called "first movers."

So important is speed in warfare that it in itself might have qualified as one of the ten winning strategies presented in this book. Sun Tzu recognized its importance, saying "Speed, surprise and deception are the primary essentials of the attack." The Duke of Wellington's victory over Napoleon at Waterloo traces back specifically to that factor.

Eisenhower in WWII recognized the benefit of swift movement—
"Speed is the essence of success," he wrote. The Confederate army,
over four years of Civil War fighting and scores of battles, was almost
always outnumbered by the blue-clad Union forces, sometimes by as
much as three or four to one. It often didn't seem to matter because the
Johnny Rebs were able to move so quickly and obtain a battlefield
position of choice, even if it was not a perfect choke point. "To git thar
fustest with the mostest men" was the key to victory for Gen. Bedford
Forrest, commander of Virginia's fearsome First Cavalry.

Speed is also crucial in the world of business. Visa with 50 percent
of the market and MasterCard with 25 percent dominate the credit card
business. The two moved quickly in the 1970s to control the choke
point between consumers on one side and banks on the other. The
more card holders they had and the more banks that signed on, the
stronger their choke point became. Dozens, hundreds of competitors
have appeared on the scene, but too late. So successful have Visa and
MasterCard been that they have recently caught the eye of Washington's antitrust people. That is the political reality of a successful choke-
point strategy. Dealing with it will be addressed in a few paragraphs.

Enron provides another example. All of its enormous success
today stems from its being a first mover in natural gas trading just as
the industry began to deregulate in the early 1990s. It has since
expanded, again as a first mover, into the trading of electricity, wood
pulp and now Internet bandwidth. By moving quickly it has collared
large numbers of buyers and sellers. That in turn has enabled the
Enron people to structure far more complex and profitable deals. "We
have a once-in-a-lifetime opportunity to establish a position for the
next 100 years,"[2] says CEO Jeffrey Skilling. Skilling is in essence
talking about a choke point. Enron has also been among the first to
gather together spirited, talented and relatively young employee
cadres that are expert at what they do: moving swiftly to a choke point.

There is much merit to an emphasis on speed and being the first
to move into position even if all preparations have not been made.
Tom Peters, the management consultant, likes to say "Test fast, fail
fast, adjust fast."[3] A similar version of this reads: "Ready, fire, aim."
Time is almost always available to make corrections on the run, and
there is the side benefit that the competition is kept in a perpetually
reactive state.

Another advantage to speed is that it sharpens the senses and increases efficiency. A driver's thoughts may occasionally wander as he or she cruises the interstate at 60 mph. But there would be no idle daydreaming if the driver was behind the wheel of a Formula One car at the Daytona 500, doing not 60 but 160 mph. Speed, of necessity, heightens the senses and rivets the concentration.

Operating at great speed does something still more: It forces an organization to be fully prepared in advance of actual combat. When the bullets begin to fly and the bombs begin to fall, there is no time to find one's weapon, make certain it is loaded and learn how to fire it. It is too late for that. That is one of the reasons why the military spends so much time, during a stand-down in combat, cleaning weapons, stockpiling ammunition, repairing equipment and training personnel: Once the battle is joined, all is ready for speedy movement and decisive action.

One last benefit of acting swiftly: "Speed exhilarates and energizes,"[4] says GE's Jack Welch. Welch initiated his company's "Workout Program" in which people bring to their manager some issue they believe needs resolution. Discussion may go on for an hour or two or more, but in the end the manager has but three alternatives in dealing with the proposal: He or she can say yes, or no or request more specific information and set a date for the next meeting. Rather than procrastinate, issues are settled and the decks cleared to address a whole new set of incoming matters. The result of this process is greatly accelerated GE decision making and much faster response to market changes, both of which are so necessary in the competitive arena.

Speed, then, however it is achieved, is crucial to the successful execution of a choke-point strategy. But beyond that, speed is often a desirable end in itself.

Antitrust Defense

No World Court or high tribunal issued an injunction against Leonidas at Thermopylae ordering him to yield up his "unfair" position. But contemporary business is another matter. A company in control of a crucial choke point must be prepared to defend itself not only in the marketplace but also in the courts.

At the height of her career, the husky-voiced, sultry and seductive Mae West of early Hollywood fame found herself completely exasperated by agents, producers and studio officials. Out of great frustration, she was heard to yell out, "I am up to my ass in midgets." Microsoft must sometimes feel like that. The Justice Department Lilliputians, spurred on by Microsoft competitors, are seeking to break Microsoft's operating system choke point. Choke point it indeed is—but a benign one that has led to the creation of trillions of dollars of new wealth and millions of jobs, to say nothing of astonishing advances in science, medicine and commerce. That was of no concern to the government's lead attorney David Boies, who, in 1999, won round one of an antitrust legal proceeding against Microsoft. But the fight is not over. A Federal Court of Appeals has decided to hear the Microsoft case. That is good news for Gates, Ballmer and Co. It means that litigation will be dragged out for at least two more years, a near eternity in the world of today's high-tech; time enough for Microsoft to position itself to seize final victory. Indeed, the new Bush White House will likely be supportive of the Microsoft position.

Bill Gates, although he may look a little nerdy, is tough as nails and epitomizes the men and women of his company. Microsoft is comprised of really smart and combative people who savor a fight. The Justice Department and a certain gaggle of politicians will discover this as Microsoft belatedly learns to play the Washington lobbying game. Already, like the omnipresent rains of Redmond, Washington, Microsoft lobbying dollars are falling upon the other Washington across the country. The president of Common Cause, Scott Harshbarger, recently whined, "Microsoft, the software giant has become the soft-money giant."[5] Microsoft was long above the fray of petty politics—but no longer. Other high-tech companies were quicker to discover the ways of Washington.

Intel, for one, has a huge legal budget to defend its own patent and antitrust positions. After losing in the marketplace, DEC has brought a triple-damages suit against Intel, claiming infringement on its Alpha chip technologies. A dozen other suits are outstanding, and the Federal Trade Commission (FTC) is always looking over Intel's shoulder. "Antitrust awareness is embedded in our culture,"[6] says an Intel spokesman. Part of that means not sending incriminating e-mails into cyberspace or using inflammatory language in memos or recording the minutes of strategy meetings. It also means schmoozing the regulators—something Microsoft had been loath to do.

Cisco, with an 81 percent share of the Internet router market, should be as much of a target for the FTC as Microsoft, but it isn't. Cisco has avoided trouble by working with the government. "We try to maintain an ongoing dialogue,"[7] says Cisco's general counsel, Dan Scheinman. That is Orwellian lobby-speak and its meaning is not entirely clear—although one can guess. What is clear is that Cisco gets slaps on the wrist or sent to its room for occasional time-outs by the Feds, while Microsoft has a belt taken to its collective behind.

One last example is Coca-Cola, which seems to be adopting a kinder-gentler, more congenial facade when working with overseas regulators. Coke was recently blocked from a major acquisition, England's Cadbury Schweppes, and underwent intense European Union (EU) regulatory scrutiny after hundreds of alleged contaminated Coca-Cola containers were reported. The new CEO, Douglas Daft, is setting aside the company's past tough, aggressive, pugnacious tone and has become more conciliatory when talking with EU antitrust people. "They [Coca-Cola] behave with contempt toward us,"[8] pouts Karl van Miert, the EU's antitrust chief. Daft, recognizing that 80 percent of his company's profits come from overseas and that he wants to grow his existing global 50 percent market share, is on a goodwill tour across Europe stretching from Brussels to Rome. "Coke will play by the 'house rules,'"[9] Daft riffs to every EU bureaucrat and politician in sight. Look for Coke rhetoric to become far less shrill in Europe and Asia for that matter, as pretentious regulators are stroked, pacified and, one way or another, co-opted. It is not pretty but it is business. Coca-Cola's brand, the most recognized in the world, is its choke point against the competition. If protecting it means donning a cloak of feigned humbleness, cooperation and obeisance when dealing with government, so be it.

Sooner or later, companies that successfully execute a choke-point strategy will run afoul of the government. Like it or not, then, in-house and outside legal counsel as well as government affairs and lobbying people play a vital role in achieving success with this choke-point strategy. Government, putatively in the business of protecting consumers, demands its levy. A company's competitors try in vain to break its marketplace choke point. But governments at the local, national and, more recently, international level can achieve through legislation, fiat or court rulings what competitors cannot. Still, the threat is modest: Government can be assuaged, but it takes some effort as well as the swallowing of corporate pride to do so.

Maginot Line Syndrome

This chapter's choke-point strategy comes with a warning: Beware the Maginot Line syndrome. As Hitler's threats and saber-rattling in the 1930s became ever more provocative, the French were comforted by their recently built Maginot Line. Named after Andre Maginot, the minister of war, and constructed at great cost, it was comprised of a string of heavily fortified concrete bunkers along the French border facing Germany. The individual bunkers were connected by an elaborate underground tunnel system. This, the French thought, was the choke point behind which they were safe. It wasn't and they weren't. In an unprecedented blitzkrieg, or lightning war, the Germans in 1939 flanked the Maginot Line, bypassing it through neutral Belgium and the thickly forested and undefended Ardennes. Then, the never-before-seen, giant, railroad car–mounted Krupp cannon pounded the forts to rubble. The entire French army capitulated to Hitler within three weeks. Nazi occupation of France followed with the formation of the puppet Vichy government. There are few better military examples of barriers thought to be impregnable choke points that when tested could not stand than the Maginot Line.

It is difficult to find historical examples of military choke points that have endured without ever having been breached or flanked—in the end even Thermopylae was taken by the Persians. Recognizing this, companies holding choke points must be ever aware of the peril of falling into Maginot Line complacency. Rather, they must constantly track competitor movements and prepare against either a direct assault or a flanking movement. When Sun Microsystems talks of "Networks being the computer," it is clear this is a strategy to circumvent Microsoft's PC operating system choke point. Microsoft is quite aware of that—there is no Maginot Line thinking at Redmond. The enmity that Scott McNealy of Sun and Bill Gates of Microsoft have for one another is based on their own individual will to shape the future unopposed by anyone else. McNealy vs. Gates

and Sun Microsystems vs. Microsoft—this is the archetype of business as war. That is a wonderful thing, it galvanizes the two companies
and the two men who lead them to the benefit of the rest of us.

Another example of what was once thought to be a choke point is
American Airlines' SABRE reservation system. In the mid-1980s, travel
agents around the country installed the computer-based system, which,
in theory, could be used to book flights with any airline, but which in
fact gave an advantage to American Airlines. Because of that, the
company enjoyed a decisive marketing edge until about 1998. From
that point on, it took less than two years for SABRE to be overtaken by
Internet technology—indeed, even Captain Kirk, aka William Shatner,
with his Priceline.com off-key singing television commercials, has
achieved cyberspace victories over American Airlines.

For decades, if a viewer wanted more than the meager and frothy
offerings of over-the-air network television, he or she had to pass through
the choke point of that ubiquitous little cable box atop the TV set. Most
cable companies were caught up in the Maginot Line syndrome—their
monthly charges were high and forever moving higher still, customer
service was infuriatingly unresponsive and programming itself was
limited. None of that mattered to the cable companies. They were safe
behind their choke points. But recently there has come the flanking
assault of DirecTV and EchoStar with their 100 channels of satellite
television offerings. Look for cable customer service to improve and for
prices to stabilize.

The country's two largest PC resellers, InaCom and MicroAge,
have just gone into bankruptcy. Their choke point, located precisely
between PC manufacturers and the retail market, was demolished as
Compaq, Hewlett-Packard and IBM moved more aggressively to
customer-direct sales. "It all changed over night,"[10] said a weary, battle-
fatigued Jeff McKeever, the MicroAge CEO. Other resellers, such as
CompuCom, saw the changes coming and transformed themselves into
service providers. InaCom and MicroAge, on the other hand, have seen
their Maginot Line breached and overrun.

Finally, the last example provides something of a twist. In the case
of Microsoft, government is working to break up a perceived monopoly.
But there are other situations where government itself creates and then
protects the choke point and resultant monopoly. Consider the world
of auto dealerships. With only a few exceptions, the consumer cannot

buy a new car factory-direct. He or she must go through a dealer. This dealer choke point has been won by raw politics. Auto dealers are among the wealthiest and most tightly politically connected of the citizenry of small and mid-size towns. The result of their influence and quite successful lobbying effort is a thicket of state laws that bar auto manufacturers from owning their own retail outlets or selling direct. This can't stand. Sooner or later inefficiencies in the current system will cause it to implode and auto dealers will find their Maginot Line choke point circumvented or simply swept away. In fact, recently, the two largest auto industry trade groups sued the state of Arizona over its franchise law, which keeps manufacturers from selling directly to customers. One way or another the auto dealership choke point will be demolished or simply bypassed, probably sooner rather than later.

It is crucial then for companies executing a choke-point strategy to be coldly objective in evaluating the strength of their position. War games are helpful in doing that. They involve an elite team within the company playing the role of the competitor and seeking a way through or around the choke point. For a company that has a perceived strong choke point, its greatest threat is its own complacency—the Maginot Line syndrome. Strategies, by definition, last a long time—years or even decades. But there are 10X events, explored in chapter 3, that call for strategic change even in the case of the highly effective choke-point strategy.

––––––––

Gen. William Tecumseh Sherman, like his superior Gen. Grant, was an advocate of total, unmerciful, unrelenting warfare. In 1864, with the outcome of the Civil War still in doubt, Sherman advanced into Georgia, where he defeated the Confederate force that had been sent to block him. He went on to sack the undefended Atlanta, leaving it a smoldering ruin. He wasn't done. Sherman led his men in a march from Atlanta to the sea. He left in his wake torched fields, slaughtered livestock and destroyed railroads. Homes, from the smallest cabin to the greatest mansion, were burned to the ground. This was a strategy of relentless warfare. It resulted in victory. It often does.

CHAPTER ELEVEN

Sherman's March through Georgia

Relentless Attack

No terms except an unconditional and immediate surrender can be accepted. I propose to move immediately upon your works.
—Gen. Ulysses S. Grant

Always attack without regard for flanks. Attack rapidly, ruthlessly, viciously, without rest.
—Gen. George S. Patton

By God sir, that man [Gen. Grant] fights!
—Abraham Lincoln

No captain can do wrong if he places his ship along side that of an enemy.
—Adm. Horatio Nelson

Hit hard. Hit fast. Hit Often.
—Adm. Bull Halsey

"A Grant Came After Him

ll we ask is to be let alone," Jefferson Davis, the president of the newly formed Confederate States of America, told the North. His CSA had just seceded from the United States. Abraham Lincoln, vowing to keep the Union together, wouldn't have it. The two sides jousted verbally for the next few months and then on April 12, 1861, Confederate forces fired upon, and seized, Fort Sumter in Charleston Bay, South Carolina. While casualties were few, nevertheless the act signaled the beginning of America's great Civil War.

The first major battle took place shortly thereafter in Virginia, near a small stream called Bull Run, just a few hours' hard ride from Washington. There, the raw Union forces were routed by Johnny Rebs led by outstanding generals like Thomas Jackson, who at the battle would earn the nickname "Stonewall" for his determined defense against repeated enemy assaults. What many in the North had expected to be a short war evidently would not be. The Union loss at Bull Run augured things to come—in ensuing battle after battle the Yanks were defeated, or, if they were able to win, their generals lacked the will to follow-up.

The North, with three times the population, twice the railroads, three times the factories and four times the bank deposits of the South, could nevertheless not put a winning army in the field. A frustrated Lincoln appointed, then was forced to fire, general after general. First there was the loyalty-torn, obese and septuagenarian Winfield Scott: "Old Fuss and Feathers" he was called. Then came the hopeless John Pope. He was followed by the diminutive George McClellan, who was more interested in parades, posturing and politics than fighting—Lincoln said he had the "slows." The incompetent butcher Ambrose Burnside came next to be succeeded by the overly cautious Joe Hooker. Then, in the summer of 1863, came Gen. George Meade, whom Lincoln hoped would be different.

Meade would face the South's brilliant, revered and much-loved Gen. Robert E. Lee. Lee's Army of Virginia was then as strong as it had ever been. It was newly refitted and numbered some 70,000 men. Knowing that Meade intended to attack Richmond, the Confederacy's capital, Lee decided on a strategy going back to the Punic wars. In the second of those wars, in 207 B.C., Hannibal, with his war elephants and Carthaginian army, had crossed the Alps and threatened Rome, the capital of the Roman Empire. Rather than make a defensive stand, the Roman General Scipio loaded his troops aboard ships, sailed to Carthage and attacked Hannibal's homeland. Hannibal was forced to withdraw and rush to his own nation's defense. A few months later, on Carthaginian soil, Scipio met and defeated Hannibal. Lee's intent was to practice a modern version of Scipio's initiative, leaving Richmond only lightly defended and advancing north through the Shenandoah Valley into Pennsylvania, threatening the very person of Abraham Lincoln and his war government in Washington. To the sounds of "Dixie" and the waving and smiling of pretty girls, Lee and his men marched out of Richmond and headed for the Union heartland.

George Meade, with his 90,000 men, moved to block him. The two armies, like a pair of blindfolded boxers, flailed about trying to locate one another. Finally, more or less by accident and fate, extensions of the two armies, a Confederate brigade and elements of the Union cavalry, collided on July 1, 1863, in a small Pennsylvania village. A firefight immediately broke out. By nightfall, like a great mischievous magnet, men, horses, weapons and supplies from both armies were being drawn to the village's surrounding rolling hills and fields. Unfolding events were about to thrust the previously anonymous Gettysburg into the history books.

The Confederates were a powerful fighting force. True, the irreplaceable Stonewall Jackson had been killed six months before at Chancellorsville, but the South, unlike the North, still had a panoply of great generals: James Longstreet, J. E. B. Stuart, Nathan Bedford Forrest, Richard Ewell, Pierre Beauregard, John Hood, J. P. Hill and Jubal Early. The men in the ranks were tough, enthusiastic veterans who were eager to test themselves once again against Lincoln's army. The Yanks, although not so well generaled, were also spoiling for a fight—especially some of the recently formed regiments of newly arrived, pugnacious Irish, Scottish and German immigrants.

By the second day, the battle lines had largely been drawn. The Union forces, facing west, stretched some four miles along Cemetery Ridge running from Gettysburg in the north to Little Round Top in the south. Across from them, about a mile away, were the Confederates. From midmorning on, both sides launched a series of probing attacks that were readily repulsed. Periodically, Southern and Northern artillery dueled without greatly harming one another. These were still preliminaries. The sun set on a virtual stalemate. That night the men, both Reb and Yank, ate a good supper, quietly smoked and talked of home, knowing that the following day would bring the decisive battle. By midnight the two armies had fallen into a restless sleep.

The men awoke on the third morning to a huge red sun; it presaged a blistering hot day with temperatures that would reach the high nineties. Perhaps the heat stirred Lee's arthritic blood. Perhaps he was simply greatly fatigued from three years of the heavy burden of leadership. Perhaps the gods of war had whispered to him as he slept. In any case, quite uncharacteristic of his style of clever strategic maneuvering, he ordered Gen. George E. Pickett and his 15,000 men to frontally assault the center of the Union line along Cemetery Ridge. Preparations to do so were begun.

At 1:30 in the afternoon, following a barrage of Confederate artillery, Pickett marched his division, in parade order, out of the protective woods where they had been invisible to Union cannon. The men were formed in two ranks: 9,000 in the first and 6,000 in the second. Across a mile of open field and up the gentle slopes to Cemetery Ridge they went. At the ridge's crest was a low stone wall. Behind it were the men in blue. Canister and grapeshot fired from Union batteries on Little Round Top arched across the sky and plunged down upon the advancing Southerners. Bits and chunks of iron tore and ripped into the men in gray. They fell by the tens, hundreds and then thousands. But still the line advanced.

The 3,500 or so Southerners who made it to and then over the wall fought bravely but could not hold. Union reinforcements quickly converged at the point of the Confederate attack. Those Rebs not killed, wounded or captured were repulsed. No one knew it then, but that wall had been the high-water mark of the ill-fated Confederacy. The battle was over. Pickett's men, what was left of them, limped back to their lines with their pride intact and with their heads held as high as their wounds and great fatigue would allow. For the survivors, there would be a lifetime of memory in the brief minutes they had just endured. Pickett himself, who had been on horseback throughout the assault—and hence a highly visible target—miraculously escaped injury. Later, alone and counting his dead, Pickett wept uncontrollably. An eerie quiet settled over the battlefield.

That night, Lee ordered the withdrawal of his army. During three days of fighting he had lost most of Pickett's command and some 20,000 men in all—almost one-third of his army was gone. The Union commander, Gen. Meade, now was handed the golden opportunity to end the war by rolling up the retreating remnants of Lee's army. The war's end was at hand. But Meade procrastinated, delayed and dithered . . . in the end nothing was done. Lee and his battered but still viable army returned safely to Virginia. Lincoln went into an apoplectic rage upon hearing of Meade's failure to pursue Lee and his letting the victory slip away. The war drifted on. Some nine months passed.

Meanwhile, quietly, with very little newspaper attention, the Union was consistently winning battles in the West. The best known of the Western generals was Ulysses S. Grant, who had won a series of victories including his latest, at Fort Donelson on the Cumberland and Vicksburg in Mississippi, where he had demanded and received unconditional surrender from his Southern counterpart. Grant had a well-earned reputation as a stolid and relentless fighter. This was the kind of general Lincoln had long sought. On March 9, 1864, Lincoln reached down into his eligibility list of generals, bypassing a dozen of them, and promoted Grant to General in Chief of the Union armies.

Upon giving Grant his command, Lincoln asked his new general what his strategy would be. Pointing to a nearby map showing the area just north of Richmond, Grant responded, "I propose to fight it out on this line if it takes all summer." It would take longer than that.

Grant's first encounter with Lee, on May 6, 1864, took place in a tangled, thickly dense and tinderbox dry forest of northern Virginia. It would come to be called the Battle of the Wilderness. It was a bitter infantryman's struggle—cavalry and artillery were useless in the constricted terrain. Hundreds of wounded men, unable to be reached, died of thirst or were burned to death by forest fires that erupted from the continuous musket fire. While Union forces outnumbered the Confederates 100,000 to 60,000, the battle's outcome was more or less a draw, although Grant suffered a somewhat greater proportion of fatalities. After the last shot had been fired, Lee moved south to lick his wounds.

Much to the amazement and joy of the Union army, when Lee withdrew, Grant pursued him. This was the first time, in three years of fighting, that the men in blue had seen such a thing. Prior to Grant, Union generals had not attacked retreating Southern forces—certainly not aggressively. In quick succession in the ensuing weeks the two armies fought again, first on May 8 to 12 in a bloody clash at Spotsylvania. Again, Grant's losses were heavy, but so were Lee's. Lee retreated. Grant came after him. Then on June 3 there was the battle at Cold Harbor, which was a kind of reverse Gettysburg. There, Union forces attacked Southern earthworks and lost 6,000 men in a single hour of combat—but once again, Lee's casualties were also high. Lee withdrew, and relentlessly Grant followed. Then on June 23 Lee settled into trenches twenty-three miles from Richmond. The Union noose was tightening—but at a high cost.

In less than two months of fighting, Lee had lost some 32,000 men; Grant's killed in action numbered nearly 60,000 men—roughly the same as the United States would experience in some *fifteen years* of fighting in Vietnam a century later. Complaints began to come to Lincoln about the inordinate Union casualties, and rumors swirled around Washington about Grant's drinking. Some called for his dismissal. Lincoln refused: "By God sir, that man fights! You just tell me the brand of whisky Grant drinks: I would like to send a barrel of it to my other generals." Grant was a bulldog of a fighter—tenacious, stoic and relentless in the face of terrible losses.

The Union siege of the Confederate capital of Richmond was not passive: Grant relentlessly jabbed, poked and prodded at Lee's lines. But that was not offense enough for Grant. Chafing at the relative stalemate, he attacked in another direction. On November 15, 1864, he ordered Gen. William Tecumseh Sherman to move eastward from Chattanooga in Tennessee into Georgia. There, Sherman's army of 90,000 would decimate the Confederate forces of Joseph E. Johnston, capture Atlanta and then continue on to the sea. That advance through Georgia covered a swath of sixty miles. Houses, barns, fields, small farms and large plantations were burned and livestock slaughtered. Railroad tracks were uprooted, piled crosswise over dry brush and set afire. The rails became grotesquely twisted and unusable—"Sherman's neckties" they were called.

Sherman, under Grant's command, showed the South the savage, cruel and relentless face of war. That "March through Georgia" broke the South's will to fight. It demonstrated the extent to which Grant was prepared to go in his dogged pursuit of victory.

After closing down the Georgia campaign, Sherman joined Grant in Virginia. His added presence enabled Grant finally to turn Lee's flank, forcing him to retreat on April 1, 1865, from the barricades before Richmond. It was the endgame. Lee sought an escape route. Grant relentlessly moved to check him. Union forces maneuvered in front of Lee no matter what direction he turned. After eight days came the surrender at Appomattox and checkmate. Grant, having obtained unconditional surrender from Lee, gave generous terms to the Southerners, and the war was over.

The United States had survived the greatest crisis of its history. The price was high—some $1 trillion in today's currency and the loss of 622,511 men. But the country was now poised to fulfill what many were beginning to call its "manifest destiny." The West was opening. A period of vibrant economic growth was about to begin. Young men named Rockefeller, Carnegie, Morgan and Vanderbilt were already at work. Within another half a century the country would become one of the world's great powers. And within a little over a century it would become *the* world's great power. None of this would have happened without Ulysses S. Grant and his successful relentless-attack strategy.

Perhaps because the relentless-attack strategy is so truly American, it has become the strategy of choice for great American companies. For those companies that have executed it well, it has almost always been a winning strategy—think of Nike, Home Depot, Microsoft, Coca-Cola, Oracle, Wal-Mart, Dell and Cisco. They are relentless competitors, singularly driven to attack and then attack again.

Doug Ivester, Coca-Cola's recently retired CEO, has been heard to say, "If a !#$%* competitor was drowning, I'd shove a hose down his throat and turn it on full blast."[1] For decades now, Coke has been a relentless battler for market dominance, both domestically and globally. Over the years, the company has given its competitors not a moment of respite.

Cisco has just won a $1 billion contract from SBC, the giant telecom provider. That should grow its already substantial 81 percent of the

Internet router and infrastructure market. John Chambers, Cisco's CEO, says, "We made literally hundreds of sales calls to SBC. No to us from SBC, or any other customer, just means that we have to come back again."[2] That epitomizes Cisco's inherent culture of relentless attack.

Thirty-nine-year-old Michael Dell has matured from a young college entrepreneur into a world-class large-company CEO. Dell relentlessly attacks the competition. Says its CEO, "We just sold our millionth server. The same thing will happen in storage. People doubted us. Bring them on. We are going right after them."[3] Dell indeed goes "right after them." The company relentlessly attacks segment after segment, competitor after competitor. Since 1996, Dell has moved from fourth to first in desktop PCs, sixth to first in portables and sixth to second in servers.

"Our new Windows for Workgroups will crush all competition and dominate the market."[4] That was Mike Maples, a Microsoft executive who exemplifies the acquisitive, aggressive and relentless character of his company. Few corporations in the world better demonstrate the obsessive quest for victory and the strategy of relentless attack to obtain it than Microsoft. It is this that makes Microsoft so hated and so feared by its competitors.

Companies like the ones just noted are driven by the relentless-attack strategy. It is a strategy that matches one company's will against another's. One of the adversaries inevitably breaks.

Strategic Choice: Prevailing Circumstances

The prevailing circumstances that call for or make possible a strategy of relentless attack are unique. The strategy is suggested when the enemy is strong, determined and capable and is waging a largely rearguard, defensive form of warfare. It is the strategy of choice when the objective is the surrender of such an enemy. The South did not have to win the Civil War; it only had to not lose it. The South's objective of independence would have been obtained if the North had simply quit fighting. For its part, the North could not compromise, negotiate or settle for anything less than complete victory.

Another prevailing circumstance involves comparative strength. To use this strategy, one's own forces need to be strong, indeed stronger than the adversary's, with substantial reserves in hand before going into battle.

With these prevailing circumstances in place, and the choice made to execute the relentless-attack strategy, what are the factors that lead to its success?

Factors of Success

There are four factors that combine to determine the success or failure of the relentless-attack strategy: leadership, mission, esprit and required resources.

Leadership

Perhaps none of the strategies presented in this book so clearly demonstrate the importance of leadership as does Grant's role in the North's relentless-attack strategy in the last year and a half of the Civil War. From the earliest days of the conflict, following Fort Sumter in 1861, the North had pursued an overall "Anaconda Plan" against the South. The Confederacy was to be surrounded, its ports blockaded, and then it was to be squeezed to death. It was a sound idea, except that, for three years, no Union general was able to do the squeezing . . . until Grant.

Grant graduated from West Point in 1843. As a cadet he had excelled at little except horsemanship. He served courageously, if not brilliantly, in the war against Mexico, after which he was stationed at various posts in Texas, Missouri, Oregon and California. He resigned from the army in 1854 but failed at farming, real estate and several other civilian ventures. He was recalled to active duty in 1861. Grant was a short, stocky man with dark hair and brooding brown eyes who had a penchant for cigars and whiskey—some said too much whiskey. A quiet man, Grant was not given to inspiring speeches. In the midst of a battle, when all decisions had been made, he could often be seen alone, sitting on a camp stool, stubble bearded, chewing on an unlit cigar, wearing a mud-spattered private's coat and whittling; perhaps he prayed.

Grant's leadership did not depend on strategic brilliance. He simply followed a strategy of relentless attack. That did not, however, translate into pointless slaughter. Grant refused to send his men en masse against the entrenched forces of Lee outside of Richmond. Instead, he redirected his relentless attack, as noted earlier, to Georgia under the trusted command of the redoubtable Gen. Sherman.

It was no accident that Grant drew excellent men to him, like Sherman and Philip Sheridan, his head of cavalry. They shared his philosophy of relentless warfare. Sherman, like Grant, believed in waging total war, saying "It [war] is hell and cruelty and horror." Leadership means, in part, attracting people of ability and like mind to the cause—whatever that might be. Grant was able to do that. From his officers to the privates on the line, his men had confidence in him and the outcome of his strategy.

A business strategy of relentless attack demands the same kind of leadership. One sees it at dozens of the best global companies: in Bill Gates at Microsoft, John Chambers at Cisco, Fred Smith at FedEx, Carly Fiorina at HP, Sir John Browne at British Petroleum, Nobuyuki Idei at Sony, Jurgen Schrempp at DaimlerChrysler, Rupert Murdoch at News Corp., Jack Welch at GE and more. Emerson once wrote that "An institution is the lengthened shadow of one man." The Civil War's Union army under Grant was such an institution. So are many of the great global companies, especially those executing a strategy of relentless attack.

Mission

Grant earned the nickname "Unconditional Surrender" while still fighting in the West. When facing an enemy army, his sole objective was to win from it unconditional surrender. That was his mission when facing Lee and his Army of Virginia. Grant never lost sight of the mission that Lincoln and the people of the North had assigned to him. With that clearly, and ever, in mind, the relentless-attack strategy naturally followed.

A strategy, any strategy, is but a means to an end. The end is the mission. A strategy of relentless attack, whether on the battlefield or in the business arena, can succeed only if the mission of ultimate victory is continuously held in mind. Carly Fiorina of Hewlett-Packard exhorts her people, "Keep our mission [of industry domi-nance] ever in your hearts, minds and spirits."[5] HP is in fact emerging as one of the world's dominant companies of the early twenty-first century.

Rupert Murdoch's mission of creating the world's greatest media empire has been four decades in the making. Starting from one small-town Australian newspaper, News Corp. has grown exponentially into a near-global newspaper, magazine and television colossus. Murdoch is now expanding relentlessly into network, cable and satellite operations to create arguably the most powerful electronic media platform in the world. Murdoch has set his sights on the DirecTV operations of General Motors. The buttoned-down, tortoise-speed executives at GM will likely be no match for the mission-driven and entrepreneurial Murdoch.

An imbued corporate mission to achieve industry leadership is basic to the success of a relentless-attack strategy.

Esprit

The relentless-attack strategy both fuels and is fueled by organizational esprit. There is cause and effect at work here. Napoleon wrote that "In war, morale is to the material as three is to one." Prior to Grant's assuming command of the Union armies, morale had been terrible. Grant's relentless-attack strategy and leadership changed that. The demands on the men were great, greater than they had ever before been, but it didn't matter—they were attacking the enemy and they were winning.

Arguably, no fighting force in WWII had greater esprit than Patton's Third Army. Patton, like Grant, was a believer in relentless attack: "Always attack without regard for flanks. Attack rapidly, ruthlessly, viciously without rest." That his men did. The Germans feared the Third Army as no other. From senior officers to privates, Patton's men were driven, relentless fighters infused with pride. Patton understood that unit esprit can come only from having been tested by fire and enduring warfare's rigors and travails, indeed, the harsher the testing the greater the esprit.

Microsoft compares well to Patton's Third Army. The lights at Microsoft facilities burn far into the night. The company's culture is austere and Spartan. Peer pressure to perform is intense and unwavering. Top-down criticism is rife: "That's the stupidest idea I've ever heard," is a favorite Bill Gates response to a colleague's suggestion. Praise is rare. This tough working environment reinforces, rather than detracts from, the organization's esprit. The relentless-attack strategy serves to raise morale and pride higher still. The Micosofties feel no shame for being called to task by the FTC for their relentless and monopolistic ways—to the contrary, they glory in it.

Organizations that can capture a level of esprit like that of Patton's Third Army, or like that of Bill Gates' Microsoft, are simply invincible. Nothing and no one can stand before them. Such organizations are nourished on the red meat of relentless attack.

Required Resources

This strategy of relentless attack takes a heavy toll on human and capital resources. Indeed, it devours both of them. It is therefore necessary that capital funding be adequate and that additional funds can be called on if necessary. The Union, in the Civil War, clearly benefited from having nearly four times the bank reserves of the South. Correspondingly, companies like Microsoft that practice the relentless-attack strategy are awash in cash and near-cash reserves.

Management reserves are equally important. General Electric, for one, has a reputation for a very deep management bench. A strategy of relentless-attack actually eases the task of recruiting and retaining talented people. Such individuals yearn for opportunity that only a highly competitive company offers. As noted, great demands are put on Microsoft people, but the company has less than half the turnover rate of Silicon Valley. Certain people, the best people, thrive in this kind of intense environment and are attracted to companies that provide it. A relentless-attack strategy in business requires a host of such men and women.

Balaclava

Only a few years before America's Civil War, the Crimean War fought itself out from 1853 to 1856. The war pitted the Russians against the combined forces of England, France, Turkey and Sardinia. On October 25, 1854, a British cavalry brigade was ordered to charge an entrenched Russian position at Balaclava in the Ukraine. While the assault was part of a larger relentless British attack strategy, it was nevertheless an appallingly foolish command; there was no chance that the Russian line could be breached.

Some 600 British horseman galloped straight forward over a few thousand yards of a flat valley floor directly into the open U of Russian cannon that had been placed wheel to wheel. The British were armed only with pikes and sabers—they were waging nineteenth-century warfare with eighteenth-century weapons. No matter, on they came. The ground thundered with the horses' hooves and the sun glittered from the men's plumed helmets and polished breast plates. The brigade closed on the Russian line: 1,000; 500; 300; then 50 yards. The Russians opened fire.

Of the 600 who raced across that plain, only a score or so made it to the Russian redoubt, and little more than 100 returned. "It is magnificent but it isn't war," wrote Gen. Pierre Bosquet of the charge. It sounds even better in French, "C'est magnifique, mais ce n'est pas la guerre."

The famed Charge of the Light Brigade, with all of its courage, gallantry, foolishness and terrible loss, has almost exact equivalents in business. Recall Iridium's misadventure in which billions of dollars were squandered in a flawed but persistent attempt, over nearly a decade, to launch a global satellite system. Then there was CEO Roger Smith of General Motors and his multi-billion plant automation folly. Smith's strategy was relentless . . . and stupid. AT&T, under CEO Robert Allen, threw billions of dollars into long-distance promotions in a relentless effort to hold market share. Allen might as well have gathered those billions into neat packages, piled them in an open field, poured gasoline over it all and lit a match. Hundreds of business examples like these exist, in which a relentless-attack strategy results only in the profligate expending of resources.

There is a dividing line between Grant's successful relentless attack strategy and the senseless ordering of the now immortalized British 600 to near-certain death at Balaclava. And there is a dividing line between Wal-Mart's relentless attack on its competitors, with its constant honing of operations on one hand and, on the other hand, the reckless waste in the Iridium, GM and AT&T examples just noted. That line is easy to see in hindsight—not so easy to recognize in real time amidst the fog and chaos of war or its business equivalent of intense market competition. Ultimately it is the experience, judgment and wisdom of the general, or CEO, in correctly reading the prevailing circumstances that determine the appropriateness of the relentless attack strategy—that, and maybe a little of the luck that is always at work in both war and business.

––––––––––

Gen. Grant's mission was the enemy's unconditional surrender. He achieved that with a blunt strategy of relentless attack. However, sometimes in war and, by extension, business, circumstances preclude such a strategy. Sometimes mere containment has to be good enough. So it was in Vietnam.

CHAPTER TWELVE

Vietnam

Containment Is Good Enough

We shall pay any price, bear any burden, meet any hardship, support any friend, oppose any foe to assure the survival and success of liberty.
—JFK Inaugural Address

The Vietnamese people will resist until they have won.
—Ho Chi Minh

We have finally achieved peace with honor.
—Richard M. Nixon

There is no finish line.
—Phil Knight, CEO, Nike[1]

"Frantic, Shameful Mess"

Radio Saigon was playing Bing Crosby's "White Christmas" on automatic loop—it was the prearranged signal to Americans still remaining in the besieged city that they should immediately proceed to their designated evacuation points. The Stars and Stripes was lowered from the American embassy's flag pole as U.S. Army helicopters, with their .50-caliber machine guns, protectively circled the compound. The Viet Cong (VC) were pouring into the city. The last

CH-46 passenger helicopter filled with evacuees lifted off from the rooftop of a CIA safe house near the embassy.

There was not enough time for everyone to escape. Some 200,000 South Vietnamese government officials, army officers, businessmen, translators as well as hundreds of young women with their Amerasian children were tragically left behind. Expecting to be taken out by plane, most had raced to Tan Son Nhut Air Force Base, only to find it closed down due to intense VC shelling. Panicking, they frantically headed for the American embassy seeking sanctuary; too late. Their lives and fortunes had been wagered on the United States, and in the end they had been forsaken. They stood beneath the wash of that last helicopter with anguished upturned faces, futilely waving money, jewelry and a variety of official-looking documents. At best, under the coming Communist regime, they would be stripped of their jobs, wealth and homes and sent away to "reeducation camps." At worst . . . well, the VC cadres were professionals at torturing, maiming and often even murdering those who opposed them.

It was April 29, 1975. Saigon, Paris of the Orient, had fallen to the Communists. America's agony of Vietnam was at an end. President Nixon told the country, in a televised address, that this was "Peace with honor." Insiders at the time, like Brent Scowcroft, the deputy national security adviser, didn't think so. He privately called those last few days a "frantic, shameful, mess." History has shown that they were both right.

Some fifteen years before that chaotic end in Saigon, John F. Kennedy, upon assuming the presidency in 1960, had declared to the world that Communism would be fought everywhere, including in Vietnam, where the Communist North threatened the non-Communist South. The first American killed in action (KIA), an adviser to the South Vietnamese military, occurred shortly thereafter. Thousands more United States Army, Navy, Marine, Air, and Special Forces personnel would lose their lives in Vietnam. The Americans who fought there faced vicious guerrilla warfare, horrendous fighting conditions and an implacable enemy. Still, they might have obtained a quick victory were it not for a larger issue out of their control: Cold War geopolitics. A postwar survey showed that 89 percent of the men who served in Vietnam agreed that "We were asked to fight a war our leaders would not let us win."[2] Fear of drawing China or Russia, or both, directly into the war in support of the Viet Cong kept America from a strategy that would achieve an unconditional enemy surrender. The result was that VC sanctuaries in Laos and Cambodia were not attacked and crucial but sensitive North Vietnamese targets, including the port of Haiphong where Russian and Chinese military supply ships rode at anchor, were not bombed. No, a strategy of all-out relentless war, as discussed in the last chapter, could not be waged. A stalemate would have to be good enough.

Early in the Cold War, George Kennan, a one-time Princeton professor, State Department foreign affairs expert, as well as former ambassador to Russia, called for a strategy of *containment* against Communism. Its objective was the blocking of further Communist expansion beyond its current existing borders. Failure at containment in one country, it was believed, would cause the domino-like collapse of a neighboring state, and then its neighbor and so on until the United States would be alone and isolated in a global sea of Communism. Containment became the prevailing American Cold War strategy for some four decades. It was the strategy in Vietnam.

When the Communists took control of all of Vietnam in 1975, it did not seem that containment had been a winning strategy for the United States. But indeed it had been. That became evident in 1989 with the fall of the Berlin Wall and the collapse two years later of the USSR. But another wall, this one black-marbled, elegantly poignant and deeply unsettling, stands in Washington, D.C., as a monument to the 58,209 Americans who fought and died in Vietnam without seeing that victory. All that they *did* see was a teeth-gnashing, frustratingly fought war with a strategy, not of winning, but of merely containing.

It is true that in 1975 Vietnam was lost to Ho Chi Minh and his black-clad cadres. But the victory for the Communists was at best Pyrrhic. VC and civilian casualties were staggering, estimates run from ten to twenty-five times those of America's. In the aftermath of the war the once-vibrant entrepreneurism of South Vietnam was eradicated and supplanted by the gross inefficiencies of Communist central planning. The economy of Vietnam, North and South, was ruined. A war-ravaged and fallow Vietnam became a firebreak against Communist expansion in Southeast Asia, although the Marxist Khmer Rouge would, in the years ahead, launch a genocidal assault on their fellow Cambodians. For a quarter of a century since Saigon's fall, Vietnam has been mired in abject poverty and the rampant corruption and oppression of a hidebound Communist government. Today, Vietnam stands economically isolated from an otherwise largely thriving, free market–oriented and democratic region of the world. It serves as an example of the bitter fruits of Communism: repression and poverty. An American strategy of containment, in the end, led to victory in Vietnam and Southeast Asia.

The Vietnam War epilogue has taken a rather bizarre twist that perhaps provides a glimpse of what the Vietnamese future might be—the benign invasion of Nike. One of the very few current bright spots in Vietnam's decimated economy is the presence of Nike factories. The Oregon-based company is Vietnam's largest and most admired employer, with some 42,000 people on the payroll. The employee turnover rate is less than 2 percent and the average salary, at $53 a month, is twice the national average. The children and grandchildren of the tough, principled, sinewy-built men who fought the Americans four decades ago now make swoosh-emblazoned shoes for less than two dollars a day, to be worn by the affluent children and grandchildren of those their grandfathers fought. The gods of irony revel in this kind of thing.

Vietnam was the most prolonged of American wars, lasting some fifteen years. It was integral to the larger Cold War that went on for nearly half a century. In both cases the underlying strategy of containment achieved final victory. Because of their longevity and unique nature, and because of America's strategy of containment in fighting them, Vietnam and the Cold War offer invaluable strategic lessons to business.

"There Is No Finish Line"

This military strategy of containment has its direct counterpart in the business wars. Pepsi and Coke, with 75 percent of the global soft-drink market between them, are essentially fighting a war of containment against one another. So, too, are Procter & Gamble and Colgate in the soap, diaper and toothpaste businesses. The PC makers—Hewlett-Packard, IBM, Dell, eMachines, Compaq and Gateway—are fighting a complex war of containment each against all the others. United Airlines and American Airlines, the world's first and second largest air carriers respectively, are in an ongoing aerial dogfight. The objective of each—at least over the next several decades—is not the defeat of the other but rather its containment. The auto industry has just over half a dozen significant and viable combatants: GM, Toyota, Ford, Daimler-Chrysler, Renault, Fiat, VW. Into the years and decades ahead, they, too, must wage business wars of containment. By way of final example, among the beer brewers there are Anheuser-Busch, Heineken, Inter-brew, Miller, Carlsberg, Asahi, Kirin and a score of smaller competitors. Each is in a war of containment against every other. So it goes for essentially every industry marked by duopoly or oligopoly.

In war, the total annihilation of an enemy is not always the immediately intended objective. Individual battles are won and lost but the war goes on, often with no end in sight. Vietnam was like that and in this chapter it serves as a military model for waging a business strategy of containment. Phil Knight, Nike's CEO, captures the essence of this strategy: "For us [Nike] there is no finish line."[3] Nike faces competition from Reebok, Adidas and a dozen others. It cannot expect to rout them all and drive them completely from the competitive arena. A strategy of containment may have to be good enough.

Strategic Choice: Prevailing Circumstances

When the enemy or, by extension, business competitor is of nearly equal strength to oneself and when escalation can lead to a kind of apocalyptic mutually assured destruction, a strategy of containment is called for. During the Cold War, Pentagon strategists were always aware of the very possible doomsday scenario of full-scale nuclear warfare between the United States and Russia. The business equivalent to this is an all-out effort to eliminate a competitor that may result in one's own destruction with shattered profit margins, mountains of debt, government wrath, media crucifixion, stockholder revolt, hostile takeover threats and in the end bankruptcy.

Another prevailing circumstance, for the strategy to be invoked, is that the enemy, if left unhindered, would continue to expand into one's own domain, using seized territories as platforms for further advances. From the earliest days of Communism with Marx and Engels and then later with Lenin, Trotsky and Stalin, and later still with Nikita Khrushchev and indeed every Russian leader until Gorbachev, there was a belief in and commitment to an ultimate global conquest. Had it not been for a steadfast United States, the world today would not be largely free but Communist. Turning to the business arena, should Pepsi lower its defenses even a bit, within five years an expansionist and unrestrained Coca-Cola would control not 50 percent of the global market but 75 percent or even more.

These then are the prevailing circumstances that call for a strategy of containment: an aggressive, expansionist enemy and a too-high risk of waging total war.

Factors of Success

Wars of containment, or of limited objectives, have historically been rather commonplace. They were typical for Prussia's Frederick the Great, and Israel has, more or less, fought such a war against its hostile Arab neighbors for half a century. But this approach has not been in the American tradition of warfare.

The American people largely supported the war in Vietnam until it became clear that it was not being fought to be won. Americans have never had much patience for halfhearted warfare. They tired of hearing of that light at the end of the Vietnam tunnel. Few in the government were able to explain the American presence in Vietnam in a rational and straightforward way that could gain popular support, especially toward the end as casualties mounted.

A strategy of containment, in war or business, is very difficult to execute. It can be bitterly confounding. Success depends on several factors involving mission, alliances, arms race, an eye for an eye, competitor intelligence, leadership and brinkmanship. Begin with mission.

Mission

Previous chapters have emphasized the importance of the mission as a factor of success in the execution of strategy. The United States struggled in the Cold War because it could not come to a national consensus on the underlying mission. There were three basic ideological camps in the country. First, the Doves believed that it was possible to live peacefully with the Communists. Second, a smaller group of people thought that the Communists would ultimately prevail. Finally, Harry Truman, John F. Kennedy, Ronald Reagan and their fellow Cold War warriors believed that Communism's Evil Empire should be contained and that in the end it would be defeated. The United States with its democracy and free markets would, thought these Hawks, triumph. For much of the Cold War it was the last view that prevailed in Washington and became the de facto U.S. mission. Still, the lack of complete national unity made fighting the war very difficult and probably prolonged it.

Clausewitz once wrote, "No war should be begun until it is first determined what is to be achieved and how it will be conducted." He was writing of mission and could have been speaking of Vietnam. What holds for war also holds for business.

Is the mission of Wells Fargo bank to "Be *one of* the world's leading customer service banks," or is it to "Be *the* world's leading customer service bank"? The distinction is crucial to strategy setting. This is equivalent to the Vietnam War's Dove vs. Hawk argument. Is containment an end in itself, or is it a means to an ultimate end of victory? A lack of mission clarity creates enormous strategic planning problems—in fact, it makes effective strategic planning nearly impossible because the underlying premise of the mission has been too compromised.

The first key factor for a successful strategy of containment is that the mission be consistent with it, clearly articulated and understood.

Alliances

United States alliances in Europe with the North Atlantic Treaty Organization (NATO) and in Asia with Japan, South Korea and Taiwan, among others, were crucial factors in the containment of Communism. Napoleon and Sweden's Charles XII, to name but two of history's military leaders, were often forced by circumstances to face multiple enemies. They both sought to confront only one adversary at a time while merely containing the others. They used alliances, albeit temporary ones, as effective expediencies to do that.

In business, a strategy of containment of one competitor may well mean an array of impermanent alliances with other competitors. Even a more complex mixed strategy might well be appropriate involving relentless attack against one competitor, containment against others and alliances with the rest.

Strategic alliances have their own factors of success, which have been detailed earlier. Here, alliances complement the strategy of containment.

Arms Race

Over the long years of the Cold War, U.S. military spending averaged about 6 percent of GDP. The Russians, on the other hand, were spending as much as 25 percent of a much smaller total. It was unclear at the time to the experts at the State Department and the Central Intelligence Agency (CIA) that this heavy expenditure was bleeding dry the Russian economy. Indeed, when Khrushchev told America that "We will bury you [economically]," many in Washington thought that was indeed possible. They were wrong. They had been duped by Russian propaganda. The reality was that Russia, spread over more than half a dozen time zones, was one vast Potemkin Village. Behind that facade was a nation wallowing in near Third World poverty.

Thus it was that the mere announcement of Ronald Reagan's Strategic Defense Initiative (SDI), or Star Wars, as its opponents derisively called it, was decisive in ending the Cold War. The intent of SDI was to provide a shield of defensive antimissile missiles against incoming nuclear-armed intercontinental ballistic missiles (ICBMs). Such a system, if successfully deployed, would make the United States invulnerable to Russian attack. Reagan preferred to bet on American scientists rather than rely on the promises of Russian leaders. The Russians knew they could not afford the vast expenditures that a missile-defense system such as SDI would require. That was much in the thinking of Mikhail Gorbachev as he moved his country to stand down against the West. Short of a shooting war, which the Russians could not win, they lacked the resources to arm themselves for future battle. They de facto capitulated. The Russians had lost the arms race and with it the Cold War. There is a direct analogy in the business wars.

A strategy of containment, in business or in war, often results in an aggressive arms race. That was the situation in the Cold War, which featured a military arms race that included the development and deployment of nuclear submarines, stealth bombers, multiple-independently-targeted-reentry-vehicle (MIRVed) ICBMs, M1A1 tanks, over-the-horizon radar, biological weapons and other ingenious and quite costly killing devices. In business, an arms race takes a more benign, but nevertheless costly, form that includes creative advertising, new product development, additional distribution channels, increased inventory, the hiring of more talented and able people, investment in information technology and more. Adversaries, in a war of containment, have no choice but to run this race. By constant upping of the ante, it is intended that the competitor will ultimately collapse if he cannot maintain the pace.

In many ways the Wal-Mart vs. Kmart competition of the last two decades mirrors that of the United States and Russia in the Cold War. Wal-Mart has continued, year after year, improving its operations in a myriad of ways, until today Kmart is barely hanging on. Since 1990, Wal-Mart's stock has increased 1,100 percent while Kmart's has declined 42 percent. The Cold War did not end with the bang of a U.S. and Russian nuclear warhead exchange. Rather, it ended quietly with a Russian whimper as the once-feared adversary limped off of the world scene. That is, more or less, how the Wal-Mart and Kmart war has ended or at least now stands.

In a real sense, then, a strategy of containment becomes something of a war of attrition. A company embarking on such a strategy must be prepared for a prolonged and costly arms race. Prolonged is the right word: General Motors and Ford, for one example, have been battling and trying to contain one another for almost a century. A strategy of containment then requires adequate retained earnings, outside funding or both.

Eye for an Eye

Israel, surrounded by enemies vowing to drive it into the sea, has survived, and indeed thrived, ever since its modern-day rebirth in 1948 by the Old Testament dictum of an eye for an eye and a tooth for a tooth—no turning of the other cheek here. A terrorist bombing in Tel Aviv is countered, within hours, by an Israeli Air Force strafing attack against Libyan targets. The murder of an Israeli diplomat abroad is quickly followed by the mysterious vanishing of a ranking Arab diplomat—the culprit is likely *Shabak*, Israel's highly effective, and quite secretive, counterterrorism unit. Rapid and certain reprisals have been key to Israel's security and an important factor in its successful containment strategy against its many enemies. While the Israeli approach has been effective, perhaps even better is the Chicago way.

In the film *Untouchables*, Sean Connery, playing a grizzled Chicago street cop, instructs Kevin Costner, who plays Elliot Ness, a young and naive FBI agent, in how to fight Al Capone and his mob control of the city. "He pulls a knife on you, you pull a gun. He sends one of yours to the hospital, you send one of his to the morgue. That's the Chicago way."[4] That is also the way to achieve success using a strategy of containment.

What works in the tinderbox of the Middle East and what worked in the untamed streets of Chicago in the 1920s works in business today. For a company executing a containment strategy, there must be an immediate eye for an eye or, Chicago style, retaliation to a competitor's effective price cut, ad blitz, new product launch, pirating away of valuable employees or any other well-thought-out and vigorously executed offensive gambit.

Competitor Intelligence

Wars fought using a strategy of containment are protracted affairs, waged on many fronts, with victory coming only after countless tactical successes. In such conflicts, adversaries search for even the smallest advantage. That advantage is gained from accurate and timely information about the enemy. In the Cold War, Russia's KGB and America's CIA waged their own behind-the-scenes war of information gathering. Today, scores of former CIA people are now found in *Fortune* 500 companies heading competitor intelligence units. Those units often report directly to the CEO in a way that parallels today's CIA head reporting directly to the president of the United States. Motorola, for one, has such a reporting structure.

Competitor information must be gathered and fed into a company's constantly updated satellite snapshot and future scan. The intent is to determine exactly what the competitor is now doing and search for clues as to what might be its future initiatives. The mere tip of the business cloak-and-dagger iceberg is seen with the *Wall Street Journal* story of Oracle hiring a well-known business intelligence firm, IGI, to sift through Microsoft trash. The somewhat amusing tenor of this story belies the underlying seriousness of it all. Competitor tracking is earnest business for companies in bitter competitive battles, especially when they are executing a containment strategy.

Sought-after information includes competitor strengths and weaknesses in personnel, marketing, technology and financing. Companies seek knowledge of, say, a competitor's new product development, scheduled IPO or upcoming advertising campaign. This kind of information must be obtained for each competitor—as noted earlier there can be a dozen and more of them. Also tracked are potential new entrants into the given industry. Albertson's and Krogers, the first and second largest grocery chains, awoke one morning a few years ago to find the colossus that is Wal-Mart suddenly invading the province of their business. That kind of thing cannot be allowed to come as a surprise. Indeed, had Albertson's and Krogers been more alert they might have been able to block Wal-Mart's entry. It is too late now. The fairly comfortable and lazy war of containment they were conducting against one another has been shaken by the greatest retailer the world has ever seen. The competitive deck for them has been shuffled by the sudden presence of Wal-Mart in their midst. They will have to develop a whole new set of strategies.

Leadership

The decades-long nature of the Cold War made staying the course crucial for the United States. John F. Kennedy's inaugural address, in which he spoke of "paying any price and bearing any burden to ensure victory," reinforced that. In a prolonged conflict, leadership succession is crucial. Democrat or Republican, from the beginning of the Cold War in 1945 to its end in 1991, every president, with the possible exception of Jimmy Carter, was a supporter of the strategy of containment against Communism.

That same kind of uninterrupted leadership must be manifest in the business wars, where a company's containment strategy may have to be in place for decades during which time numerous CEOs will hold the leadership post. Without individual and continuous leadership, the containment strategy will fail. This is especially so because battling for a lifetime with an objective of mere containment seems so dissatisfying for Americans, whether in war or in business. Asian and European countries, perhaps because they are so much older than the United States with its comparatively short 200 years of history, seem to have far more patience for this kind of thing. In general, a succession of CEOs, each serving relatively short three- to five-year stints, militates against a containment strategy. Often a CEO's ego causes him or her to stray from former policy in an attempt to leave a unique legacy, perhaps by seeking rapprochement with a hated competitor or conversely by launching a full-scale, damn-the-torpedoes, competitive war. Beware such a CEO. If containment is to be a winning strategy, continuity of leadership is necessary. That leadership must stand as a guardian, protector and preserver of the mission and, with it, the strategic plan.

Brinkmanship

In the Cuban missile crisis during October 1962, the world came as close as it ever has to the Armageddon of all-out nuclear war. Russian nuclear-tipped missiles were being assembled in Cuba to be primed and targeted at the United States, only ninety miles away. At the same time, American missiles in Western Europe were poised for response. The U.S. Navy stood ready to interdict and board Russian cargo ships carrying missiles and missile parts that were steaming to Cuba. The young chevalier, President John F. Kennedy, issued an ultimatum to Russia's ursine premier, Nikita Khrushchev: Remove the missiles from Cuba and turn around the ships already at sea, or else. The status quo with Russian missiles so close to American shores was unacceptable to JFK. The world teetered on the very brink of annihilation as intense negotiations went forth among the Americans, the Russians and a host of well- and not-so-well-intentioned intermediaries. Kennedy learned to endure long days and even longer nights of forbearance. Finally, an out-of-breath high-level adviser rushed into the Oval Office and sputtered to the president, "Sir, I think the other fellow just blinked." Khrushchev, and the Kremlin, had backed down—although, not much publicized, the United States gave up some Turkish missile sites in something of a quid pro quo. At any rate, the crisis was over. The United States had taken the Russians to the brink and the latter had folded.

A defensive posture in waging a war of containment is not enough. Periodically the enemy must be driven back with offensive initiatives—sometimes driven back even to the very brink of catastrophic, all-consuming warfare. Wars of containment are not static affairs. They are marked by sporadic offensive actions that risk expanding the conflict. Brinkmanship is a most dangerous gambit, but it is a crucial factor in successfully executing a strategy of containment. That is true in war, as just discussed. It is also true in business where, for example, Coca-Cola in a bold, and surreptitiously planned, Venezuelan initiative recently convinced that country's only bottler to defect from Pepsi and join its ranks. That aggressive and provocative Coke action was at least a 7.5 Richter scale shaking of the Cola war status quo between the two companies. Would Pepsi retaliate, thus testing the limits of an all-out global competition? In the end, after much Pepsi bluster, threats and lawsuits, nothing was done—probably a mistake in a war of containment. In war or in business, a strategy of containment calls for these kinds of high-risk offensive moves and countermoves as situations and opportunities dictate.

———

The Cold War turned hot many times over its half-century duration. There was the Berlin blockade, Korean War, U2 incident, Cuban missile crisis, Six Day War, Hungarian uprising, Sandinista putsch and of course Vietnam. Even though most of those situations arose with little or no warning, America's military responded quickly and decisively. How can a nation's armed forces, and by extension a business enterprise, be ever combat-ready and able to respond instantly to a threat from wherever it may come and in whatever form it may take? America's Rangers, Green Berets, SEALs and Delta Forces are trained to do exactly that and serve as a model for business to emulate in obtaining a strategy of combat-readiness.

CHAPTER THIRTEEN

Black Hawks Down!

Forging the Combat-Ready Company

> *!@#$%, let's go out there and kill [people].*
> —Sgt. Paul Howe, Delta Force[1]

> *We are talking about life and death in every piece of e-mail.*
> —Bill Gates, chairman, Microsoft[2]

> *Only the paranoid survive.*
> —Andy Grove, chairman, Intel[3]

> *Our esprit is at the core of our success.*
> —Herb Kelleher, chairman, Southwest[4]

> *When you leave your gate, act as though an enemy is in sight.*
> —Code of Bushido

> *To be prepared for war is one of the most effectual means of preserving peace.*
> —George Washington

FUBAR

Some 100 of the Special Forces unit, made up of Rangers, SEALs and Delta Force personnel, grimly stripped down and cleaned their weapons. That was standard operating procedure following combat. Only minutes before, they had returned from the bloody streets of Mogadishu, where they had been in pursuit of the war lord Moham-med Farah Aideed. But the hunter had become the hunted. Somalis, thousands of them, armed with Russian AK-47s and rocket propelled guns (RPGs) had attacked the Americans. "Black Hawks down! Black Hawks down!" crackled the radio at American command headquarters. The Somalis had shot down two supporting Sikorsky-built MH-60 Black Hawk helicopters; one of the surviving pilots was captured and dragged naked through the town, taunted and pelted with rocks by a frenzied mob. A heavily armed convoy of Humvees and person-nel carriers had been ordered to rescue the Special Forces assault unit. That had been done but at an overall cost of eighteen American dead and scores of wounded.

A Third World rabble had humiliated the U.S. Armed Forces. Aideed was still at large, his whereabouts unknown. Somali gangsters continued to roam the streets, firing their weapons, raping and looting at will. The situation, for the Americans, was f——ed up beyond all repair, or FUBAR for short. Nevertheless, one of the Delta Force noncoms spoke for all of them: "!@#$%, let's go back out there and kill [people]." It was October 4, 1993, in far-off Somalia.

Somalia was an ugly and very dangerous assignment for Amer-ican Special Forces. It wasn't their first. Special Forces can be traced back to WWII. In 1942, Col. William Darby formed the 1st Ranger Battalion, which went on to carry out daring commando raids behind German lines in occupied Europe. Then there was the specially trained 2nd Ranger Battalion that scaled the sheer heights of Pointe du Hoc, with German gunfire pouring down on them, at the Normandy D-Day landings. In Burma the unconventional, com-mandolike warfare of Merrill's Marauders against the Japanese contributed greatly to American victory in the region. Specially recruited and highly trained underwater demolition teams (UDTs) played a decisive role in the Pacific war against the Japanese, where they removed or defused mines and reconnoitered beach defenses just prior to U.S. Marine D-Day landings. From those beginnings, in the post-WWII years, came the SEALs (U.S. Navy SEa-Air-Land special warriors). The SEALs were followed, in 1961, by President Kennedy's initiated Green Berets, and later still came the Sigma, Omega and Delta Forces.

Special Forces played a crucial role in the Vietnam War, especially on recon missions behind enemy lines in Laos, Cambodia and the Northern Highlands. They were in Iraq, gathering information, days before the actual Desert Storm attack. Special Forces have been in Grenada, Kosovo, Panama, Colombia, Nicaragua, Peru, Afghanistan and a dozen other hot spots around the world. Some missions are only whispered about—drug lord assassinations, hostage extractions, terrorist camp attacks and more. The personnel of these units are the elite of American Armed Forces and the most outstanding of their kind in the world. And here is the crucial point: *Whatever* the situation might be, *whenever* it occurs and *wherever* in the world it might be unfolding, the strategy of combat-readiness renders the Special Forces fully prepared to immediately respond and "Go out there and kill people." A strategy of combat-readiness is important in warfare and crucial in business.

Microsoft, Cisco and Enron

The best of American companies have built combat-readiness into their corporate DNA. There are a score or so of such companies but three especially come immediately to mind: Microsoft, Cisco and Enron.

Microsoft's rapid response to the Internet challenge posed by Netscape and its browser is a quintessential example of business combat-readiness. A single, thoughtful memo by Bill Gates issued to his people on December 7, 1993, outlined both the Netscape threat and the larger opportunity posed by the very real new world of the Internet. Amazingly, for an organization of some 30,000 people, it took the galvanized Microsofties only some six months to come up with a competing product and begin to integrate the Internet into existing and planned software product offerings.

In a second example, Cisco has developed elite cadres to quickly assess, acquire and then assimilate small and midsize Internet and telecommunications companies. Recently the rate of acquisition has been nearly one company every two weeks. Each acquisition serves to strengthen Cisco's technology and advance its dominant position in the Internet hardware infrastructure business. Beyond Cisco's ever-ready acquisition team, nearly all of its people throughout the company are among the industry's best, most work-obsessed and combat-ready.

Finally, few companies demonstrate combat-readiness better than Enron. The company, which annually ranks among the leaders in *Fortune*'s list of most admired, rose to prominence as a trader of natural gas following deregulation of the industry in the 1980s. Enron flourished in the fast moving, no-holds-barred industry where there was no sheriff in town. Profits soared. But then the market abruptly collapsed in 1993. That did not matter to the Enron people who rapidly adjusted to the new situation by applying their trading skills to other commodities. Today, Enron is highly successful in trading not only natural gas but wood pulp, water and even Internet broadband. Indeed, some 43 percent of the company's market value stems from businesses it was not even in three years ago. That ability to move quickly and effectively characterizes a combat-ready company. More about Enron in a few paragraphs.

Strategic Choice: Prevailing Circumstances

Many of history's wars seem to have developed in slow motion. After declaration of hostilities, there has generally been ample time for methodical preparation. WWI broke out in 1914 yet America was not drawn into the conflict until 1917. The United States entry into WWII came with the Joint Congress declaration of war against the Axis powers on December 8, 1941. But nearly a year passed before there was actual American combat against German fortifications in North Africa. More recently, in 1991 Gen. Schwarzkopf took six months to build his forces in the Middle East before launching Desert Storm against Iraq. But the times and circumstances of warfare are changing.

America's unique role today as the sole world superpower requires it to be ever combat-ready. Even without a major shooting war, there are rogue states, terrorists, totalitarian gangsters, drug lords and even pirates in and about the Strait of Malacca, all of whom must be dealt with. Relatively quiet situations suddenly explode into violence and potentially very dangerous escalation. Trouble arises with almost no warning and must be responded to immediately. This is a change in warfare as it has been fought over the centuries.

Business, too, once operated at a leisurely, antebellum, mint-julep pace, but today is another matter. Events occur with unprecedented warp-speed. A new technology, alliance, lawsuit, industrial accident, top executive resignation, product recall or merger can completely and instantly reshuffle the competitive deck. The resulting changed situation likely calls for a quick response. That in turn requires organizations—or at least smaller elite units within them—to be always combat-ready.

For business, then, the prevailing circumstances that call for a strategy of combat-readiness are, with few exceptions, *always* and *everywhere*, no matter the business or industry. Even if no threat appears on the satellite snapshot or the future scan, this combat-ready strategy should be in place. Indeed, the strategy is most necessary when the situation, both current and projected, appears to be quite calm. So combat-readiness should almost always be one of a company's limited number of strategic building blocks.

Factors of Success

It is appropriate that combat-readiness is the last strategy presented in this book. In many ways it is the most important strategy and it is certainly the most difficult to implement. A number of factors are crucial for its success. Among them are people, training, atmosphere of danger, rewards-punishments, esprit, competitor tracking, flexibility, acceptance of bad news, instant communication, leadership and zest for battle. These factors must be successfully addressed if a military, or business, unit is to react instantly and successfully to a crisis. Consider each factor in some detail.

People

A strategy of combat-readiness depends greatly on having the best people. That starts with effective recruitment, training and retention programs. American Special Forces draw recruits from only the best among the military services. Even among those candidates nominated, the washout rate during intense training exceeds 70 percent. The Special Forces are as good as they are largely because their people are the best the U.S. military has—a selective recruiting process supplemented by intense training and a gung-ho culture of esprit de corps assures that this is so.

Business has been slow to understand this most basic point about the importance of people. In decades past the rhetoric was "People are our most important asset." Then would come a few bad financial quarters and 15 percent or so of this supposed most valuable asset would suddenly become expendable and be laid off. But the chasm between rhetoric and reality regarding the importance of people is narrowing. Jobs are requiring ever more expanded skill sets, and the labor force, especially the educated and trained labor force, is in short supply, growing at only half the rate of the economy. An ever-increasing number of companies are recognizing that people indeed are their most important asset. America's outstanding companies recognize that a combat-ready strategy depends on their people.

John Chambers, Cisco's CEO, says, "Recruiting and retaining good people to implement our strategy is crucial. I rank each VP and senior VP each quarter."[5] Chambers' concern for his people extends beyond senior management to include everyone in the organization, including working parents. Cisco employees with children have access to the company's day care center, one of the largest in the world, where nearly 500 wee Ciscoites frolic. Web-cams track the movement of the little folks so that Mom or Dad, from their work areas, can check up on them. Only Type A people can sustain the very high performance levels Cisco demands. People are constantly moved around the company and new business units are periodically formed not only for reasons of efficiency but also in order to maintain a high level of excitement and challenge. As a result of all of this, Cisco has become one of the world's most combat-ready companies.

Bill Gates has said that "One of our core philosophies is that when you bring a bunch of smart people together, great things happen. Our people have a maniacal work ethic."[6] In hiring new recruits, Gates looks for ambition, IQ, technical expertise and business judgment. Nothing has been more basic to the success of Microsoft's combat-readiness than its human resource policy.

General Electric is known for its Nine-Step Talent Plan that focuses on the development of top managers. The some 600 senior managers, making up GE's Praetorian Guard, are carefully monitored by Jack Welch himself. Those managers are frequently moved from division to division. Scott McNealy, Sun's CEO, is a member of GE's board of directors. He says of GE, "They can spin on a dime because they have black-belt and Green Beret types infiltrated throughout the organization."[7]

Southwest hires only some 3 percent of 140,000 annual applicants. Few companies are so selective. Herb Kelleher has built the world's most profitable airline around his people. The men and women of Southwest are immediately ready to deal with the vicissitudes of the airline industry, including bad weather, engine malfunction, sick passengers, lost luggage, closed airports, passenger rage and crying children. The people of Southwest are uniquely persevering, indefatigable and proud. *They* are the reason that Southwest, unique among all the airlines, has remained profitable year after year.

"We prefer a smart person to a physical asset,"[8] says Enron's COO, Jeffrey Skilling. That principle is at the core of the company's success and combat-readiness. In practical terms, it means several things. First, titles and salaries stay with a person no matter what job change within the company he or she might choose to make. This is a highly effective way to encourage healthy movement of people around the organization and assure that knowledge is widespread. Job appraisal is done not by one's senior only but by a committee familiar with the person. Another factor is that a substantial portion of compensation is risk oriented. Finally, every job offers constant challenge and development. The result of all this is that new MBAs from the best schools prefer Enron as a place to work as opposed to the more glamorous investment banks and consulting firms.

Procter & Gamble, like Enron, recruits from among the top business schools for midlevel positions. Promotion from then are only from within. That is consistent with the recruiting and promotion approach of the nineteenth-century British army. The Duke of Wellington, in command of British forces at Waterloo, wrote in his memoirs, "The battle of Waterloo was won on the playing fields of Eton." By that he meant that his officers had been educated, trained and played highly competitive athletics at the elite boy's school of Eton. It was there that their character had been molded. They were the best of English gentlemen and so, thought Wellington, made the best of officers.

Napoleon, on the other hand, believed that "Every French soldier carries a marshall's baton in his knapsack." Indeed, with only a few exceptions, his generals rose through the ranks from humble beginnings. They were men hungry for fortune and fame. This, unlike Wellington's belief, is consistent with Wal-Mart's approach, at least in its earlier days, of able and motivated people working their way up from stocking shelves to management positions.

In fact, if properly executed, either of these two approaches can be effective in identifying and promoting outstanding people. Both separate wheat from chaff, men from boys, women from girls. What is crucial is that, when they are most needed, at times of crisis, the best people are at hand.

Special Forces, with their instant combat-readiness, comprise a relatively small proportion of America's military personnel. They are the elite cadres within the larger U.S. Army, Navy, Marine and Air Force commands. A similar kind of structure is appropriate for business. An entire corporation should ideally be combat-ready, able to change direction and adjust to new circumstances quickly. At the least, within the company there must be smaller units of uniquely qualified and trained people, equivalents of the military's Special Forces, who can instantly be injected into just-breaking hot spots. Success depends singularly on the people—their strengths, skills and character.

Training

Another important factor in Delta, Ranger, SEAL or other Special Forces readiness is training. Fort Bragg in North Carolina is home to much of that training. Courses, always taught by experienced veterans, are intense, team-oriented, ongoing and tailored to simulate future missions. The introductory training course is fifteen weeks long. The first seven days, known as Hell Week, is physically and mentally brutal. Survivors share the highest levels of esprit, pride and team identity.

Few WWII commanders dedicated more time and effort to training than did Gen. Patton. Immediately after the outbreak of hostilities on December 7, 1941, Patton set up a nearly hundred-square-mile training center outside of Indio in the bleak deserts of Death Valley in California. There, man and machine were tested nearly beyond endurance in 120-degree temperatures. That training would later pay off in the deserts of North Africa.

General Electric spends some $700 million annually for its various training programs. A good portion of that goes to GE's in-house university at Crotonville. Located on fifty campuslike acres in New York's Hudson Valley, Crotonville is thought of as the Harvard of corporate America. Six classes composed of sixty executives each are run during the year. The instructors are mostly experienced senior GE people. The instruction is specific to the problems the company faces. GE is not alone in having an in-house university. Intel University offers some 5,000 courses. Then there is Southwest's University of People in Dallas, Dell University, Toyota University, Motorola University and dozens more. Some 40 percent of the *Fortune* 500 have similar in-house universities. That percentage will likely grow, especially as dissatisfaction with business schools increases.

DaimlerChrysler's chairman, Jurgen Schrempp, introduced his 2+2+2 program into the company a few years ago. Says Schrempp, "To qualify for top management here you have to have served in two quite different jobs in two different divisions in two different countries."[9] Daimler, quite evidently, uses real-world experience as an important complement to conventional training for its senior people. That's a good idea although it does require delicate monitoring. If too heavy-handed the learning experience is lost, but if too light-handed, an entire division could be badly damaged.

Julius Caesar, writing in the third person, noted in his journal: "In the winter, Caesar trained his legions in all manner of warfare so that in the spring when he committed them to battle against the Gauls it would not be necessary to give them orders for they knew what to do and how to do it." Some 2,000 thousand years have passed since Caesar penned those words. The value of training in the military, and by extension business, is as great now as it was then.

In summary, simulated real-world training is essential to maintaining individuals and organizations at a high level of combat-readiness. Indeed, the quality and extent of a corporation's training program provides an immediate barometer of overall combat-readiness.

Atmosphere of Danger

An atmosphere of mortal threat, real or imagined, adds to an organization's state of readiness. Hernando Cortés instinctively knew that. He was commissioned, early in the sixteenth century, by the Spanish crown to subjugate the New World. Landing in 1519 on the east coast of Mexico, Cortés offloaded his men, horses and supplies. That completed, he pointed to his ships lying at anchor and ordered, "Burn them." That was done. From that moment on he and his men knew there was no turning back—they had to be ready to fight with whatever resources they had at hand. They were in a terribly dangerous situation with no one to rely on but themselves.

Combat-ready companies capture, one way or another, the emotional intensity that Cortés and his fellow conquistadors must have felt. Intel's chairman, Andy Grove, likes to say "Only the paranoid survive," and Bill Gates observes that "We are talking about life and death in every piece of e-mail."[10] A TimeWarner executive says of the company's president, Robert Pittman, "He [Pittman] operates as though there is always a crisis."[11] The best business leaders are able to create this mind-set of heightened threat even when none is visible. GE's Jack Welch achieved that in the mid-1980s. Ford's Jaq Nasser does that now. He is having to deal with a very real threat involving the recall of millions of Ford Explorer tires; the company's combat-readiness will be severely tested.

It is when victory is in hand that one must be most vigilant. An old Japanese military maxim exhorts, "After victory, tighten your helmet cord." It is perhaps human nature to relax after victory, but it is dangerous doing so. After Hannibal had defeated a large Roman army at Cannae, he whiled away his time at Capua allowing his men to rest, drink and fraternize with the lovely and quite accommodating

214 FROM BATTLEFIELD TO BOARDROOM

local maidens. Hannibal had not tightened the cord of his helmet after victory; indeed, the helmet had been removed along with his armor. The result was lost momentum and, later, loss of the war.

Combat-ready companies are never complacent even following a victory. An atmosphere of mortal danger, of eternal vigilance, is demanded. While a company may not be able literally to burn its ships, it assuredly can make every effort to create an environment that closely emulates the one Cortés and his men faced.

Rewards, Recognition and Punishment

At the top of the chapter, the story of Special Forces in Somalia on October 3, 1993, was told. Today, we do not celebrate October 3 as a national holiday commemorating the men who fell in Somalia. It is likely that not 1 in 1,000 Americans would recognize the significance of that date. That doesn't matter to Special Forces. They do not look to the civilian world for praise and recognition. Their reward is a quiet word, nod or wink of approval from a comrade. Sometimes recognition comes in the form of a medal or ribbon bestowed by one's unit commander. Napoleon noted that "For no amount of money will a soldier sell his life. Yet he will gladly give it up for a piece of ribbon." Napoleon understood his men—rewards and recognition are powerful motivators.

In the business arena, recognition of combat-ready individuals and units also is important. Mary Kay, FedEx and Southwest, for example, have excellent merit-recognition programs. Mary Kay awards top performers with ostentatious pink Cadillacs. FedEx lavishes praise and rewards on outstanding people. Wal-Mart's twice-a-year manager's convention features education, encouragement and especially recognition of top performing people. At the last Wal-Mart clan gathering, the head of Canadian operations wept upon receipt of the prestigious Sam Walton Entrepreneur of the Year trophy. It brought down the house.

The Romans provided retired soldiers pieces of land, and historically, most victorious armies have let their men loot and partake of the spoils of war. Still, financial reward matters more in the business arena than in the military. Money as a reward in business is very important. Cisco's CEO John Chambers says, "I've learned that stock options are the best way to incentivize employees."[12] Cisco's top 500 executives average $15 million in net worth from their accumulated company stock.

"Uh, I'm sort of thinking of leaving." When a talented employee says that to a Disney or FedEx manager, the manager is authorized to immediately offer a predetermined pay raise without going through the Human Resources department. Other companies have developed similar means of holding on to good people in a tight labor market.

Surprisingly, even in staid Japan, incentive, or reward, pay is making inroads. The largest market cap company, DoCoMo, and the world-class Sony use it. A growing number of European telecom, Internet and financial services companies are also introducing a version of this kind of compensation. Still, the United States leads the way with some 70 percent of companies offering incentive pay—up from 40 percent in 1990. Not only do more companies offer stock options, they also are distributing them more deeply into the organization. Part of the attraction Enron has for its outstanding people is the phantom equity it provides for start-up operations—the result is a possible lotto-like payoff for participating employees. There is growing evidence that this form of incentive-based financial compensation adds greatly to combat-readiness. Microsoft, like Enron, believes that to be so.

Largely as a result of its ongoing Justice Department battle, Microsoft's stock has taken a hit. Employees have found their stock options reduced in value or in some cases, for newer employees, rendered worthless—the options are "underwater," goes the jargon. For a company that compensates disproportionately with equity, as Microsoft does, that can be disastrous. But Microsoft has moved quickly to protect and preserve its singular most valuable asset, its people. Some 70 million new repriced options have been issued at reduced strike levels. A slew of new promotions to "Vice President" and "Distinguished Engineer" have been announced, and across-the-board salary has been increased. This point should not be taken lightly. Most companies under attack would do the reverse of this by cutting back on salaries and benefits as part of a broad retrenchment. Microsoft knows better. In the end, its people *are* the company.

"Rewards and punishments provide the basis for control," wrote Sun Tzu. Thus far the discussion has focused on reward. That's good, but too often it is forgotten that *punishment* can also be a highly motivating force. The Greeks and Romans used it to great effect.

The Greeks dealt severely with military misconduct. There is a story of the Athenian general Iphicrates who coming upon one of his sentries asleep, whipped out his sword and cut the man's throat. "I only left him as I found him," the general said with a shrug. Thereafter it was rare indeed for an Athenian sentry to be anything but alert.

The Romans were no less harsh. The penalty for a soldier's poor military performance was often death. Even entire units were punished. One effective way to deal with a malingering, cowardly or simply unassertive cohort or legion was called decimation. Every centurion in the unit under disgrace was made to draw straws, one in ten of which was short. Those who drew the short straws were beaten to death by their own comrades. Anyone refusing to participate in the beatings was himself killed. For centuries, Roman legions were all but invincible. Punishment of various kinds, including decimation, was part of the reason why.

Nowadays we think of ourselves as too advanced, too enlightened, to resort to punishment as a means of controlling behavior. Corporate America today is even reluctant to raise its voice in employee criticism let alone hand out long and short straws. But that is a mistake. Demotion, pay cuts and firing should be used as punishments for poor performance. Granted, the ever-vigilant, paternalistic government is concerned with employee rights and firing and then hiring a replacement comes at a high cost. But the cost is higher still of keeping non- or poorly performing people in an organization. Even a small number of them can damage organizational esprit. It takes but one incompetent person in a position of authority to ruin an entire organization. GE, for one, is constantly winnowing its ranks, eliminating those it designates as subpar employees.

Esprit

The great military leaders of the past are in accord about the important role of morale. Napoleon thought it to be of vital importance. So did Gen. George Marshall who said, "It is not enough to fight. It is the spirit which we bring to the fight that decides the issue. It is . . . morale that wins the victory." Mao Zedong, China's long-time leader, went even further: "Morale is the sole decisive factor in war." Morale, or esprit, as noted in chapter 11, is indeed of great importance to an armed force, especially for elite units that are always in a state of combat-readiness. This notion carries over to the world of business.

"Competitors can buy physical assets but not our employee dedication, devotion, loyalty and feeling part of a crusade," says Herb Kelleher of Southwest. "Our esprit is at the core of our success."[13]

There are many outside of Microsoft who speak pejoratively about the company's arrogance and truculent, belligerent nature. That is one reason why some competitors feel such visceral antagonism toward Microsoft. But at Redmond, Washington, at Microsoft's headquarters, among the people of the company it isn't arrogance, it is pride, and it isn't truculence, it is esprit. Outstanding organizations, whether they are military units like Special Forces or corporations like Microsoft, always have their jealous and whining detractors.

The business world cannot quite match the adrenaline rush of life-threatening combat, but it can approach it. Microsoft, certainly in its early days, with its order-in pizzas, all-night work sessions and sleeping bags under the desks, came close. To stir and excite emotions, companies can give people stretch goals and large responsibilities that have the potential for great victories. Enron achieves that; so does GE and DaimlerChrysler at least for their top executives who are moved frequently into challenging new situations.

There is no entry on a balance sheet for esprit: too bad, since it is more important than cash flow, Economic Value Added (EVA) or any other financial statistic that can be conjured to measure the viability of a company. There are a myriad of ways to achieve corporate or unit camaraderie, bonding, solidarity or esprit de corps. However it is achieved, it is a basic determinant of success for a strategy of combat-readiness.

Competitor Intelligence

Sun Tzu wrote, "Know your enemy and know yourself and you can fight a hundred battles without disaster." Combat-readiness for a military unit requires having accurate and updated enemy intelligence. The military is quite good at this, and business is getting better.

Motorola, in 1982, was one of the first large companies to form a corporate Intelligence Unit. It was headed by the retired CIA veteran Jan Herring, who reported directly to senior management. "The concept was to mirror the interaction between the CIA and the White House,"[14] says Herring, referring to the Motorola operation. As noted earlier, today, nearly all companies, especially those in high-tech, have similar units involved in seeking out upcoming competitor mergers, new technologies, patent filings and more.

Oracle has admitted to hiring outside people to sift through Microsoft's trash. "There is a lot of dumpster-diving that goes on,"[15] quips Eddie McClain of Krout and Schneider, whose firm deals with this kind of thing—presumably it is within the law. This information gathering is referred to as "competitor intelligence," which is something of a euphemism for what can sometimes be a rather tawdry undertaking. Although companies don't like to say much about this publicly, one way or another, combat-readiness requires aggressive intelligence gathering so as not to be caught off guard by a surprise competitor initiative.

Flexibility

A strategy of combat-readiness requires flexibility of action so that quick response to a new situation can be achieved. Special Forces can be air-dropped into a volatile situation or injected by fast-moving water craft or ground transport. Personnel are trained for desert, jungle, urban and even Arctic warfare. They have available to them a rich variety of weaponry that fit the given circumstances. Most conventional military units are one-dimensional in their functional abilities: artillery, infantry, motorized and so on. Special Forces, on the other hand, are far more flexible with a spectrum of fighting skills. Combat-, or competitor-, readiness in the business world also demands flexibility.

In manufacturing, maximum flexibility can be obtained by delaying the freezing of a product's design as long as possible to incorporate last-minute changes. Modularizing and component standardizing wherever possible adds further to manufacturing flexibility. So, too, does the introduction of demand-flow manufacturing methods and semicircular work cells rather than conventional production lines.

Computer technology has made possible great flexibility in product and service pricing. Applying that technology is called yield management. The airlines were the first to use it, and hotels have followed. Simply, yield management means that prices are constantly updated—raised or lowered—to maximize revenues and profits. Expect to see more of this pricing flexibility in the years ahead. Companies will have to be cautious, however, as Coca-Cola discovered: a plan to automatically raise prices at cola dispensing machines on hot days was withdrawn after a clamorous public outcry.

The U.S. Navy has just struck a $7 billion outsourcing deal with EDS to have the latter manage its computer network. That should free up personnel and capital resources for added battle flexibility. Outsourcing has the same desirable result in business. With careful monitoring, outsourcing adds greatly to a company's flexibility. Focus can be brought to bear on what have come to be known as core competencies. Another benefit here is that outsourcing breaks the mooring that fixed assets have on a firm. By outsourcing manufacturing, Hewlett-Packard does not need to tie up billions of dollars in factories. And by outsourcing logistics, Saturn does not need to invest millions of dollars in warehouses, trucks and equipment to handle parts and finished inventory. With outsourcing, assets become more liquid and can be more readily redeployed.

Most military bases feature ubiquitous Quonset huts. These easy-to-construct and tear-down semicylindrical metal shelters can serve as offices, barracks or storage areas. They add appreciably to the military's flexibility of movement. They are reminiscent of Dell's dozens of non-descript one-story buildings sprawled over the company's Round Rock campus in Texas. The office interiors are high-tech but Spartan. The architecture, quips a Dell engineer, is "prison modern."[16] Those practical and efficient buildings baking under the Texas summer sun are consistent with what one would expect from a fast-moving and nimble global company. Dell is at war with its competitors, and every aspect of its operation, including the flexibility of the buildings that house its people, is a reflection of that.

A company's corporate headquarters, whether it is located in New York, Chicago, London, Paris or Tokyo is generally a magnificent edifice. Its architecture is intended to be a reflection of the very spirit and soul of the company. It may be all of that. It is also obsolete, unnecessary and quite irrelevant in today's business world. A headquarters, or any building for that matter, is fixed in location. But the battlefields of contemporary business competition are forever changing from one place on the globe to another. JDS Uniphase is a world leader in fiber optic technology. To meet the demands of ever shifting markets, the company's CEO operates out of Ottawa; the CFO, San Jose; the COO, Santa Rosa. The rest of the Operating Committee is scattered at locations around the United States and Canada, depending on need. In a real sense, JDS Uniphase has no headquarters—that is as it should be.

Business is war, and war is not conveniently fought in a single location in proximity to a fixed headquarters. In combat, a field general, with his senior staff, is likely to move headquarters many times over the course of even a single battle. Headquarters are understood to be temporary, always changing depending on the flow of combat. Business is becoming like that. It is no longer limited to a single region, as it was until late in the twentieth century. Deloitte Touche is one of hundreds of companies that has introduced the concept of hoteling. Working space—with telecommunications and computer hookups—is provided at various facilities around the country for traveling executives, managers and staff to catch up on administrative or other work. "It is like checking into the Ritz-Carlton,"[17] says Susan Zaffiro, director of national facilities.

Fully armed with cell phones, Internet access devices, laptops and, if necessary, a Gulfstream on the tarmac ready for takeoff, a large company CEO does not need a permanent headquarters—indeed, he or she should not have one. Literally and symbolically a fixed headquarters is inconsistent with a combat-ready company—it too greatly limits flexibility.

Every means available—from outsourcing to hoteling and more—should be used to increase corporate flexibility, which in turn adds to combat-readiness.

Acceptance of Bad News

In the last two years of WWII, when the tide had clearly turned in favor of the Allies, Hitler hunkered down first in his Wolf's Lair in the forests of Austria and later in his concrete bunker fifty feet below ground in Berlin. He was surrounded by sycophants, like Generals Keitle and Jodl, who were terrified to bring their leader bad news. They were justified in their fear: Hitler was known to go into a rage when brought a negative or pessimistic situation report and often lashed out at the messenger with a demonic, screaming harangue. The result, happily for the Allies, was that German decision making became ever more divorced from reality simply because Hitler's officers withheld crucial information from him. Toward the end, Hitler was shuttling about on his situation maps SS and Panzer divisions that had weeks or months before been captured or wiped out. No one was willing to tell him that the divisions no longer existed.

In a real sense there is no bad news. Shakespeare wrote, "There is nothing either good or bad, but thinking makes it so." Combat-readiness requires that kind of perspective. Incoming information is to be viewed as neither positive or negative. It is simply information that must be acted upon. The best companies, and their leaders, understand that.

"Under no circumstances should you ever shoot the messenger,"[18] admonishes Andy Grove, Intel's chairman.

Douglas Daft, Coca-Cola's new CEO, says, "I don't just want to hear good news."[19]

"For every piece of good news, send me bad news,"[20] demands Microsoft's Bill Gates of his people.

John Chambers, Cisco's CEO, observes, "Compliments are nice and I always need them, but I really listen to what we need to do better very, very carefully."[21]

Following the report of a fire in a major supplier's factory, Nokia's top trouble-shooter, Pertti Korhonen, made certain the information was disseminated to key personnel. "We encourage bad news to travel fast [within the company],"[22] he later said.

Two other pertinent stories are much in the news at this writing. One deals with Mitsubishi Motors. For a decade now, its midlevel management has kept reports dealing with leaky fuel tanks, faulty engines and defective brake systems from senior executives. Managers secretly repaired vehicles to avoid publicity, government recall and their own punishment. The second story involves another Japanese company, Bridgestone. Defective tread on its Firestone brand tires have been associated with over 100 fatalities in the United States.

CNBC reports that some people at Bridgestone likely knew about the problem as long as two years ago. If top management was indeed informed, nothing was done. Evidently, Mitsubishi and Bridgestone did not have a corporate culture whereby information, good and bad, moved freely through the organization.

Mitsubishi and Bridgestone will not escape the consumer, legal and regulatory firestorm that has been ignited. Bridgestone may disappear from the American marketplace, and Mitsubishi may lose its independence to DaimlerChrysler, which already owns a substantial share of it. Quite clearly, disasters of such scope could never have fallen on the likes of Cisco, Microsoft, Coca-Cola and Intel. The management of those companies understand that problems are inherent to business and are to be acknowledged and quickly dealt with. One snippet of bad business news is like a single cockroach spotted on the kitchen floor—it is a very good bet that neither is an isolated event. Better to deal with such situations immediately. The acceptance of bad news is an important factor for the successful execution of a combat-ready strategy.

Instant Communication

For almost two weeks, in the summer of 1863, Gen. Robert E. Lee, while marching into Pennsylvania, lost contact with his cavalry that was under the command of J. E. B. Stuart. Stuart was Lee's eyes and ears. Without communiqués from him, Lee had no idea where the enemy was. This put him at a great disadvantage. As a result, Lee stumbled onto the Union army, which held the high ground, at Gettysburg. There, history played itself out with a disastrous Confederate defeat. Contrast that to today, where the chairman of the Joint Chiefs, in a Pentagon war room, can speak directly to a platoon leader who is under fire at some street corner in Kosovo. American military communications in warfare are now instantaneous and able to reach every corner of the battlefield. That must be so for any combat-ready military or business organization.

"If you don't dotcom your business . . . things will come back to get you,"[23] says Scott McNealy of Sun Microsystems. He was referring to the instantaneous communication that the Internet brings to a company's competitive readiness. Employees, customers and suppliers should all be put online.

As late as 1995, a company's accounting department would cloister itself for two or three weeks in December to close the year's books. Today, Cisco is able to close its financial records in one day, any day. Its CFO, Larry Carter, says, "The earlier we get information disseminated, the easier it is to fix any problem there might be."[24] Real-time information is available throughout Cisco, which allows decision-making power to be devolved deep within the organization, indeed to the very front lines. This in turn contributes greatly to the company's overall combat-readiness.

High-tech, state-of-the-art equipment is not always the key to effective communications. Here is a Dell story. Moe Grzelakowski was recently hired as the company's new Senior Vice President of Wireless. On her first day on the job, she was given the names of the fifty people in the company who were most knowledgeable about wireless technology. Over a period of one month she met with them all. "They did brain dumps on me," she later said. "That is how Dell transfers knowledge and power. It is most effective."[25]

The leader of a combat-ready military unit must have knowledge of real-time battlefield conditions. In addition, every member of the unit must be able to communicate with every other member. A strategy of combat-readiness for a business unit, be it a department, division or entire corporation, requires the same level of communication. Today's technology makes such communication possible. Combat-ready companies exploit that technology.

Leadership

Brig. Gen. Theodore Roosevelt Jr., son of the turn-of-the-century intrepid president, commanded the 4th Army Division at the Normandy D-Day landings on June 6, 1944. He and his men were scheduled to go ashore on a particular stretch of Utah beach just after dawn. It had all been worked out beforehand down to the minute and yard in the greatest detail. Everything went wrong. Communications were lost, covering off shore naval fire was missing, supporting armored units had not yet landed, and most important, the division had been put ashore several thousand yards away from its designated area. Roosevelt found his men cowering behind sand berms while they were being shelled and mortared by the Germans, who were dug in and concealed above them. Fear, uncertainty, helplessness, panic was setting in. The men were all but paralyzed. Above the clamor of battle, a perfervid young lieutenant shrieked to Roosevelt, "Sir, we've landed in the wrong place." The general calmly looked about him and replied, "Son, that doesn't matter, we will start the war right here." Under Roosevelt's leadership they did.

Juxtapose that story with the situation that Bill Gates faced with the earlier-noted Internet challenge. Gates addressed that situation with his now-famous, memo. The Gates message to his people was in essence the same as Roosevelt's: "Look, the past doesn't matter. This is where we are and this is where we will start the [Internet] war."[26]

Roosevelt was a general and Gates a CEO. Their leadership at a crucial moment was decisive in reversing a potentially disastrous situation for their respective organizations. This is leadership at the highest level and is of crucial importance. But when it comes to combat-readiness, leadership must come from all levels of the organization.

Special Forces are very team oriented. In any particular set of combat circumstances, leadership can come from any team member. A typical Special Forces combat team is composed of two officers and ten sergeants. Each individual has a specialized role, say communications, demolitions, or first aid, but each is also capable of assuming the specialty role of every other. Every team member is capable of leading should others be killed or wounded. A strategy of combat-readiness requires that kind of team leadership as well.

Leadership, then, from the top of the organization down through the ranks, is vital for the successful execution of strategic combat-readiness.

Zest for Battle

Colonel, later president, Teddy Roosevelt led a charge up San Juan Hill on a hot, steamy summer day in Cuba during the Spanish-American War of 1898. Roosevelt's men were all on foot while he himself was on horseback. Teddy, with a red bandanna around his neck and sunlight reflecting from his spectacles, was an extraordinary and inspirational sight for his own men, to say nothing of being a prominent target for the sharp-shooting Spaniards. With sweat pouring from him and bullets buzzing all about, Roosevelt grinned his huge toothy grin and advanced up the hill. Later, Roosevelt wrote of it, "All men who feel . . . any joy in battle know what it is like when the wolf rises in the heart."

The greatest of America's generals have had this zest for battle. The young major, George Washington, wrote of a battle during the French-Indian War in which he fought: "I heard the bullets whistle; and believe me, there is something charming in the sound." George Patton had similar feelings: "Compared to war, all other forms of human endeavor sink to insignificance. God how I love it." Even the warrior-gentleman Robert E. Lee wrote: "It is well that war is so terrible or we should grow too fond of it."

A combat-readiness strategy requires this kind of zest for battle among its organization's leaders; the people of the organization will respond immediately to it. Sgt. Dan Daly yelled to his men at Belleau Wood in 1918, during the closing months of WWI, "Come on you sons of bitches. Do you want to live forever?" No doubt they did, but they followed him anyway out of the relative safety of their deeply dug trenches and charged forward against German fortifications.

"Pardon one offence and you encourage the commission of many," wrote Publilius Syrus. Bill Gates manages his Microsoft by that credo. Microsoft, like other combat-ready companies, is notoriously thin-skinned and relishes a fight. The men and women of Redmond will not be passively led to the Justice Department's abattoir. The company, absent from previous political campaigns, is now throwing money everywhere around Washington to counter the influence of IBM, Oracle and Sun Microsystems on the Justice Department. "We aren't going to let them define us or the debate,"[27] growls a Microsoft spokesman.

Clausewitz wrote "Whenever boldness encounters timidity, it is . . . the winner." That is probably mostly true. But the issue here is not so much military or combat boldness. The issue is the love for combat as an end in itself—fighting for the sheer joy of it. That zest for battle characterizes the combat-ready organization.

Instant Response

An old samurai maxim says, "When you leave your gate, act as though the enemy is in sight." That is, the warrior must be ever vigilant and ever ready for combat. Similar counsel is appropriate for today's business professional. For perhaps a decade now there has been much talk of "global competition" and more recently the "Internet revolution." Both are now realities and call for a whole new way of doing business, requiring instant response to rapidly changing situations. Only companies with well-executed strategies of combat-readiness can survive. This chapter has highlighted the importance of that strategy and the crucial factors that go into executing it.

———————

The strategy of combat-readiness is the last of the ten winning strategies presented in this work. The next, and final chapter, serves as a quick summary, or debriefing, of the book's highlights.

CHAPTER FOURTEEN

Debriefing

What Was Learned?

We must learn from the past.
　　　　　　　　　—Gen. George S. Patton

Those who cannot remember the past are condemned to repeat it.
　　　　　　　　　—George Santayana

We spend a lot of time looking back to find out what was learned and how to apply it.
　　　　　　　—Harry Longwell, SVP Exxon Mobil[1]

After Action Reviews

George Patton suffered from dyslexia as a boy and young man but overcame it to graduate from West Point. He went on to become a lifetime scholar of past wars. Throughout WWII, when in North Africa, Sicily and Europe, Patton, by that time a general, would regale his officers with stirring accounts of battles fought hundreds, even thousands, of years before on the same ground where they then stood. Patton studied those past battles and applied what he learned to his present efforts against the Nazis.

In 1924, when Patton was almost forty years old, he was posted to the prestigious Army War College at Fort Leavenworth in Kansas. The War College was to military training then what the Harvard Business School is to business training today. It was designed for midlevel officers thought to have the potential for high rank. At Leavenworth, major battles of the past became case studies to be analyzed for insights and best practices to apply to future wars. Patton excelled there.

The military does a much better job evaluating past actions, whether strategic or tactical, than does the business world. Brig. Gen. William Wallace, who commands the U.S. Army's National Training Center, refers to these evaluations as After Action Reviews and believes them to be powerful learning tools for military professionals. In contrast, corporations do not review completed major capital, advertising or research projects frequently enough to discern key lessons learned. Nor are those involved in various tactical operations debriefed often enough to learn what worked and what did not. The situation is beginning to change somewhat. General Electric, for one, makes a point of reviewing past efforts from throughout its various divisions to determine a set of best practices to be used company-wide in the future. GE also utilizes actual past situations as case studies that are presented at its in-house university. In academia, a growing number of business schools are using case studies as effective means of learning from the past. Reviewing the past is invaluable in dealing with the future.

The great poet and philosopher George Santayana wrote of the importance of learning from the past if its mistakes are not to be repeated. Looking back to past wars, battles and even minor skirmishes to learn appropriate lessons can be invaluable in waging future warfare more efficiently. The same reviewing process holds for business case studies at the corporate, division or department level. It also holds for this book. This last chapter serves as a kind of book review or debriefing to discern what was learned.

Ten Key Points

Different readers take away a different set of lessons from any book, including this one. Recognizing that, here are the author's intended ten most important points to remember: leadership, people, women, tactics, mission, competition, business-war nexus, strategic planning model, winning strategies and *strategia*. Each relates to the book's core topic of strategy. The reader can match the list against his or her own.

Leadership

In presenting Japan's attack-strength strategy at Pearl Harbor, it was noted that one of the crucial factors of success was the leadership of Adm. Isoroku Yamamoto. When recounting Russia's victory over Napoleon in 1812, the decisive role played by Gen. Kutuzov was underscored. For the execution of the choke-point strategy at Thermopylae, Sparta's King Leonidas was of vital importance. After so many others had failed, Grant's leadership in the Civil War with his relentless-attack strategy led to a Union victory. With only a few exceptions the design and execution of most strategies depends greatly on leadership.

The team is certainly important in warfare, especially at the tactical level. And certainly, Special Forces are known for their team approach in combat. Much has also been written in the management literature regarding teams in the workplace—especially cross-functional teams. Honda was among the first companies to make use of such teams in designing and bringing to market new vehicles; people were brought together from the marketing, engineering, purchasing, manufacturing, design and accounting departments. This approach has now become something of an industry standard. Today, teams do indeed play an important role in business. But that does not mean that the team is a replacement for leadership, especially when it comes to strategic planning.

The first important point, then, to carry away from this book is that in war, and to an even greater extent in business, the setting of strategy and the oversight of its execution requires outstanding leadership. The winning strategies of GE, Microsoft, Cisco and Disney, by way of example, have come in no small part from the leadership of Welch, Gates, Chambers and Eisner respectively.

Let it not be forgotten that the Greek roots of the word "strategy" refer to generalship, or the military *leader*. Strategy and leadership are inextricable almost by definition.

People

Warren Buffett's Berkshire Hathaway is essentially a holding company comprised of large blocks of stock of a dozen or so companies. Buffett's long-held policy as chairman has been to acquire a position in a company only if it has a straightforward and easy-to-understand business that outsiders can quickly grasp. Among Buffett's holdings for example are Coca-Cola, the *Washington Post,* Gillette, Dairy Queen, Geico, See's Candies and American Express. Interestingly, Buffett holds no shares of Microsoft, even though Bill Gates is a best friend—the two are among the five wealthiest men in America and they share a myriad of social interests. Buffett does not own shares in Microsoft because he believes the business is too complicated for him to understand.

Indeed, the business of Microsoft is not readily understood. There must be times when even Bill Gates and Steve Ballmer, as Chairman and CEO respectively, do not entirely comprehend it. Still, there is something that an outsider like Buffett, or anyone else, *can* understand about Microsoft, and that is its hiring and people strategy. Microsoft recruits only the brightest, most passionate and tough-minded people. It has retained them by providing challenging assignments, an invigorating and pride-filled corporate culture as well as very generous stock options. Gates says, "One of our core philosophies is that when you bring a bunch of smart people together, great things happen."[2] The logic of this is incontrovertible: A company composed of smart, tough and intensely dedicated people will likely prevail no matter the industry or the current status of the company.

That logic suggests an alternative acquisition or investment approach for Buffett. Forget about understanding the underlying business that is to be acquired. Instead, make acquisition decisions based largely on the people of the business, from most senior to most junior. Indeed, doing this is by no means far-fetched, venture capitalists do it all the time. This focus on the people in an organization also suggests a crucial matter relating to strategy. It is the people of an organization who execute strategy. A strategy's ultimate success or failure depends on them and their abilities, drive, intellect and perseverance. Even a flawed strategy can lead to victory if the people of the organization are dedicated, smart and able. "This [Hewlett-

Packard] is a company whose people can do things no one else can do,"[3] says HP's CEO, Carly Fiorina. It is the people of a company, division or department who translate a strategic plan into actions. It is they, not the plan itself, that are the crucial factors in determining victory or defeat.

Women

The role of women in strategic business planning was not specifically raised in the book. It was not thought necessary to do so. Women are no different from men in their ability to think and act strategically in the business world. This should be obvious. Still, here in closing the book, it is of value to underscore the point.

"The face of war is almost always that of a man,"[4] wrote Tom Brokaw in a recent best-seller, *The Greatest Generation*. Indeed, it is a fact that women have not played a very large historic role in warfare . . . at least not on the battlefield itself. Is that fact relevant to the success of women in contemporary business, given the nexus between war and business especially regarding strategic planning? The answer is an unequivocal no. Here is a straightforward argument.

Women have indeed been absent from history's battlefields. Why is this so? Women lack neither the courage nor the intellect necessary for warfare. Nor do they lack the killing instinct if the motivation is strong enough. What women have lacked, and what warfare has always demanded, is physical prowess. Men, overall, are bigger, stronger and swifter and have more stamina. The United States military's current double standards in physical requirements—higher for men, lower for women—attest to this. Some might argue that there is also a socializing dimension that should be explored—little Spartan boys were trained for warfare from an early age while little Spartan girls were not. While there may be something to that, the primary explanation for why war has been the domain of men is simply that its physical demands can far better be met by men than women. But here is the key point: There are *no* such equivalent physical demands in business.

The one dimension that limits women in warfare, superior physical ability, is not relevant in the world of business. Recall Clausewitz' observation that "War is a paradoxical trinity of primordial violence, chance and reason." Now replace the term "primordial violence" with "extreme competitiveness." The result is a good working definition of domestic and global business today: "Business is a paradoxical trinity of extreme competitiveness, chance and reason." Business so defined is an ideal environment within which women can excel; it is war but without the physical imperative.

Regarding the extreme competitiveness of today's business world, look to any American high school or college athletic field or classroom and it is immediately apparent that young women are more than a match for young men in competitive spirit and heart. As for the laws of chance, Julius Caesar wrote, "Fortune in war favors the bold." Well, boldness is gender free. Finally, the third component of the above definition of business is reason or intellect. This book has underscored the fact that intellect is crucial for strategy setting, which in turn is crucial for the success of a business organization. Here, once again, women and men are essentially equal. Scholastic Aptitude Tests (SATs) show that women do a little better at reading than men while men do a little better at math, but the differences are barely statistically significant.

It was really only one generation ago, beginning about 1975, that women in significant numbers began to enter the management ranks of business. The results have been good and will get even better. Even in the manufacturing sector, which has historically been dominated by men, about one-third of executive and management positions today are held by women. More and more women are obtaining the most senior positions in the best companies. Among them are Carly Fiorina of Hewlett-Packard, Andrea Jung of Avon, Shelly Lazarus of Ogilvey & Mather, Jeanne Jackson of Wal-Mart, Meg Whitman of eBay, Marissa Peterson of Sun Microsystems, Stacey Snider of Universal Pictures, Cynthia Trudell of Saturn, Ellen Hancock of Exodus, Abby Cohen of Goldman Sachs and scores more. These women can compete with anyone.

War since the beginning of time has been the province of men. Business, which uses the strategic principles of warfare, is not so constrained. Implicit in this book's presented material is the verity that women can be expected to reach the highest levels of business and finance. Indeed, as the above paragraph indicates, they are already doing so. At last count 2 of the *Fortune* 500 CEOs were women.

Expect that to increase to 100 and more over the next decade or so. This is a wonderful time to be a businesswoman.

Tactics

Tactics were briefly introduced in chapter 3 and touched on here and there afterward. The fact that they were not discussed in more depth in no way minimizes their importance as related to strategy.

Tactics are present-oriented, immediate actions taken by individuals or small units at the very point of contact with the enemy. They are flexible, depend on rapidly changing circumstances, and have modest and localized objectives. Tactics can be thought of roughly as little strategies. But "little" in no way indicates their importance; tactics are crucial in achieving success in war or business. Recall Patton's observation that "Good tactics can save even the worst strategy. Bad tactics can ruin even the best strategy." But the reverse probably also holds true. In reality, both strategy and tactics matter. Indeed, they complement one another.

Even though this book has focused almost entirely on strategy, readers must not lose sight of the importance of effective tactical maneuvering in executing strategy.

Mission

Strategies are not designed and executed in isolation. They are action blueprints intended to achieve a clearly understood mission. Mission has been identified often as a factor of success for the ten strategies discussed in this book. For a company, division or department, the mission is the starting point of a strategic plan. Strategies are means; the mission is the end. Lose sight of the mission and strategy becomes chaotic and, in the end, meaningless.

The mission should identify most basically what business the organization is in as well as its underlying principles of operation, its ultimate objectives, what it is and what it is not—indeed, its very reason for being. Whether written in a lengthy statement or in a few trenchant words, the mission is the essence of the organization. It is the overarching, guiding North Star. Strategy setting always begins with the mission.

Competition

"War and violence are the crucible of human progress," wrote Immanuel Kant, the German philosopher. Some might take issue with Kant's assertion although at least some historical evidence can be found to support it: WWII brought us jet aircraft, radar, advanced telecommunications, nuclear energy, wonder drugs and so on. But what cannot be argued is that "Vigorous, tough business competition is the crucible of *economic* progress." Over much of the twentieth century, Communism battled Capitalism. The world itself served as the laboratory and some 6 billion people of every culture, race and ethnicity served as participating lab animals. The experiment ended with the collapse of the Berlin Wall in 1989 and the implosion of the Soviet Union two years later. Capitalism won over a thoroughly discredited Communism.

Implicit in Capitalism is the fierce battling among competitors and the Darwinian nature of free enterprise. Just as armies battle one another for control of a land mass, businesses compete against one another for control of a specific market segment. And, just as military strategies are directed at the enemy, business strategies are directed at competitors. Every functional activity of a company, be it marketing, manufacturing, finance or any other, must in the end take account of the competition. This is a crucially important point of the book: Strategies, to be meaningful, must be competitor directed.

For a decade now, business has heard the know-the-customer mantra. That's OK but not enough, not when there are competitors fighting for the same customer. Appropriately, the strategies developed in this book have all been directed toward the competition. Defeat the competitor, and the prize, the customer, will fall easily into one's grasp. Harvard's Michael Porter writes, "A strategy not grounded in competitive rivalry will fail."[5] A comprehensive strategic plan certainly takes the customer into account, but it is the competitor, the adversary, against whom strategies must be designed. So they have been in this book. Sun Microsystems, for example, is challenging the market leader EMC in storage devices. It is doing so with smaller and cheaper units where EMC is not strong. Sun has adopted the attack-weakness strategy discussed in chapter 5. While there is of course a marketing dimension here for Sun, the strategy is not a marketing one per se. Rather, it is a strategy directed at EMC, a competitor, that includes an important marketing component.

It would have been absurd for Desert Storm's supreme military commander, Norman Schwarzkopf, to have an infantry, artillery, tank, air force and naval strategy that failed to take account of the enemy, the Iraqis. It would be equally absurd for a company's business strategy, whatever that strategy might be, to take no account of the competitor or competitors. Absurd as it may be, too often such omissions occur. Consider the example of Nissan.

Carlos Ghosn was recently brought in as CEO to oversee a much-needed turnaround at Nissan. The company, Japan's second largest automaker, had been afflicted with problems that went uncorrected for decades. One of those problems dealt with the matter considered here—competitor awareness. Ghosn has said, "Don't laugh. When I first came here we had no detailed intelligence about how we were faring against the competition."[6] Strategic planning must *always* be competitor directed.

Business-War Nexus

The book's approach of introducing great military battles and extracting from them winning strategies for application to the business arena reinforces the nexus between business and war. That nexus is a good thing for readers to keep constantly in mind.

Too much dopiness has been written about smiley-face, win-win, love-thine-enemy kinds of business thinking. Business, like war, is basically a zero-sum adversarial game with economic and professional stakes of the highest order. It requires the same deadly serious mind-set as does war. The higher one rises in the business world, the more evident that becomes; this book has reinforced that point. Readers will surely benefit from perceiving of business as war and then thinking and acting accordingly.

While the links between war and business are many and strong, the focus of this book has been on only one of them: strategy. Still, the other links are important. Understanding them gives readers a decided career edge in the brutal and warlike world of business competition.

Strategic Planning Model

The starting point for the design of any strategic plan is the model developed in chapter 3, which included the elements of mission, satellite snapshot, future scan, strategic building blocks, performance targets and required resources. The entire plan probably can be completed in a dozen pages with any necessary details appended.

For readers now in senior positions, strategic planning is probably already a primary responsibility. For those not in such positions it is suggested that they proceed on their own to forge their version of a company or business unit strategic plan and present it, unsolicited, to the most senior management. This might involve some bypassing of authority and should be handled with some sensitivity. But still, Peter Ueberroth, the erstwhile baseball commissioner, once noted that "Authority is 20% granted and 80% taken." While those percentages may vary somewhat from company to company, it has been said that it is "better to ask for forgiveness than permission." Readers are encouraged to take that authority and develop a department, division or entire corporate strategic plan. Doing that, their prominence in and knowledge of the organization will be raised substantially. Career advancement may well follow.

In the years ahead, thinking and acting strategically will be key to achieving top professional ranking in business. The strategic planning model offered here has been used as the basis to wage great military campaigns. Readers can also use it for their own business campaigns in the rigorous competition of domestic and global business.

Winning Strategies

This book has presented ten winning strategies taken from history's greatest battles and brought them to the business arena. The strategies deal with attacking strength, concentration of forces, controlling a choke point, bringing change to a failing company, alliances, containment, combat-readiness, attacking weakness, patience and relentless attack. Companies that have effectively used the strategies are noted for the reader to benchmark. A rich bibliography is also included to help in further researching the presented strategies.

Strategic building blocks for readers' companies likely will include several of the ten strategies presented in this book. General, later President, Eisenhower, once wrote that "Strategic principles are largely unchanged over time." He might have added that they are also relatively few in number. As complex as war, and by extension business, is, there are probably no more than a score of underlying strategies. Depending upon prevailing circumstances, one or more of those strategies will likely become the readers' own.

The next time the reader is in a planning meeting and there is a pause in the discussion, as the group seems uncertain about what to do, he or she might interject, "You know, I've been thinking. Our situation is a lot like that which faced the Spartans at Thermopylae." The reader would then go on to briefly describe the Spartan choke-point strategy, being as vivid in the telling as possible, and translate it directly to the prevailing circumstances currently confronting their own firm. Out of the ensuing discussion may well come a winning strategy. That is exactly how this book is to be used.

Strategia

The Greek *strategia*, or our strategy, is the centerpiece of this book. Alexander's military-oriented *strategia* of 2,300 years ago has evolved to today's quite sophisticated and complex strategy of modern warfare—the Gulf War, with its Operation Desert Storm, being a recent example of its use. The book's underlying theme has been the relatively new application of military strategy to business competition.

The strategic plan is an organization's—be it military or business—action blueprint. It puts into motion substantial human and capital resources with the intent of driving the adversary from the field. There is enormous power in this setting and execution of strategy. Indeed, the great sages, philosophers and theologians have long spoken of it: When the mission is clear and the strategies are well conceived and tenaciously executed, then life, fate, luck and even adversaries yield. More often than not, the sought-after mission is made a reality. This is breathtaking in its implications. Machiavelli understood that. Though he died centuries ago, he could have been speaking directly to readers at this moment when he exhorted, "Be audacious in [strategic plans] . . . and persevering in their execution . . . and fate will crown your brow with shining glory."

At the core of strategic thinking there is a profound idea: The fate of a nation, army, business enterprise or indeed an individual is self-determined. Destiny is within one's own control. There is cause and effect. First there is the mission—bold and audacious. Then there is the strategy: the who, what, where, when and how for achieving it. Next there is the resolute and steadfast execution of the strategy. Finally, there is victory and the realization of the mission. The linchpin to it all is strategy.

Winning strategies on military battlefields have changed the course of history. Readers can use those same strategies to compete in today's world of global business. The author wishes them the best of fortune.

Maxims and Quotes

Even death is afraid of him because he has the heart of a lion.
—Arab proverb

There is no such thing as a fair fight.
—SEAL Cmdr. T. L. Bosiljevac

Fortune [in war] favors the bold.
—Julius Caesar

It is magnificent [Light Brigade charge] but it is not war.
—Gen. Pierre Bosquet

When you leave your gate act as though the enemy is in sight.
—Code of Bushido

The Samurai thinks not of victory or defeat but merely fights insanely to the death.
—Code of Bushido

War is the ultimate test of a man's character.
—Gen. Lawrence Chamberlain

Battles are won by slaughter and [strategy]. The greater the general, the more he contributes in [strategy], the less he demands in slaughter.
—Winston Churchill

There is no logical self-imposed restriction on waging war. International law is irrelevant. Victors are the strongest not the most ethical. It is childish to talk of wars as just or unjust. They are simply wars.
—Carl von Clausewitz

There is no higher, or more basic, strategy than keeping one's forces concentrated at the point of attack.
—Carl von Clausewitz

There is an imperative need for pursuit after victory.
—Carl von Clausewitz

War is a paradoxical trinity of primordial violence, chance and reason.
—Carl von Clausewitz

A great part of information obtained in war is contradictory, a still greater part is false, and by far the greatest part of a doubtful character.

—Carl von Clausewitz

War and commerce are entirely alike in terms of human conflict, strategy and sought objectives.

—Carl von Clausewitz

Strategy . . . takes [circumstances] as it finds them.

—Carl von Clausewitz

Whenever boldness encounters timidity, it is . . . the winner.

—Carl von Clausewitz

War is an act of force to compel the enemy to our will.

—Carl von Clausewitz

No war should be begun until it is first determined what is to be achieved and how it will be conducted.

—Carl von Clausewitz

War . . . divides itself into strategy and tactics.

—Carl von Clausewitz

Not territorial or economic gain, but destruction of the enemy is the objective.

—Carl von Clausewitz

Today is a good day to die.

—Crazy Horse

Come on you sons of bitches. Do you want to live forever?

—Sgt. Dan Daly

The best way to predict the future is to create it [yourself].

—Peter Drucker

Strategic principles remain unchanged through time.

—Gen. Dwight Eisenhower

Speed is the essence of success.

—Gen. Dwight Eisenhower

When you strike at a king, you must kill him.

—Ralph Waldo Emerson

[The god of war] hates those who hesitate.

—Euripedes

My centre is giving way, my right is in retreat, situation excellent. I attack.
                                    —Gen. Ferdinand Foch

Machine guns are overrated, airplanes silly and tanks mere toys.
                                    —Gen. Ferdinand Foch

War means fightin' and fightin' means killin'.
                                    —Gen. Bedford Forrest

Git thar [the battlefield] fustest with the mostest [men].
                                    —Gen. Bedford Forrest

We are talking about life and death in every piece of e-mail.
                                    —Bill Gates

One of our core philosophies is that when you bring a bunch of smart people together, great things happen.
                                    —Bill Gates

If I live, I will fight, wherever I must, as long as I must, until the enemy is defeated.
                                    —Charles de Gaulle

We fight, get beat, and rise and fight again.
                                    —Gen. Nathanael Greene

Only the paranoid survive.
                                    —Andy Grove

Under no circumstances should you ever shoot the messenger.
                                    —Andy Grove

You need a high tolerance for ambiguity but must strive to order that which is around you.
                                    —Andrew Grove

Hit hard. Hit fast. Hit often.
                                    —Adm. Bull Halsey

A strategy not grounded in competitive rivalry will fail.
                                    —Gary Hamel

War, business, life, demands one thing from you . . . not to have run away.
                                    —Dag Hammarskjold

We must either find a way [across the Alps] or make one.
                                    —Hannibal

There are worse things than war; and all of them come with defeat.
                                    —Ernest Hemingway

Never take counsel of your fears.

—Gen. Thomas "Stonewall" Jackson

To capture the baby tiger you have to go into the mother tiger's lair.

—Japanese military maxim

After victory, tighten your helmet cord.

—Japanese military maxim

War and violence are the crucible of human progress.

—Immanuel Kant

Competitors can buy physical assets but not our employee dedication, devotion, loyalty, and feeling part of a crusade.

—Herb Kelleher

There is no finish line.

—Phil Knight

Patience and time, time and patience.

—Gen. Mikhail Hilarionovich Kutuzov

It is well that war is so terrible or we should grow too fond of it.

—Gen. Robert E. Lee

War, by definition, means a suspension of rules, laws and civilized behavior.

—Gen. Robert E. Lee

If we first knew where we are and whither we are going we could better judge what to do and how to do it.

—Abraham Lincoln

Disregard the immaterial and perfect the few things one does best.

—Vince Lombardi

Nothing stokes that fire [in you] like hate.

—Vince Lombardi

I will not take by sacrifice of men what I can take by strategy.

—Gen. Douglas MacArthur

Councils of war breed timidity and defeatism.

—Gen. Douglas MacArthur

Surprise is the most vital element for success in war.

—Gen. Douglas MacArthur

Leadership is the key to victory.

—Niccolo Machiavelli

Be audacious in planning and persevering in execution and fate will crown your brow with shining glory.

—Niccolo Machiavelli

There is nothing more difficult, nor dangerous nor doubtful of success than to initiate a new order of things.

—Niccolo Machiavelli

It is not enough to fight. It is the spirit we bring to the fight that decides the issue. It is . . . morale that wins the victory.

—Gen. George Marshall

If you get the objectives right, a lieutenant can write the strategy.

—Gen. George Marshall

It makes no difference what we think of war. War endures.

—Cormac McCarthy

War is the inevitable fate of mankind.

—Count Helmuth von Moltke

Circumstances. I make circumstances.

—Napoleon

When you start to take Vienna . . . take Vienna!

—Napoleon

In war, morale is to the material as three is to one.

—Napoleon

Every French soldier carries a marshall's baton in his knapsack.

—Napoleon

No captain can do wrong if he places his ship alongside that of the enemy.

—Adm. Horatio Nelson

We have no eternal allies and no perpetual enemies . . . Our interests are eternal and perpetual.

—Lord Palmerston

Always attack without regard for flanks. Attack rapidly, ruthlessly, viciously without rest.

—Gen. George S. Patton

Shoot them in the belly and cut out their living guts.

—Gen. George S. Patton

Good tactics can save even the worst strategy. Bad tactics can ruin even the best strategy.

—Gen. George S. Patton

May God have mercy on our enemies . . . they will need it.
—Gen. George S. Patton

Compared to war, all other forms of human endeavor sink to insignificance. God how I love it.
—Gen. George S. Patton

Never fight a battle when nothing is gained by winning.
—Gen. George S. Patton

Only the dead have seen the end of war.
—Plato

People are reluctant to change. The more senior they are, the more reluctant.
—John Reed

Always use the chain of command to issue orders . . . but never to gather information.
—Adm. Hyman Rickover

We will start the war right here.
—Gen. Teddy Roosevelt, Jr.

When confronted with a challenge, immediately take the offensive.
—Teddy Roosevelt

Every man takes the limits of his own field of vision for the limits of the world.
—Arthur Schopenhauer

Be excited about change, don't fear it, be part of it.
—Juergen Schrempp

Our strategy for going after this [Iraqi] army is very, very simple. First we are going to cut it off and then we are going to kill it.
—Colin Powell

War is cruelty and you cannot refine it.
—Gen. W. T. Sherman

No one can command an army from the rear.
—Gen. W. T. Sherman

War should be long in preparing in order that you may conquer the more quickly.
—Publilius Syrus

Pardon one offence and you encourage the commission of many.
—Publilius Syrus

If you don't have a strategy you will be . . . part of somebody else's strategy.

—Alvin Toffler

The strongest of all warriors are these two—Time and Patience.

—Leo Nikolaevich Tolstoy

All men can see these tactics whereby I conquer but what none can see is the strategy out of which victory evolves.

—Sun Tzu

Warfare is a matter of deception.

—Sun Tzu

Know your enemy and know yourself and you can fight a hundred battles without disaster.

—Sun Tzu

To be certain to take what you attack is to attack a place the enemy does not protect.

—Sun Tzu

Rewards and punishments provide the basis for control.

—Sun Tzu

When the foe is desperate do not exceedingly press him.

—Sun Tzu

Speed, surprise and deception are the primary essentials of the attack.

—Sun Tzu

To be prepared for war is one of the most effectual means of preserving peace.

—George Washington

I heard the bullets whistle; and believe me, there is something charming in the sound.

—George Washington

Speed exhilarates and energizes.

—Jack Welch

The battle of Waterloo was won on the playing fields of Eton.

—Duke of Wellington

When men take up arms to set other men free there is something sacred and holy in warfare.

—Woodrow Wilson

Business is like war . . . If the grand strategy is correct, any number of tactical errors can be made and yet the enterprise proves successful.

—Gen. Robert Wood

Morale is the sole decisive factor in war.

—Mao Zedong

Don't let victory intoxicate you.

—Mao Zedong

Notes

Chapter 1

1. Mark Borden, "Thinking About Tomorrow," *Fortune*, November 22, 1999, p. 170.

Chapter 2

1. Pui-Wing Tam, "Competitive Drive: Palm Puts Up Its Fists as Microsoft Attacks Hand-Held PC Market—Smaller Firm Stays Ahead, Thanks to Michael Mace, Paranoid Corporate Spy—Bill Gates, Phantom Shopper," *Wall Street Journal*, August 8, 2000, p. A.1.
2. Patricia Sellers, "The 50 Most Powerful Women in Business; Secrets of the Fastest-Rising Stars," *Fortune*, October 16, 2000, p. 130.
3. Gene Bylinsky, "Look who's doing R&D," *Fortune*, November 27, 2000, p. 231.
4. Cormac McCarthy, *Blood Meridian, or The Evening Redness in the West* (New York: Vintage Books, 1992), p. 248.
5. Robert Frank and Jonathan Friedland, "Cola-War Casualty: How Pepsi's Charge Into Brazil Fell Short of Its Ambitious Goals—Trying to Beat Coke Quickly, It Failed to Build Brand, Had Executive Problems—'A Key Bottler Is in Trouble,'" *Wall Street Journal*, August 30, 1996, p. A.1.
6. Andrew Grove, *Only the Paranoid Survive* (New York: Doubleday, 1996).
7. Lee Smith, Cindy Kano and Edward A. Robison, "Hitachi Gliding Nowhere?; The Japanese Behemoth Is Looking to PCs to Boost Its Meager Profits. Good Luck, Say the Experts," *Fortune*, August 5, 1996, p. 80.
8. Betsy McKay, "Juiced Up: Pepsi Edges Past Coke And It Has Nothing to Do with Cola—The Company Now Capitalizes on a Growing Thirst for Drinks without Fizz—Tropicana's Vitamin Punch," *Wall Street Journal*, November 6, 2000, p. A.1.
9. McCarthy, *Blood Meridian*, p. 248.
10. Pui-Wing Tam, *Wall Street Journal*, August 8, 2000.
11. Gene Bylinsky, *Fortune*, November 27, 2000.

12. See "Leadership Tip of the Day," October 6, 2000 at www:emazing.com/archives/leadership/2000-10-06.

Chapter 3

1. Mark Borden, "Thinking About Tomorrow," *Fortune*, November 22, 1999, p. 170.
2. Kara Swisher, "Boom Town: Why Is Jeff Bezos Still Smiling?—Amazon's Stock Has Plunged, But He Thinks It's Poised to Profit from a Shakedown," *Wall Street Journal*, April 24, 2000, p. B.1.
3. Scott Thurm, "Boss Talk: How to Drive an Express Train—At Fast-Moving Cisco, CEO Says: Put Customers First, View Rivals as 'Good Guys,'" *Wall Street Journal*, June 1, 2000, p. B.1.
4. Thomas Peters, *In Search of Excellence* (New York: Harper & Row, 1982).
5. Rebecca Buckman, "Boss Talk: Keeping on Course in a Crisis—Microsoft CEO Stresses Need to Simplify Goals, Heed Key Employees' Concerns," *Wall Street Journal*, June 9, 2000, p. B.1.
6. "Dick Kovacevich Does It His Way," *Fortune*, May 15, 2000.
7. Alex Taylor III, "Kellogg Cranks Up Its Idea Machine," *Fortune*, July 5, 1999.
8. Gary Hamel, *Competing for the Future* (Boston: HBS, 1994).
9. Alex Taylor III, "Wrong Turn at Saturn," *Fortune*, July 24, 2000, p. 371.
10. Stanley W. Angrist, "What We Don't Have Here Is a Failure to Communicate," *Wall Street Journal*, June 14, 2000.
11. David Kirkpatrick, "Why We're Betting Billions on TV," *Fortune*, May 15, 2000, p. 256.
12. Sally Beatty and Carol Hymowitz, "Boss Talk: How MTV Stays Tuned into Teens, Teenagers—CEO Recommends Hiring Staff That Appreciates Kids' Tastes and Doing Lots of Research," *Wall Street Journal*, March 21, 2000, p. B.1.
13. Bernard Wysocki Jr., "Power Grid: Soft Landing or Hard? Firm Tests Strategy on 3 Views of Future," *Wall Street Journal*, July 7, 2000.
14. Grove, 1996.
15. Rob Norton and Jane Folpe, "The Motley Crew That Hates Rate Increases," *Fortune*, January 24, 2000, p. 44.
16. Howard Fineman, Michael Isikoff and Martha Brant, "Dixie Donnybrook," *Newsweek*, February 21, 2000, p. 18.
17. Geoffrey Colvin, "The Ultimate Manager," *Fortune*, November 22, 1999.
18. Alex Taylor III, "Is the World Big Enough for Jurgen Schrempp?" *Fortune*, March 6, 2000, p. 140.
19. Jack Welch, Scott McNealy, John Huey, and Brent Sclender, "The Odd Couple," *Fortune*, May 1, 2000, p. 106.
20. Marc Gunther, "These Guys Want It All," *Fortune*, February 7, 2000, p. 70.
21. Joseph Nocera, "The Men Who Would Be King," *Fortune*, February 7, 2000, p. 66.
22. Jeremy Kahn, "How Gartner Got Snagged by the Net," *Fortune*, December 6, 1999, p. 365.

23. Scott Thurm, "Boss Talk: How to Drive an Express Train—At Fast-Moving Cisco, CEO Says: Put Customers First, View Rivals as 'Good Guys,'" *Wall Street Journal*, June 1, 2000, p. B.1.
24. Joseph Nocera, "The Corporation Comes Home," *Fortune*, March 6, 2000.
25. Gary Hamel, *Competing for the Future* (Boston: HBS, 1994), p. 100.
26. Kara Swisher, "Boom Town: Why Is Jeff Bezos Still Smiling?—Amazon's Stock Has Plunged, But He Thinks It's Poised to Profit from a Shakedown," *Wall Street Journal*, April 24, 2000, p. B.1.

Chapter 4

1. Rudy Abramson and John Broder, "Four-Star Power; Colin Powell's Career Has Proceeded With the Certainty of a Laser-Guided Missile. How Much Higher Will He Go?" *Los Angeles Times*, April 7, 1991.
2. Leslie Cauley, "Losses in Space—Iridium's Downfall: The Marketing Took a Back Seat to Science—Motorola and Partners Spent Billions on Satellite Links for a Phone Few Wanted—Counting on 'User Dexterity,'" *Wall Street Journal*, August 18, 1999, p. Al.

Chapter 5

1. Sam Walton, *Made in America* (New York: Bantam, 1992).
2. Ibid.
3. Walton, 1992.

Chapter 6

1. Patricia Sellers, "Behind the Scenes at Citigroup," *Fortune*, March 20, 2000, p. 27.
2. Mark Heinzl, "Boss Talk: Buying into the New Economy—CEO Uses Acquisitions to Turn Nortel into a Huge Player in Technology for the Web," *Wall Street Journal*, July 25, 2000, p. B1.
3. Robert Slater, *Jack Welch and the GE Way* (New York: McGraw Hill, 1998).
4. Ibid., p. 93.
5. Katrina Brooker, "New blood for an old brand," *Fortune*, February 21, 2000, pp. 289-290.
6. David P. Hamilton, "H-P Chief Shuffles Top Roles, Says Server Sales May Pinch Net," *Wall Street Journal*, October 4, 1999, p. A4.
7. Ibid.
8. Calmetta Y. Coleman, "Kmart's New CEO Outlines Plans For Fast Changes—Conaway Shakes Up Senior Management, Moves to Revamp Store Operations," *Wall Street Journal*, July 27, 2000, p. B4.

9. Evan Ramstad, "Circuit City's CEO Gambles to Galvanize the Chain—Decision to Drop Major Appliances, Overhaul Stores Aimed at Keeping Up," *Wall Street Journal*, September 18, 2000, p. B4.
10. Todd Zaun, "Japan's Nissan Sends Out Bullish Signals—President Says Rebuilding Is Ahead of Schedule, Expects Profit This Year," *Wall Street Journal*, October 20, 2000, p. A17.
11. Katrina Brooker, "Plugging the Leaks at P&G," *Fortune*, February 21, 2000, p. 44.
12. Matthew Rose, "Indigestion: Mr. Ryder Rewrites The Musty Old Book at Reader's Digest—Cost Cuts and Other Shocks Lift Profits, Sap Morale; A Wary Internet Strategy—Mr. Bohane Receive a '360,'" *Wall Street Journal*, April 18, 2000, p. A1.
13. Robert C. Alexander and Douglas K. Smith, "Can Xerox Duplicate Its Original Success?," *Wall Street Journal*, May 17, 2000, p. A26.
14. Ibid.
15. Gary McWilliams, "Gateway Says PC Sales Plunged and It Plans to Lay Off 3,000," *Wall Street Journal*, January 12, 2001, p. A.6.
16. Katrina Brooker, "New Blood for an Old Brand," *Fortune*, February 21, 2000, p. 289.
17. *Empire of the Sun*, directed by Steven Spielberg, based on the novel by J. G. Ballard, screenplay by Tom Stoppard, 1987.

Chapter 7

1. John Barry and Evan Thomas, "Probing a Slaughter," *Newsweek*, May 29, 2000, p. 28.
2. Carol J. Loomis, "Sam Would Be Proud," *Fortune*, April 17, 2000, p. 135.
3. Geraldine Laybourne and Katrina Brooker, "My Sober Year," *Fortune*, June 26, 2000, p. 150.
4. Lisa Bannon, "Mattel's New Boss Promises a Leaner and Meaner Firm—Eckert Plans to Focus on Toy Business and Renegotiate Licensing Accord," *Wall Street Journal*, August 10, 2000, p. B2.
5. Jennifer Ordonez, "Will Big Mac Find New Sizzle in Shoes, Videos?" *Wall Street Journal*, April 14, 2000, p. B1.
6. Jennifer Ordonez, "McDonald's Cites Waning Promotion for Weak Earnings," *Wall Street Journal*, July 26, 2000, p. B8.
7. Margaret Studer and Jennifer Ordonez, "The Golden Arches: Burgers, Fries and 4-Star Rooms—McDonald's Plans to Open Two Hotels in Switzerland; Will Business Travelers Bite?" *Wall Street Journal*, November 17, 2000.
8. Katrina Brooker, "My Sober Year," *Fortune*, June 26, 2000, p. 150.
9. Robert L. Simison and Joseph B. White, "Reputation for Poor Quality Still Plagues Detroit—Ratings Show U.S. Car Makers Lag Behind Foreign Rivals Despite Years of Efforts," *Wall Street Journal*, May 4, 2000, p. B1.
10. *Wall Street Journal*, August 10, 2000, p. B2.
11. Suzanne Koudsi, "Beat It," *Fortune*, May 29, 2000, p. 34.

12. David Maraniss, *When Pride Still Mattered* (New York: Simon & Schuster, 1999).
13. Carol Loomis, "Sam Would Be Proud," *Fortune*, April 17, 2000, p. 134.
14. Jack Welch, Scott McNealy, John Huey, and Brent Schlender, "The Odd Couple," *Fortune*, May 1, 2000, p. 106.
15. Andy Serwer, "The next richest man in the world," *Fortune*, November 13, 2000, pp. 98-124.
16. Robert A. Guth, "Japan's Toshiba To Place Focus On Computers, Not Appliances," *Wall Street Journal*, March 22, 2000, p. A17.

Chapter 8

1. Betsy McKay, "Coke's Think Local Strategy Has Yet to Prove Itself," *Wall Street Journal*, March 1, 2001, p. B2.
2. Robert L. Simison, Gregory L. White and Deborah Ball, "GM's Linkup With Fiat Opens Final Act of Consolidation Drama for Industry," *Wall Street Journal*, March 14, 2000, p. A3.
3. Gary McWilliams, "Compaq Buying Custom-PC Lines of Inacom, With Dell in Mind," *Wall Street Journal*, January 5, 2000, p. B2:3.
4. David Kirkpatrick, "Competition comes to Enterprise Software," *Fortune*, December 7, 1998, pp. 102-112.
5. David Kirkpatrick, "The New Player," *Fortune*, April 17, 2000, pp. 162-168.
6. Ibid.
7. Robert Slater, *Jack Welch and the GE Way* (New York: McGraw Hill, 1998).
8. Philip Siekman, "Building 'em better in Brazil," *Fortune*, September 6, 1999, p. 246C.
9. Lisa Bannon and Joseph Pereira, "E-Business: Toy War II: Holiday Cyber Battle Begins—Two Big Online Toy Sellers Fight Over Delivery Speed and Exclusive Products," *Wall Street Journal*, September 25, 2000, p. B1.
10. Steve Liesman, "BP Amoco Is Set to Outsource Accounting in $1.1 Billion Deal," *Wall Street Journal*, November 10, 1999, p. A4.
11. David Whitford, "The Two-Headed Manager," *Fortune*, January 24, 2000, p. 147.

Chapter 9

1. Stuart F. Brown, "How to Build a Really, Really, Really Big Plane," *Fortune*, March 5, 2001, pp. 150-151.
2. Katrina Brooker, "Survival of the fittest," *Fortune*, July 24, 2000, pp. 34-36.
3. Joseph B. White and Gregory L. White, "GM's Pearce Pans Market-Share Efforts—Vice Chairman Bluntly Says Company's Management Has Failed to Deliver," *Wall Street Journal*, December 9, 1999, p. A3:1.
4. Robert L. Simison and Scott Miller, "Scrap Heap: Widening Losses Force BMW to Sell Rover; Ford Nabs the Big Prize—Land Rover Goes to

Detroit and German Maker Goes Back to Drawing Board—Dithering, Dissent in Munich," *Wall Street Journal*, March 17, 2000.

5. Paul Ingrassia, "Car Companies Consolidate, and Wall Street Yawns," *Wall Street Journal*, March 22, 2000, p. A22.
6. David Kirkpatrick, "Eckhard's Gone but the PC Rocks On," *Fortune*, May 24, 1999, pp. 153-158.
7. Amy Merrick, "Northern Trust, Shunning Mergers, Sticks to Its Last—Chicago Firm Thrives by Focusing on Private Banking for the Wealthy," *Wall Street Journal*, October 9, 2000, p. B6.
8. Ibid.
9. Steven Lipin and E. S. Browning, "Is New Chase the Bank of the Future?—A Bigger Model Isn't Necessarily the Better Way," *Wall Street Journal*, September 14, 2000, p. C1.
10. Daniel Roth, "Surprise! Yahoo Goes Broadband," *Fortune*, May 29, 2000, pp. 182-192.

Chapter 10

1. Rebecca Smith and Aaron Lucchetti, "Sink or Swim: Rebecca Mark's Exit Leaves Enron's Azarix Treading Deep Water—Venture's Troubles Vindicate Her Rival, Who Pushed Parent in New Directions—A Bad Smell in Argentina," *Wall Street Journal*, August 28, 2000, p. A1.
2. Ibid.
3. Thomas Peters, *In Search of Excellence* (New York: Harper & Row, 1982).
4. Robert Slater, *Jack Welch and the GE Way* (New York: McGraw Hill, 1998).
5. John R. Wilke, "Microsoft Is Source of 'Soft Money' Funds Behind Ads in Michigan's Senate Race," *Wall Street Journal*, October 16, 2000, p. A3.
6. Scott Thurm, "Safe Conduct: Microsoft's Behavior Is Helping Cisco Learn How to Avoid Trouble—Lesson No. 1: Seek to Charm Antitrust Regulators, Don't Try to Bully Them—There Isn't 'a Secret Sauce,'" *Wall Street Journal*, June 1, 2000, p. A1.
7. Ibid.
8. Betsy McKay, "New Formula: To Fix Coca-Cola, Daft Sets Out to Get New Relationships Right—He Woos European Officials and Lets Managers Adapt Tactics to Their Markets—Lessons from Old Masters," *Wall Street Journal*, June 23, 2000, p. A1.
9. Betsy McKay, "Spanish Officials Raid Coca-Cola Offices," *Wall Street Journal*, September 21, 2000, p. B14.
10. Gary McWilliams, "Big Computer Dealers Feel Mail-Order Bite," *Wall Street Journal*, July 13, 2000, p. B6.

Chapter 11

1. Robert Frank, "Heard on the street: Pepsi losing overseas fizz to Coca-Cola," *Wall Street Journal*, August 22, 1996, p. C1.

2. Andy Serwer, "There's Something About Cisco," *Fortune*, May 15, 2000, p. 114.
3. Betsy Morris, "Can Michael Dell Escape the Box?" *Fortune*, October 16, 2000, p. 95.
4. Paul Andrews, *How the Web Was Won* (New York: Broadway Books, 1999), p. 92.
5. David P. Hamilton, "Soul Saver: Inside Hewlett-Packard, Carly Fiorina Combines Discipline, New-Age Talk—Some Executives Lost Sleep, But Now H-P United Work with Each Other on Deals—Big Kudos for 'Ann Amazon,'" *Wall Street Journal*, August 22, 2000, p. A1.

Chapter 12

1. Patricia Sellers, "Big, Hairy, Audacious Goals Don't Work," *Fortune*, April 3, 2000, pp. 39-44.
2. Stanley Karnow, *Vietnam* (New York: Viking, 1983).
3. Sellers, *Fortune*, April 3, 2000.
4. *The Untouchables*, novel by Oscar Fraley, Eliot Ness, Paul Robsky; directed by Brian DePalma, 1987.

Chapter 13

1. Mark Bowden, *Black Hawk Down: A Story of Modern War* (New York: Atlantic Monthly, 1992).
2. Paul Andrews, *How the Web Was Won* (New York: Broadway Books, 1999).
3. Andrew Grove, *Only the Paranoid Survive* (New York: Doubleday, 1996).
4. Katrina Brooker, "Can Anyone Replace Herb?" *Fortune*, April 17, 2000, p. 186.
5. Scott Thurm, "Boss Talk: How to Drive an Express Train—At Fast-Moving Cisco, CEO Says: Put Customers First, View Rivals as 'Good Guys,'" *Wall Street Journal*, June 1, 2000, p. B1.
6. Andrews, 1999.
7. Jack Welch, Scott McNealy, John Huey, and Brent Schlender, "The Odd Couple," *Fortune*, May 1, 2000, p. 106.
8. Thomas A. Stewart, "Taking Risk to the Marketplace," *Fortune*, March 6, 2000, p. 424.
9. Alex Taylor III, "Is the World Big Enough for Jurgen Schrempp?" *Fortune*, March 6, 2000, p. 142.
10. Andrews, 1999.
11. Martin Peersand and Julia Angwin, "Internet Time: AOL, TimeWarner Are Already Putting Operations Together—Collaboration Is Watchword, And That Means Change for Some Division Chiefs—Regulators Delay a Decision," *Wall Street Journal*, November 10, 2000, p. A1.
12. Andy Serwer, "There's Something About Cisco," *Fortune*, May 15, 2000, p. 114.

13. Katrina Brooker, "Can Anyone Replace Herb?" *Fortune*, April 17, 2000, p. 186.
14. Neil King Jr. and Jess Bavin, "Call It Mission Impossible, Inc.—Corporate Spying Firms Thrive," *Wall Street Journal*, July 3, 2000, p. B1.
15. Ibid.
16. Betsy Morris, "Can Michael Dell Escape the Box?" *Fortune*, October 16, 2000, p. 96.
17. Lauren Goldstein, "Whatever Space Works for You," *Fortune*, July 10, 2000, pp. 269-270.
18. Grove, 1996.
19. Betsy McKay, "New Formula: To Fix Coca-Cola, Daft Sets Out to Get Relationships Right—He Woos European Officials and Lets Managers Adapt Tactics to Their Markets—Lesson from Old Masters," *Wall Street Journal*, June 23, 2000, p. A1.
20. Andrews, 1999.
21. Scott Thurm, "Boss Talk: How to Drive an Express Train—At Fast-Moving Cisco, CEO Says: Put Customers First, View Rivals as 'Good Guys,'" *Wall Street Journal*, June 1, 2000, p. B.1.
22. Almar Latour, "Trial by Fire: A Blaze in Albuquerque Sets Off Major Crisis for Cell-Phone Giants—Nokia Handles Supply Shock With Aplomb as Ericsson of Sweden Gets Burned—Was Sisu the Difference?" *Wall Street Journal*, January 29, 2001, p. A1.
23. Brent Schlender, "The Odd Couple," *Fortune*, May 1, 2000, pp. 106-126.
24. Thomas A. Stewart, "The Leading Edge: Making Decisions in Real Time," *Fortune*, June 26, 2000, p. 332.
25. Betsy Morris, "Can Michael Dell Escape the Box?" *Fortune*, October 16, 2000, p.100.
26. Andrews, 1999.
27. Ibid.

Chapter 14

1. Patricia Sellers, "Rising from the Smoke," *Fortune*, April 16, 2001, p. 158.
2. Paul Andrews, *How the Web Was Won* (New York: Broadway Books, 1999).
3. David P. Hamilton, "Soul Saver: Inside Hewlett-Packard, Carly Fiorina Combines Discipline, New-Age Talk—Some Executives Lost Sleep, But Now H-P United Work with Each Other on Deals—Big Kudos for 'Ann Amazon,'" *Wall Street Journal*, August 22, 2000, A1
4. Tom Brokaw, *The Greatest Generation* (New York: Random House, 1998).
5. Gary Hamel, *Competing for the Future* (Boston: HBS, 1994).
6. Norihiko Shirouzu, Joseph B. White and Todd Zaun, "U-Turn: A Revival at Nissan Shows There's Hope for Ailing Japan Inc.—Carlos Ghosn Is Overhauling Culture by Challenging Suppliers and Assumptions—Bringing Back the 'Z' Car," *Wall Street Journal*, November 16, 2000, A1

Bibliography

Agawa, Hiroyuki. *The Reluctant Admiral.* Tokyo: Kodansha, 1969.
Ambrose, Stephen. *D-Day.* New York: Simon & Schuster, 1994.
Andrews, Paul. *How the Web Was Won.* New York: Broadway Books, 1999.
Arquilla, John. *Troy to Entebbe.* University Park, MD: University Press, 1998.
Behr, Edward. *Hirohito.* New York: Vintage, 1990.
Bierce, Ambrose. *Civil War Stories.* Toronto: Dover, 1994.
Blumenson, Martin. *The Patton Papers.* New York: Houghton Mifflin, 1974.
Bowden, Mark. *Black Hawk Down: A Story of Modern War.* New York: Atlantic Monthly, 1992.
Brokaw, T. *The Greatest Generation.* New York: Random House, 1998.
Capodagli, Bill. *The Disney Way.* New York: McGraw-Hill, 1998.
Cate, Curtis. *War of the Two Emperors.* New York: Random House, 1985.
Champy, James. *Reengineering Management.* New York: Harper, 1995.
Chernow, Ron. *Titan.* New York: Random House, 1998.
Churchill, Winston. *The Grand Alliance.* New York: Bantam, 1974.
Clausewitz, Carl von. *On War.* New York: Penguin Books, 1968.
Cook, Don. *Charles de Gaulle.* New York: Putnam, 1983.
D'Aveni, Richard. *Hyper-Competition.* New York: Free Press, 1994.
D'Este, Carlo. *A Genius for War.* New York: Harper Collins, 1995.
Drucker, Peter. *Management.* New York: Harper Collins, 1973.
Farago, Ladislas. *Last Days of Patton.* New York: Berkley Books, 1981.
Farago, Ladislas. *Ordeal and Triumph.* New York: Astor-Harbor, 1964.
Fialka, John. *War By Other Means.* New York: Norton, 1997.
Gates, Bill. *Business @ the Speed of Thought.* New York: Warner, 1999.
Griffin, Nancy. *Hit & Run.* New York: Simon & Schuster, 1996.
Griffith, Samuel B. *Sun Tzu.* London: Oxford Press, 1963.
Griffith, Samuel B. *Mao Tse-Tung Guerrilla Warfare.* New York: Praeger, 1961.
Grove, Andrew. *Only the Paranoid Survive.* New York: Doubleday, 1996.
Hagstrom, Robert. *The Warren Buffett Way.* New York: Wiley, 1994
Hamel, Gary. *Competing for the Future.* Boston: HBS, 1994.
Hando, Kazutoshi. *Japan's Longest Day.* New York: Kodansha, 1980.
Harrigan, Stephan. *The Gates of the Alamo.* New York: Knopf, 2000.
Hastings, Max. *Military Anecdotes.* New York: Oxford, 1985.
Hemingway, Ernest. *Men at War.* New York: Branhall House, 1979.
Herr, Michael. *Dispatches.* New York: Vintage, 1991.
Hirshberg, Jerry. *The Creative Priority.* New York: Harper Business, 1998.
Howard, Michael. *On War.* Princeton, NJ: Princeton Press, 1976.
Jakes, John. *Love and War.* New York: Signet, 2000.

Jakes, John. *North and South.* New York: Signet, 2000.
Jones, James. *Whistle.* New York: Delta, 1978.
Jones, James. *Thin Red Line.* New York: Delta, 1962.
Jones, James. *From Here to Eternity,* New York: Delta, 1951.
Jones, Virgil. *Gray Ghosts.* New York: Galahad Books, 1956.
Jordan, Robert. *Fallon Pride,* New York: Forge, 1981.
Karnow, Stanley. *Vietnam.* New York: Viking, 1983.
Keegan, John. *First World War.* Toronto: Key Porter, 1998.
Kelly, Orr. *Never Fight Fair.* Novato, CA: Presidio Press, 1995.
Leckie, Robert. *Okinawa.* New York: Viking, 1995.
Lewis, Jon. *True War Stories.* New York: Carroll & Graf, 1999.
Lewis, Jon. *War.* New York: Galahad, 1993.
Ludwig, Emil. *Napoleon.* New York: Modern Library, 1953.
Machiavelli, Niccolo. *Art of War.* New York: Da Capo, 1965.
Mailer, Norman. *Naked and the Dead.* New York: Owl Books, 1948.
Manchester, William. *American Caesar.* Boston: Little, Brown, 1978.
Manchester, William. *The Arms of Krupp.* New York: Little, Brown, 1964.
Manes, Stephans. *Gates.* New York: Touchstone, 1994.
Maraniss, David. *When Pride Still Mattered.* New York: Simon & Schuster, 1999.
Marcinko, Richard. *Echo Platoon.* New York: Pocket Books, 2000.
Massie, Robert. *Peter the Great.* New York: Knopf, 1981.
Meier, Christian. *Caesar.* New York: Basic Books, 1982.
Mishima, Yukio. *Way of the Warrior.* New York: Basic Books, 1977.
Morris, Edmund. *Rise of Theodore Roosevelt.* New York: Ballantine, 1979.
Myrer, Anton. *Once an Eagle.* New York: Holt-Rinehart, 1968.
Peters, Thomas. *In Search of Excellence.* New York: Harper & Row, 1982.
Prange, Gordon. *At Dawn We Slept.* New York: McGraw-Hill, 1981.
Pressfield, Steven. *Tides of War.* New York: Doubleday, 2000.
Pressfield, Steven. *Gates of Fire.* New York: Doubleday, 1998.
Riker, Jay. *The Warrior Breed.* New York: Avon, 1996.
Riley, Pat. *Winner Within.* New York: Berkley Books, 1993.
Ryan, Cornelius. *A Bridge Too Far.* New York: Popular Library, 1974.
Sadler, A. *Code of the Samurai.* Rutland, VT: Tuttle 1941.
Sawyer, Ralph. *Military Classics of Ancient China.* Boulder, CO: Westview, 1993.
Scott, Leonard. *Charlie Mike.* New York: Balantine, 1985.
Shaara, Jeff. *The Last Full Measure.* New York: Ballantine, 1998.
Shaara, Michael. *Gods and Generals.* New York: Ballantine, 1996.
Shaara, Michael. *The Killer Angels,* New York: Ballantine Books, 1974.
Shirer, William. *Rise and Fall of the Third Reich,* New York: Simon & Schuster, 1960.
Slater, Robert. *Jack Welch and the GE Way.* New York: McGraw Hill, 1998.
Speer, Albert. *Spandau.* New York: Macmillan, 1976.
Speer, Albert. *Inside the Third Reich.* New York: Macmillan, 1970.
Steiner, George. *Strategic Planning.* New York: Free Press, 1979.
Strouse, Jean. *Morgan.* New York: Random House, 1999.
Thomas, Emory. *Robert E. Lee.* New York: W .W. Norton, 1995.
Toland, John. *No Man's Land.* New York: Konecky & Konecky, 1980.
Toland, John. *The Rising Sun,* New York: Random House, 1970.
Tolstoy, Leo. *War and Peace.* New York: Barnes & Noble, 1983.
Turnbull, Stephan. *Book of the Samurai.* London: Magna, 1986.

Uris, Leon. *Exodus*. New York: Doubleday, 1981.

Walton, Sam. *Made in America*. New York: Bantam, 1992.

Webb, James. *The Emperor's General*. New York: Bantam, 1999.

Wiley, Peter. *Yankees in the Land of Gods*. New York: Viking, 1990.

Williams, Ben. *House Divided*. Boston: Houghton Mifflin, 1947.

Williamson, Porter. *Patton's Principles*. Tucson, AZ: MSC, 1979.

Williamson, Murray. *Making of Strategy*. New York: Cambridge University Press, 1994.

Wouk, Herman. *War and Remembrance*. New York: Little, Brown, 1985.

Wouk, Herman. *The Winds of War*. New York: Little, Brown, 1971.

Zhisui, Li. *Private Life of Chairman Mao*. New York: Random House, 1994.

Index

Civil War, 177-190: battles, 178, 181-183; Confederate generals, 179; Davis, Jefferson, 178; Gettysburg, 179-181, 222; Jackson, Stonewall, Gen., 178-179; Meade, George, Gen., 178-179, 181; Pickett, George E., Gen., 180-181; Sherman, W.T., Gen., 182-183, 186; Union generals, 178. *See also* Grant, Ulysses, Gen.; Lee, Robert E.; Lincoln, Abraham
Clausewitz, Carl von, 1, 30, 34, 36, 114, 146, 147, 197, 231-232: boldness, 225; force concentration, 3, 98, 100, 102; prevailing circumstances, 48; pursuit after victory, 61; tactics, 23; war and commerce, 9
Coca Cola, 1, 3, 10, 11, 183, 194, 203, 219: Daft, Doug, 132, 133, 172, 221; Dunn, Jeffrey, 11; Goizueta, Roberto, 91; Ivester, Doug, 42, 183
Cohen, Abby, 232
Cold War, 132, 192-195, 197-198
Colgate, 108, 194
combat-readiness, 204-226
command structure, 143-144
common cause, 172
communication, 114-115: for combat-readiness, 222-223; upward, 88-89
Compaq, 60, 122, 134-135, 175: Capellas, Michael, 118, 137; Channel conflict, 134
competition, 234-235
competitor intelligence, 32
conglomerates, 100-101
Cortes, Hernando, 138, 213-214
Crate & Barrel, 113
Crimean War, 5, 188
Croesus, 144-145
Custer, George, Lt. Col., 104-105

Daewoo, 116
Daimler (or DaimlerChrysler), 16, 92, 120-121, 155, 195, 217: Mercedes, 96; Schrempp, Jurgen, 36, 186, 212
de Gaulle, Charles, 129, 136
Dell, 10-11, 60, 134, 184, 219: Grzelakowski, Moe, 223; Michael, Dell, 5, 134, 184; Rollins, Kevin, 151
Deloitte Touche, 220
Denso, 120-121
Desert Storm, 47, 99-100, 235, 237
Deutsche Telekom, 129
Diageo, 154
DirecTV, 35, 175, 187

Disney Corp., 1, 25, 43, 90-91, 215: Disney, Walt, 90-91; Eisner, Michael, 90-91, 229; integrity, 140; Touchstone Pictures, 155
Disraeli, Benjamin, 130
Drucker, Peter, 22, 27
Duke Energy, 33: Priory, Richard, 33

EchoStar, 35, 175
Eisenhower, Dwight, 129: SHAEF commander, 143-144; speed, 170; strategic principles, 237
EMC, 132, 234-235
Emerson, Ralph Waldo, 46, 58, 186
Encyclopaedia Britannica, 35, 161
England, 4, 47, 139, 144, 188: Blitz, 119; Chamberlain, Neville, 160-161; Far East WWII, 49, 133
Enron, 33, 170, 206-207, 210, 215, 217: Skilling, Jeff, 163, 170, 210
espionage, 32
esprit, 187-188
eToys, 122, 141-142: Lenk, Toby, 142
Exxon, 26, 111, 149: Longwell, Harry, 227

FedEx, 1, 25, 48, 62, 104, 110, 122, 214-215: Smith, Fred, 186
Fiat, 121, 195
Financial Times, 3
Fingerhut, 122, 142
first mover, 169-171
First Union, 152
flexibility, 218-219
Flextronics, 110
Foch, Ferdinand, Gen., 41
Ford Motor, 16, 26, 123, 130, 149, 151, 195: alliances, 120-121; Ford, Henry, 90; Nasser, Jaq, 5, 82, 86, 213; outsource to Bridgestone, 111, 130; Premier Auto Group, 95, 151; Visteon Div., 120
Forrest, Nathan Bedford, Gen., 12, 170, 179
Fortune, 11, 32, 62, 142, 200, 207, 212, 232
France (or French), 71, 75, 174, 188: Far East colonies, 49, 133; Munich Accord, 161; *poilu,* 16
FTC, 172, 188
Fuchida, Mitsuo, Cmdr., 46, 55
future scan, 32-36, 58: strategy of patience, 155-156

game theory, 33
Gap, 112, 113: Old Navy, 112, 155
Gartner Group, 42